A Slight and
Delicate Creature

A Slight and Delicate Creature

The Memoirs of
MARGARET COOK

Weidenfeld & Nicolson
LONDON

First published in Great Britain in 1999 by
Weidenfeld & Nicolson

© 1999 Margaret Cook

A CIP catalogue record for this book is available
from the British Library.

ISBN 0 297 84293 5

Typeset by Selwood Systems, Midsomer Norton

Printed in Great Britain by
Butler & Tanner Ltd, Frome and London

Weidenfeld & Nicolson
The Orion Publishing Group
Orion House
5 Upper Saint Martin's Lane
London, WC2H 9EA

To dearest Mum, with thanks for your powerful influences: genetic, social and spiritual.

Contents

Illustrations ix

Prologue 1

1   *Maiden Voyage* 7
2   *Wanderers Return* 14
3   *The Ewe Lambs* 20
4   *Cultural Conflicts* 31
5   *The Gleam* 39
6   *Fold, Fallow and Plough* 47
7   *Pangs of Pubescence* 53
8   *Metamorphosis* 60
9   *Sacred and Secular* 68
10   *And so to Bed* 80
11   *Celtic Twilight* 89
12   *My Intellectual Lover* 101
13   *Learning to Take the Reins* 115
14   *Nest-Building* 127
15   *Problems for the Working Mum* 136
16   *Careers Intertwine* 146
17   *Pastoral Interlude and a Winning Move* 156
18   *Living with Ambition* 167
19   *Two Disasters and the Aftermath* 177
20   *Health and Horses* 187

21 *The Invisible Barrier* 199

22 *Encounters with the Pale Horse* 212

23 *Family Crises and Celebrations* 222

24 *Betrayal and the Beginning of the End* 236

25 *The Acme of a Political Career* 248

26 *High Profile* 257

27 *Protection and Privilege* 268

28 *Media Mistress* 275

Epilogue 292

Illustrations

Between pages 86 and 87
First portrait, Pretoria 1944
Dad and two-year-old Jenny in the garden, Pretoria
Mum with her daughters outside the rondavel, Pretoria
With Clive and Jenny at Topcliffe
German prisoners of war make up a band for the New Year party,
    Topcliffe 1947
The RAF Christmas Party, Warton 1950
Brownies and Guides, Warton 1952
At sixteen
The Red Queen and the White Queen with Alice, Sunny Hill, 1960
Edinburgh Students Chanties' week, 1966
With Morag and Rod, Sennen Cove 1964
Graduation Day 1968. With Barbara and Anne
'The world's at our feet!' 15 September 1969
Chris, 1973
With Chris, Kirkcudbright 1973
Big Peter and wee Peter, Buckland, Cotswolds 1975

Between pages 150 and 151
Bedtime routine with Peter and Chris
Chris and Peter, Dalkeith 1985
At Bangour General Hospital, 1987
Robin carves the Christmas goose, Edinburgh, early-1990s
Gala Day in the constituency, Livingston, mid-1980s
Chris, Robin, Peter in the New Forest, 1989
A wet Easter in the New Forest
Fox Sanctuary, New Forest
Free-roaming sow and piglets, New Forest 1987
Peter and Chris, New Forest 1991
With Peter, Robin, Kate, Chris at Eyeworth Lodge, New Forest 1989

Chris on Wendy, Kirkliston 1986
With Liz, Bean and Phyllis, Dunbar, 1995
Robin and hunter, Kirkliston
On Carrie holding Lucky. The Grange, West Calder 1988
With Phyllis, Douglas 1990

Between pages 214 and 215
Fiftieth birthday, St John's Hospital, Day Bed Unit, 3 August 1994
Fiftieth birthday party
Golden wedding celebration for Granny and Grandpa Cook
Golden Wedding Celebration for Granny and Grandpa Whitmore
Peter's graduation, Newcastle 1996
Chris's graduation, Aberdeen 1995
Water sports. Peter on the offensive, Sarthe, France
Breakfast at Helmcken Falls Lodge, Canada 1993
With Kate and Iain on the Great Wall of China, 1995
Peter and Robin near Grenoble, France 1995
Climbing in Connemara, 1995
After a morning's ride in the Picos de Europa, Spain, 1996
In exalted company, on the royal yacht *Britannia*, Hong Kong 1997[1]
Gorky, Gary and Mike painted for hunting in the Amazon forest
Taking a bath with pirhanas in the Amazon
Portrait, 1998[2]

Sources
[1] Associated Press
[2] Rex Features (Photograph by Jeremy Sutton-Hibbert)

All other photographs supplied by the Author

Prologue

During the last weekend of July 1997 Robin and I sat down together in our Edinburgh home with our diaries. The new Labour government was just three months old and in that time he had been exploring his new role as Foreign Secretary, which had given us both a taste of the demands of our prospective lifestyle. We were accustomed to our lives only converging intermittently, but appreciated that even more forward planning was now necessary. We pondered over the coming action-packed weeks. His London base was the gracious, official Foreign Secretary's residence in Carlton Gardens, and his country retreat the gloriously beautiful Chevening, a mansion, garden and estate in rural Kent, which had enchanted us both so much at first encounter that we wanted to be there as much as possible. We identified a number of dates for this purpose, marked in other weekend events such as the Ayr races and the Parisian Arc de Triomphe race, for which we had been invited to stay with the Aga Khan, and not least the Commonwealth Heads of Government meeting in Edinburgh. At this event I would act as hostess to other Foreign Secretaries' wives, conveying them on sightseeing and shopping trips, while Cherie Blair shepherded the Prime Ministers' wives. There were to be banquets, too, attended by members of the royal family, a marvellous excuse for buying new gowns. Looking at these plans, amidst all the excitement and anticipation I experienced a certain sorrow because Sparrow, my young horse, would certainly get less of my attention. Should I sell him? I really had to entertain the thought.

The next Friday we were due to leave on holiday. Robin, who had as usual an overfull day's programme, had begged me to pack his case which I did, including the expensive new suede chaps I had bought him for riding in Montana. He arrived home at the last possible moment. Time marched on relentlessly, and still he was frantically dashing from room to room, groaning and sighing and trying to sort out papers or to find missing items.

'Did you cancel the papers?' I ventured.

He exploded, 'No, of course not, how—'

I interjected calmly, 'Okay, I'll do it.'

Finally, with only forty minutes till take-off time, we bundled into the car. The driver was obviously but effectively keeping the lid on his impatience, as I was. I was too taut to begin enjoying the prospect of the holiday. He would not begin to unwind until we had left the country and he had had a good long sleep, probably on the transatlantic flight.

As we stepped out of the car in the unwonted heat at Edinburgh airport, we were immediately aware of a foul, nauseating, sewage-like stench which was almost unbearable and which propelled us into the fresher air of the airport building as fast as possible. But later I was to think back to that moment as an omen of the disaster that was about to befall me.

On the flight to Heathrow Robin went through his accumulated mail, passing a few bills, receipts and other items to me as was our custom. A light meal was served and I relaxed a little. After arriving we were escorted from the plane by a fast-track route to the waiting security cars. The usual entourage was there, driver, Harry the body-guard and other assorted security staff; also one of his personal assistants, David, with whom Robin had business to discuss on the way to Terminal Four. David and Robin began to move to another car in order to conduct this business, then Robin had second thoughts.

'You come too, Margaret,' he said. 'We'll manage three in the back. It's more friendly that way.'

David was on edge, trying to tell Robin that Alastair Campbell (Tony Blair's press officer) had tried to contact him urgently. Robin impatiently lifted the car phone and dialled. David and I fell into conversation. I was pleased to have an ordinary, relaxed and cheerful conversation with someone, about holidays, travel, languages. It was only in retrospect that I recalled Robin becoming very still and very silent.

The cars stopped outside a VIP lounge and we were decanted inside with our hand baggage. Coffee and biscuits were laid out invitingly. The room was milling with various people, including a waiter. I was startled to hear Robin brusquely telling everyone to get outside. The waiter hovered and was told very sharply to remove himself.

Then Robin said, chillingly, 'I am afraid there won't be any holiday,

Margaret. It's cancelled. The *News of the World* is running the story of my affair with Gaynor on Sunday. I can't leave the country. I think you and I should part.'

I was calm. The prospect of newspaper exposure was not of course new. I was incredulous that he had been continuing the affair ... but yes, he confirmed it was true. I did not at first take seriously his statement that we should part, thinking it was part of a 'mea culpa' trip from which he wanted to be dissuaded. His response then and several times through that long evening was, 'I can't imagine why you would want to stay.' The hidden agenda seemed to be that it would be very convenient if I were to take responsibility for the split.

The events of the next two hours, during which we remained in the lounge, are rather confused. Robin spoke to Tony Blair on the phone and I tried to make out the substance of the discussion. He kept saying, 'I understand ... I understand.'

When he hung up I asked, 'He wants you to resign?'

'No,' said Robin complacently. 'I shan't lose my job.'

I must have become progressively convinced that he meant to leave me, but I was bewildered and could not understand why. After all, I didn't believe his love for Gaynor had any depth, and if he was thinking of his political survival, surely he would want to keep his marriage intact? I recall pacing to and fro, trying to grasp what was happening and how I should deal with it. I glanced at my watch and realised the time for our Boston flight was close. Various people had been despatched to rescue our luggage. I couldn't help wondering inconsequentially what the waiting staff were making of all this.

Stung by his impassiveness, I asked, 'What would you do if I went into a deep depression and committed suicide?'

He paused, cool and aloof, as if posed a question on a public platform. 'I should, of course, be sorry ...'

I turned away with disgust and didn't listen to the rest.

Peter our younger son, had planned to be at Heathrow to see us off to Boston, so there was a certain amount of phoning and scurrying to and fro to try to locate him. I drank some coffee, dreading his appearance. At last Peter walked in looking worried and perplexed.

'What is this heavy scene?' he asked.

'Peter,' I said, getting up to hug him. 'Come and sit down.' I held him close, looked at Robin and said curtly, 'Tell him!'

Robin said, without any emotion, quite matter-of-fact, 'Peter, I've been having an affair with my secretary. The *News of the World* have got hold of the story and are running it on Sunday.'

'And worse than that,' I said. 'Peter, he is leaving me!'

And then I let go and the flood of sobs and tears held back for so long were unstoppable. I held on to Peter with everything I had. At that point I felt a terrible failure. This was the end of my ability to protect my sons. Poor lad, he couldn't begin to take it all in; he had absolutely no warning of this. He held me tight and muttered in a voice of extreme distress, 'Oh, Mum, don't . . . don't. Oh, Mum!'

Things are misty after that, though I remember the waiter coming back and bringing fresh coffee. Robin, who had sat unmoved through the scene of my emotion, vanished. We phoned Chris, our elder son, because he had to know, and I was more composed. I told them both there had been other affairs, going back twenty years or more, and that till now I had tried to protect them and had never been able to talk of this to a single soul. Their support then and afterwards was of immense importance and it might have been easy to forget that their shock and destabilisation was in some ways greater than mine. Robin had been a greatly admired and respected father and now had to be completely rethought. I knew, however, how close they had all been and emphasised that, come what may, they should remain on reasonable terms with him.

Eventually some move had to be made and someone was sent to acquire a ticket for me to travel back to Edinburgh. At several points during the tortuous and unsatisfactory exchange with Robin I had tried to establish his reasons for wanting to part, and had not received a straight or satisfactory answer. Now, at the eleventh hour, I rallied. I thought of the self-destruct tendency he had, and made up my mind to make a last and final effort to save my marriage. I announced that I would go back to London with him that night and travel up to Edinburgh the next day. More messengers were despatched to change my ticket and provide Peter with one to accompany me. I should mention that the security staff had all been expecting their holidays at this time, all of which had to be cancelled. They were asked to change my home phone number to an ex-directory one, with immediate effect. I made no protest, but it occurred to me that as well as keeping the press at a distance it would also mean that no friends could make contact.

So the staff were gathered, the car packed with luggage. We dropped Peter at the bus stop for Slough and sped into London. Not a word was spoken, but the driver behaved like someone possessed. He manoeuvred dangerously and at speed, swerving in and out of lanes, accelerating ferociously, taking turns sharply. No one reacted, no one spoke. In London, Robin asked to be dropped at a late-night grocer's for milk and coffee. While he and Harry were gone shopping, the chauffeur turned to me and said courteously, 'I hope that wasn't too uncomfortable for you.' I realised he meant his driving.

In the grand splendour of his residence at Carlton Gardens the two of us sat down with a bottle of whisky (which I normally seldom touched), and talked. Robin went on his usual ego trip and expanded on his career, his dissatisfactions and things he wished he had done differently; none of which was relevant. He repeated that he couldn't understand why I wanted to stay with him. Perhaps it would have suited him very well to say, 'My wife is leaving me.' He wanted to talk through why I still loved him. I felt I was being put on trial. If he expected me to talk eloquently of the breadth and depth of my love at that juncture, he was sadly mistaken. I said that if the events of the last year had not proved my love, nothing would. I also spoke of my perception that he really did need more of my support now, and that I had been fully prepared to make changes: to alter my own priorities, stick my heels in hard at work for more help and greater flexibility, possibly even sell Sparrow and liberate weekends. That really stopped him in his tracks, for he knew what a sacrifice I was considering. 'I wish I'd known this before,' he said. He continued that the last three months had been wonderful and what a pity we hadn't been able to go on holiday and have just a few weeks, because then we might have made it.

I was sickened to the core at such a superficial reckoning of the legacy of our partnership. Perhaps that was when I let go. I thought then, that if I abandoned my pride and self-esteem and fell at his knees with fulsome words of adoration, he might have changed his mind. But that I would never do. Even then, though I loved him, I despised much about him; and he knew it. Somehow I eventually got a definite statement out of him: something to the effect that, yes, he really wanted to leave me and make Gaynor his partner.

I got up and placed my glass on the table, observing quietly that there was then no more to be said, and left the room.

I'd like it to go on record that I never pleaded or begged him to stay. I merely tried to get him to examine his true feelings. And I lost.

Probably I was too cool. True feeling runs deep and is not easy to describe. Also I suppose that over the years each time he inflicted a significant hurt I have withdrawn more and more from expressing my affection. The love was still there though, and was very apparent from the pain of the following weeks.

I slept poorly and had no appetite the next day. Robin showed me the statement he intended to issue on the doorstep that evening. It began, 'I am separating from my wife.' I insisted that he change this to, 'I am leaving my wife.' There was no mention of the affair. It seemed to me that the presentation was intended to put a respectable gloss on his deception.

He told me that a safe house in Edinburgh could be arranged to protect me from the press. For once I reacted with temper. 'Don't be so bloody melodramatic. What would I do in a safe house? I want to go home.' He withdrew sharply.

When it was time to leave I carried my own bags down the stairs. He did not dare to offer to do it. The waiting staff in the entrance hall must have felt uncomfortable, and none of them could meet my eyes. They helped me silently into the car which swept me through the wrought-iron gates and past the attendant policeman for the last time. I did not look back.

I

Maiden Voyage

I was born on 3 August 1944 in Pretoria, South Africa. My mother, already having a two-year-old daughter, was longing for a son, and on hearing I did not conform to expectation exclaimed, 'Send her back!' But when she saw me – and I was, they said, very beautiful – she loved me dearly and decided to keep me after all. I was wise enough to be extremely well-behaved, which gave me a huge advantage over my sister who was rather inclined to be the opposite. My eyes were intensely blue, they said in tones of admiring wonder. Probably I was no different from other babies in this or other respects, but I'm happy they thought so. My father even made up a song about my eyes. Fortunately I've forgotten it.

My earliest memories merge with stories told me by my parents about the surroundings and events which influenced my generation. So I'll go further back than my birth. Neither of my parents had a conventionally happy childhood and it is to their credit that they managed to give me one.

My father was born in India in 1912 into a middle-class family. I believe his father was in the civil service. As was the custom in that situation my father and his older sister Mary were sent back to England for their schooling. My father was brought up in London by his Aunt Chris to whom he was warmly attached. His parents eventually returned to the UK permanently and at the age of twelve he was transplanted to their home, where he was miserably unhappy. He was tormented about his London accent, expected immediately to adopt middle-class mores and restrictions and to develop instant affection for his unknown family. He had little freedom in his choice of social or academic activities and, instead of being allowed to follow his fascination with chemistry to university standard, was forced to leave school and join the Royal Air Force.

My mother's start in life was even more unpromising. Her father was wounded in the First World War, had a leg amputated and returned home a hero and an invalid. He had no doubt developed wandering habits in France, and finding his wife perhaps no longer attractive, seduced a beautiful young woman who bore his child, Joyce: my mother. Adopting the child, he took her home to his wife to rear and nurture. A year later he fathered a legitimate daughter, Grace.

Joyce and Grace were very fond of each other. But Joyce was treated as a social outcast by her stepmother and denied the simple treats and pleasures of the family. Grace always had a tasty snack to take to school; Joyce had none. One day a big red apple was placed on the table for Grace. Joyce was overcome with envy, snatched the apple and ran off. She was severely punished. To make matters worse each child took after her mother in looks: Grace was plain, straight-haired, mousy; Joyce was very pretty with a mop of dark brown curls.

Eventually the family broke up and Joyce went to live in Nottingham with her father. Without a mother's care she had to learn to deal with puberty and her periods all by herself. She left school at fourteen and earned her living in an underwear factory. Every evening, walking home, she would look back at the red glow on the horizon and hope it was the factory burning down. Religion in the shape of the Anglican Church provided solace and contacts. She must have won the respect and admiration of the vicar, Mr Brooker, who persuaded the College of Nursing in Lincoln to take her on as a student nurse.

Life at first was hard, though she was very happy. Student nurses were paid eight pounds per year, two pounds every three months, so they were always broke. Discipline was very strict indeed, though as the years went by they learned how to evade it and have a good time. They relied on gifts of cigarettes from patients which they concealed in the complex folds of their butterfly caps.

My parents' first encounter, which took place in the early stages of the Second World War, was an unromantic nurse–patient one. My father had been brought in with a broken nose following a car crash and was not in good humour. He said, 'Would you shut that damned window, nurse. There's a hell of a draught blowing.' My mother snapped, 'Don't you swear at me!' But afterwards they forgot their differences. My father must have been a romantic figure as a fighter pilot. The accident prevented him from taking part in an air-raid over Germany – in which all the participants met their ends in the North Sea. Thus, much history depends on the consequences of high spirits and a damaged nose!

Meeting was difficult in wartime as there was no transport. My father walked sixteen miles to see Mum on his day off — and then walked back again. In after years we would tease him, 'You wouldn't do it now, would you, Dad?' To which he grunted, 'I've proved my devotion.'

So in 1940 they married in some haste as Dad expected to be sent abroad, in the rather arbitrary way that service personnel were posted round the world in those days. Three months after the wedding on his return home in the evening, without a word he tossed his standard-issue tropical sunhat on the floor at my mother's feet. Within days he was aboard ship, bound for South Africa.

Mum was determined that she would follow her man to South Africa if it lay within her power. She agitated as much as she could, firing off letters to all quarters of officialdom and even writing to the Prime Minister, Winston Churchill. Eventually she received notice to prepare herself to travel. Each day for a week or more she received a different set of instructions which was apparently a ploy to confuse any spies interested in transport routes and shipping. At last she took a train to Glasgow, arriving in the black-out and having nowhere to stay, a daunting prospect for a twenty-two-year-old girl. Near the station she located a cheap boarding-house and rang the bell. The matronly woman who answered had no vacancies, but regarded with concern this young, inexperienced and extremely pretty girl wandering the streets alone. She summoned one of her lodgers, a hefty soldier, and instructed him to escort Mum to a nearby friend of hers who did have room. Mum's abiding impression of Glasgow from this briefest of encounters is of a warm, courteous and caring community.

She left early the next morning by taxi to join her ship. Sailing down the Clyde was an emotional experience as all the dock workers stopped to wave and shout good-luck messages, with unexpressed thoughts on all sides about how uncertain the future was. This was the last passenger ship to sail from the Clyde in 1941.

Mum was almost immediately adopted by a group of missionaries who clearly intended to preserve her from sin and temptation. On sitting down to dine at the end of her first full day, an officer came to ask respectfully if she would care to join the captain's table. Her friends tutted and whispered and advised against it. But Mum said, 'I rather think I will.' And so she embarked on a time of fun, entertainment and frivolity as well as lavish standards of wining and dining hitherto undreamed of in wartime Britain, and unknown to Mum at any time in her life.

The voyage gave rise to almost daily anxieties about U-boats being sighted, and the ship followed a circuitous route which traversed the Atlantic almost as far as New York in order to avoid this threat. Mostly they were aligned with a military convoy, which could be seen on the horizon. But the warships were fast movers and vanished from sight when enemy activity was reported. Mum's ship trudged slowly on alone. These tense moments only served to enhance the euphoria of ship-board life. We discovered many years later that a cousin of my father's was aboard one of the convoy ships, so he received much gratitude for his token gallantry.

The three-month journey was a cause of great anxiety to family and friends at home. As soon as she arrived in Cape Town and was reunited with Dad, Mum cabled to her friend Vera in Keyworth the news of her safe arrival. Vera received this one Sunday morning before setting off to early church service. The excitement of opening and reading the missive made her a little late and the service had already begun when she arrived. As she knelt down with the rest the cable burned a hole in her pocket.

Mr Brooker, full of foreboding and anxiety, put up a heartfelt prayer for 'Our sister Joyce, sailing the high seas in dire peril and at constant risk of her life, and from whom no word has been heard for three months.'

Vera was consumed with impatience and rushed into the vestry as soon as she decently could at the end of the service, gasping out the news: 'She's safe, she's arrived,' waving the cable frantically. Mr Brooker then and thereafter regarded this as a direct answer to his prayers. I suppose an ardent faith suspends any need to regard the limits of time and space.

My parents had been apart for over a year and had some difficulties adjusting to each other again. One example of the tensions that arose occurred on the two-day journey from Cape Town to Pretoria, when at dinner Mum took a peach for dessert. As she lifted the fruit to bite into it my father muttered, looking disapproving, 'Peel it and cut it!' Mum, who didn't want to do this and, even more, didn't want to be told to do it, accused him of making a fuss. But Dad had thoroughly imbibed the middle-class dictates – and even more the service-driven requirements – to conform to certain behaviour patterns, so insisted, probably rather rigidly, 'I know these people, and how one is expected to behave here.'

In Pretoria they were adopted by the English RAF community and at first enjoyed an active social life revolving around sport and elitist clubs but soon found that, on Dad's junior officer's pay, they were living way beyond their means. They moved away from the hub of society and rented a picturesque round house called a rondavel. Included in the rent was the service of a house boy to clean and tend the garden. Mum took up nursing again. However with the white Afrikaans community very pro-Nazi in 1941 she found herself cold-shouldered, even insulted. One day as she performed some duty in the ward sluice a nurse came in and remarked, 'What a filthy English smell!' Mum walked out of the ward and out of the hospital and never went back.

My sister Jenny was born in November 1942. This was a world in which labour was cheap and Mum's acquaintances were astonished when they realised that she planned to look after her own child. The issue of child care was raised one day when Mum was out shopping in Pretoria with an older lady friend.

'My dear, why work yourself to the bone when there's no need? You can get a good healthy native girl to work as nanny; do a few jobs around the house as well. It will cost you next to nothing, really. Let me help you.'

The lady – let's call her Gwen – had an imperious manner and a strident voice. She glanced along the street. Coming towards them was a well-built young black woman.

'Hey! You there!' shrilled Gwen. 'Come here!'

Minnie – for so she was called – calmly and with dignity came to the two white ladies, stood silently and without expression as they inspected her, one critically, the other with a degree of alarm.

'What's your name?'

'Minnie, madam.'

'Are you married?'

'Yes, madam.'

'Do you have a job?'

'No, madam.'

'This lady here needs someone to look after her baby. Have you worked as a nanny before?'

'Yes, madam.'

'Would you like to work for Mrs Whitmore?'

'Yes, madam.'

And so it was arranged. Minnie came to the rondavel and took over the care of Jenny. She endeared herself to Dad as she could make an excellent mixed grill. Mum tolerated her but they were not especially close. Maybe mothers and nannies never are.

I was conceived during a holiday in the Drakensberg mountains, a place, I understand, of breathtaking beauty. It is pleasant to know that that momentous collision which resulted in my being took place amidst especially glorious surroundings. Thereafter Minnie had her work doubled with two of us on her hands. Photographs show her as a strongly made but well-proportioned girl, very neat in white overalls, white turban and shoes, holding me, a shapeless little bundle, on one arm and competently restraining a wayward Jenny with the other. Pictures of my parents portray a very handsome pair in tropical clothes. Mum mocked the English officers' gear as they wore baggy khaki shorts hanging in shapeless redundancy to the knee, whereas the South African officers wore neat, tightly fitting short shorts. The winters must have brought cool weather, for Jenny and I are pictured clad in pixie hoods and scarves.

Mum recalls listening to the war news at the worst moments of the war. The fall of Singapore in 1942 was a particular time of despair. 'What was there now to stop the Japanese invading South Africa?' She had perhaps forgotten the whole width of the Indian Ocean, for one thing. But at the time they must have seemed horrifyingly invincible. By the time I was born in 1944 the balance of power had changed and so had attitudes, though Mum recalls an Afrikaans acquaintance teaching Jenny to do the Nazi salute about this time. Still, the anti-British stance became more muted. In Britain the church bells had been silent throughout the war, being held in reserve as a means of alerting the country in the event of an invasion. But when the news came of a major victory and it really seemed as though the tide had turned, it was decreed that the bells should be rung in celebration. I presume that everyone was forewarned. My father heard a recording of the resonant and evocative peals in a state of intense emotion, tears freely coursing down his cheeks.

The day came in 1945 when a carrier brought Mum the unexpected news that they were to catch the evening train to Cape Town, thence to be posted back to the UK on the next available ship. Quailing at the momentous task ahead, Mum sent a message to Dad at his office, acquired trunks and boxes which had to be packed even as the directions were being painted on them, and began giving away many household goods, including many to Minnie and her husband, Cain. Then there were friends to be contacted, many living at a distance and who probably would never be seen again, equipment for the two-day journey to be acquired. After lunch, so that Mum could get a clear run with the packing, Minnie took Jenny and me to the park.

The afternoon passed in a flash, the hands of the clock advancing at an alarming rate towards eight o'clock when the taxi was due. Mum began to be anxious when teatime came and went and there was no sign of Minnie with us children. She was visited by the dreadful thought that Minnie had run away with us. Dad pooh-poohed the idea. Mum had reached the stage of fear-induced paralysis and total inability to co-ordinate action when Minnie returned with us. Poor girl! I hope Mum was not too harsh with her, for she was by now in a state of deep sorrow at the realisation of losing us. She sat down in the kitchen and wailed. The taxi came, boxes and cases were piled in. Minnie sat at the table with her head in her arms sobbing passionately. Mum found Cain sitting on the pavement outside, for he normally did not enter the house, and told him to go to comfort his wife. Meanwhile the loaded taxi bore the family and all its transportable goods away.

The train journey was rather a trial with two young children snatched from their normal comfortable routine and inclined to be fractious. Milk and other baby food had to be warmed on a spirit stove. On arrival in Cape Town it became apparent that the haste had been quite unnecessary. We were met by a charming WRAF officer who asked, 'Would you like the good news first or the bad?'

The good news – so-called – was that bombs had been dropped on Japan and that it was VJ Day: that is, the war was over. The bad news – very bad – was that the ship's stokers were on strike so the ship could not move out of dock. Wearily the family installed itself in a hotel, where celebrations were beginning as the news sank in. But the tedium of waiting was short-lived. Anti-aircraft gunners, suddenly finding themselves superfluous and longing to be at home celebrating with their families, undertook to stoke the ship home.

The voyage home was expeditious indeed compared with the tortuous outward journey and was accomplished in three weeks.

2

Wanderers Return

Our ship docked at Newcastle. Plans had been hastily made on the journey to impose ourselves on Mum's family near Nottingham as we had no home of our own. With so many service personnel moving about at that time people had to shift for themselves. My parents agreed that Dad's family were unlikely to welcome us with open arms. Mum's father had died some years previously and I'm not sure at what point she had made peace with her stepmother. Maybe her middle-class marriage had made her respectable.

The voyage had not been unalloyed pleasure this time for Mum. Jenny had found the change unsettling and had required some managing. So the parents were weary enough when they were greeted by officials who came to smooth our way at the entry port. Somehow lines had been crossed and arrangements had been made – including tickets bought – which directed us not to Nottingham, but to Frome, via London and the dubious welcome of Dad's family. There was no option but to accept the proffered sandwiches and milk along with these plans. Things went well as far as Swindon where delays caused a missed connection and we faced a night in the station waiting room. Tempers were decidedly frayed, most of all mine on waking next morning and finding no warm milk ready when needed. I believe I howled piteously.

Dad, ever the good hunter-gatherer, set out in quest of relief along the early morning streets. Milk bottles stood invitingly in ones and twos at the terraced doorways. Without hesitation he lifted one, made a muttered apology and left some coins. Back at the station he was greeted like a hero, especially by me. It was not the only time in my life I had occasion to be deeply grateful to him.

As predicted we were not at all warmly received by Dad's family (as welcome as snow in spring, Mum comments acidly), and after an uncomfortable and tense week were asked to leave. This time of displacement, of not belonging anywhere, must have been altogether unpleasant. The next move took us to Nottingham where Mum's family, more accustomed to roughing it and accepting a degree of overcrowding, made us comfortable enough. Later a rented cottage was found, though as Dad's leave was nearly over and he was to be posted we knew not where, it was likely to be a temporary arrangement. At Christmas 1945 the owner, with true seasonal generosity, gave us a week's notice to quit as he wished to prepare the cottage for his son's forthcoming marriage. Fortuitously Dad had got his posting to the Isle of Man so we moved to a slightly more permanent home in Ramsey.

This point of my narrative is noteworthy as a watershed because my memories start here. People express astonishment that I should be able to remember things from the age of two, but so it is. In particular I recall vividly lying in a cot beset by an unpleasant sensation which in retrospect I recognise as boredom. Beside the cot stood a wooden wardrobe and I tried to make sense of the woodgrain patterns. I expect I expressed my frustrations vocally as I remember Dad looking anxiously out of the window – no doubt wanting help to restore my good humour. But in general I was good and docile. Photographs of the time show us enjoying the beach, the park, swings and sailing boats. I was a dumpy little girl in a knitted spotted cover-all swimsuit – pink, I think – and a pixie hood.

We left Ramsey after little more than a year. I recollect the sea trip, sitting on a bunk, watching the sailing boats through the porthole. I used to attribute a lifelong freedom from seasickness to having done so much sea travel as a youngster.

Our next home was in Topcliffe in Yorkshire from where the memories multiply exponentially. Photographs show me as a solemn child with light brown wispy hair in pigtails. In 1947 German prisoners of war were still held in the UK, although under fairly unrestricted conditions, and one of their number, a young man from Berlin called Walter, came to our house daily to help with domestic chores. He had fairly rudimentary English. We were all on friendly, easy terms. He would clean the kitchen floor so thoroughly he declared we could eat our dinner off it. He would make cocoa for Jenny and me which we loathed, so instead of drinking it we would pour it into our saucers and stand our skittles in it. The POWs in our camp got together a band which played at a New Year's dance. I have a photograph showing saxophones, fiddle, bass and percussion, the men themselves looking so young that they seem barely out of their teens. The backdrop, which is clearly hand-painted, shows an old, bald, bearded man – 1946 – holding a small cheeky boy – 1947. The depiction of this still point in time by these displaced men seems especially poignant.

Walter would talk longingly of his home and family and soon he was able to return to them. He promised to write, and he did. Mum kept his letters for years and I read them long before I understood anything about the war and its consequences. When I did it seemed so strange that Walter whom we loved had been an enemy. He wrote in terms of great affection: 'My little Jennifer and Margaret, I love you always,' and assured us that he told his wife and children all about us. At the corner of one letter he pinned some dried flowers which were the first to bloom in the Berlin spring that year.

And then the Wall went up and we received no more letters.

One of my most loved possessions was a tricycle but it had many other uses. When we went to the Naafi with Mum I was fascinated by the bacon-slicing machine. The swing, the rhythm, the production of a sinuous pink slice with each pulse, and all effected by a vigorous turning of the handle; all this was minutely observed as I stood staring open-mouthed. Then back at home the tricycle was turned upside down, the pedal used as a handle and imagination supplied the rest.

I was also deeply attached to my dummy, I am ashamed to say. Once I was engaged in a friendly chat with a window cleaner who thought we'd understand each other better if he removed the dummy from my mouth, but I screamed so loudly that he hastily replaced it. When it came to my own children I disapproved of dummies and they had to suck their thumbs instead.

There is no doubt that an enduring love of the countryside started here. I don't recall many details: mainly green, bedewed undergrowth where we collected wild raspberries and the powerful aromas both of the berries and the wet earth. To this day the scent – not the taste – of raspberries carries me back to this time. Once when we were out walking with Mum we came across a small grey rabbit caught in a snare. Mum was unable to release it and on our return called on a neighbour to help. Jenny and I were upset and wanted to know that it was safe and well. The neighbour swore under his breath and hastened away. In after years I gathered he had to kill the rabbit but I don't suppose we were told that then.

One of my most vivid memories from this time was a very violent one. Jenny and I were sitting just inside the French windows of our sitting room, playing at afternoon tea with tiny cups of orange juice and our dolls all politely assembled. Mum was in the bath upstairs. Out of nowhere came an immense roar as a plane dived out of the sky with a deafening crash and a huge fireball exploded, expanded, filling our vision. Oddly we weren't upset, only startled, not knowing the human implications. Mum leaped out of the bath and careered downstairs to see if we were unscathed. We were more interested in the sight of her, nude and wet, than in the plane crash. The visual memory remains with me to this day, and I sometimes shudder at low-flying noisy aircraft. The camp suffered a series of flight disasters, possibly to do with a policy of round-the-clock flying which my father opposed. Though he was probably right, his habitual inflexibility caused him problems which did not enhance his career prospects.

I had my first sexual experience at the age of three. This was not so shocking as it sounds. I was playing with my sister and two or three other children in a sand-pit, trying to build castles. The sand was too dry, so one of the boys, Clive, pulled down his shorts and peed on his sand. I admired his initiative, as well as his anatomy, and responded with remarkable aplomb. Perceiving even at such a tender age that girls should behave with more reserve, I asked him to come and moisten my sand also; which he obligingly did.

My parents were rather ambivalent with us about handling personal matters. I recall only one occasion when I was with them in the bedroom and they moved about freely and easily with no clothes on. It seemed very natural but then it never happened again and I absorbed the message that nude bodies, especially certain parts of them, were off-limits. Possibly the single occasion happened when I was supposed to be too young to notice.

Happenings that stapled themselves firmly on my memory did so no doubt because of the intense impression made at the time. I was a naturally good and amenable child, surrounded with all the love, kindly words and gentle attention I could desire, quite a contrast to my sister who was rather a passionate creature and seemed to muster contrary emotions in others and generally attract trouble. I was accustomed to sitting on the sidelines while she and Mum had a battle of wills. However the moment was bound to arrive when I found myself at odds with authority. It happened like this.

On our trips to the shops Mum conveyed me in a pushchair while Jenny walked, which must have given me an innate sense of superiority.

One day Jenny cut her heel which bled profusely. Mum weighed up the situation, deciding fairly enough to dispossess me of my seat and install Jenny in it. My sense of outrage was huge and quite ungovernable and made worse by the queenly and dignified mien of my sister. My furious screams were treated promptly with a slap and sharp rebuke which astonished me so much, never having been in trouble before, that I stopped yelling but wept quietly while clinging to the pushchair and reflecting on this my first serious reverse in life. Other lessons learned the hard way included a sharp shock from sticking my finger in an electric socket, and also the fact that Mum could get pretty cross about things over which one had no control, like soiling one's bed during sleep.

Soon it was time for the family to move on again, this time to the lovely town of Bath in Somerset. Here I had my fourth birthday and soon began primary school. I was very happy there. This impression is borne out by photographs of mainly outdoor activities, presumably taken by Mum, so even in 1948 the concept of community schools was practised, making schools feel like an exciting extension of home. Maybe the benign atmosphere was influenced by the new welfare state. We are pictured dressed as nurses bathing and tending dolls with an array of nursery equipment; in pants and vest doing synchronised exercises in the playground. Boys are shown in canvas aprons doing things with wood, saws and nails. Sex-typing was very much in evidence, as it was even twenty-five years later when my children started at school! We played percussion instruments and had a shop. Some of the prices are surprising, remembering that the abbreviation 'd' for penny was half the value of the current 'p'.

Carrots   4d a bunch
Potatoes   3d a lb
Cauliflowers   6d each
Rhubarb   5d a lb
Peas   6d a tin
Oranges   4d each
Lemons   2d each
Flowers   3d

Mum delighted in dressing Jenny and me in identical clothes, particularly for special occasions. We looked very demure in fawn coats coming to the knee and bonnets to match, white socks and sandals and stick-thin bare legs in between. Intricate smocking allowed party dresses to fall in beautiful gathers – and all done by hand.

The flat we occupied in Bath seemed pleasant and roomy enough but Mum told me in later years that she hated it and felt very uneasy there. She discovered as we were leaving that someone had committed suicide on the top floor so maybe there was cause for her instinctive dislike. During the summer holidays she took every opportunity to take us out, Dad too when he was home. I recall many happy exploratory outings to such places as Cheddar Gorge, Weston-Super-Mare, Combe Down Woods. The vertical rocks of Cheddar held a particular fascination for me; maybe this was a reverberation from my origin in the Drakensberg mountains.

3

The Ewe Lambs

When I was five the family moved to Warton in Lancashire where we stayed in a square brick terraced house with the imaginative address: 5 Officers' Married Quarters. The RAF camp was intimately inter-twined with an English Electric factory and frictions between the two were rife. It was a rather ugly, functional place with our homes overlooked by rectangular concrete and metal buildings and our gardens fenced around by massive lagged pipes running above ground, sup-ported by unadorned brick buttresses. The road in front of the house was hectic with RAF lorries, electric workers' buses and vans. A little further off was the wide-open space of the parade ground delimited by vast hangars on one side, ancient air-raid shelters on the other. In secluded sites – but readily discovered by us marauding youngsters – were disorderly dumps with broken glass, aluminium frames, sheets of metal and plastic, parts of old aircraft, including entire cockpits, and other assorted and unidentifiable debris.

It was a child's paradise and we loved it.

As my father had decided that in due course he was going to leave the RAF, he was no longer posted so frequently and frenetically, and we actually stayed here for four years, long enough for us to exploit the potential of our environment for mischief to the full; and on the whole without being discovered.

Except for one occasion at least. Dad, whose rank was flight lieuten-ant, sat working at his desk one morning when he was interrupted by a diffident and uneasy junior, who had some difficulty getting his message out.

'Yes, come on, man, out with it!'

'Well, sir, the dump at the back of hangar 108 has been interfered with ...'

'Have you any information about the perpetrators?'

'Yes ... ah ... sir ... it seems to be that some children have been seen playing there.'

'And whose children are they?'

'Well, sir, actually, sir ... they're yours, sir!'

Neither history nor imagination is able to complete this conversation.

We had an assortment of friends who belonged to the camp and together we roamed where we pleased. The air-raid shelters were ideal for games of Dare, being pitchy dark, damp, smelly, with unseen obstacles and probably rats, and a general air of nastiness. We split off into factions and had dens as headquarters, often in trees in the few available green areas. We broke into the canteen and drew faces in the vats of yellow cooking fat. When hush-hush developments in aircraft were revealed with great ceremony to visiting officials with much pomp and shiny brass, our little group of scruffy friends as often as not were present ex officio, having found a back entrance. Sometimes we would be noticed by a uniformed minion who hustled us out again. We were never punished on these occasions; no doubt the lapse in security was too much of an embarrassment to those in charge to worry about small fry like us. We would have passions for swings and somehow the bigger boys would sling a rope over one of the massive pipes where it reared overhead many yards from the ground. The launch pad was a trailer from which we would queue and swing for hours together until the rope cut so deeply into the lagging around the pipe that one of the RAF cadets would have to climb up and remove it. Once we made our headquarters in the back of a lorry, but the air-force blue felt lining of the truck insinuated itself into our ears and stuck to our clothes and so we were discovered. That was the only time my father spanked me.

Dad at this time cut a very fine figure, being tall, erect and slim with sleek black hair and trim moustache. He looked especially handsome in his dress uniform with shining buttons and buckles, black bow tie with shirt cuffs just showing by the regulation degree, complete with circular cap, RAF wings echoing the shape of his moustache, and medal ribbons. There he stands; I see him now among his night-scented stock in the back garden, his pipe clamped as always between his teeth. Periodically we would see him on parade or marching to and from the parade ground with his men, when he would studiously ignore us. On one occasion he took the ceremonial parade on the King's birthday, shouting out three cheers for the monarch; and was deeply hurt because not one of us had turned out to watch.

My parents enjoyed an active social life and dress evenings were a source of excitement to us children, not only because we could plan mischief with the baby-sitter, but because we loved to see the adults in their fancy clothes. Mum had some very glamorous outfits and possessed a fine figure in which to appear décolleté. I remember a black and turquoise striped gown, a black skirt with silver wrap-around top, a wispy net shawl, and one very daring dress which was strapless, ivory silk with bright scarlet and gold flowers. With her magnificent mane of dark curly hair, radiance and vivacity, I felt she far outshone the other mothers and was very proud of her. There is a group picture of one of these evenings taken at a late hour, with the wing commander, a dark stocky man, ordering the assembled company to 'Say Cheeeeese,' but the camera clicked at the wrong moment and he was caught for all time with lips protruding and teeth bared threateningly. My parents were assiduous in seeking to protect us from baneful influences but we readily picked up that behind the hilarity there was much alcohol flowing and a degree of gossip and scandal. My father was not a keen dancer and preferred to prop up the bar most of the evening but Mum loved to dance and was much in demand. She tells me there was the usual complement of Lotharios who would dance attendance on her one evening and foresake her for someone else another time. The parents had a conversation code for warning each other that certain things were not for our childish ears, particularly an exclamation, 'Not forebe the renchild!' We were privy to this of course and pricked up our ears instantly we heard these words.

The children on the camp were given a sumptuous Christmas party organised by the young RAF recruits who were detailed to give us a splendid time, in addition to hand-making our presents. One of mine was a beautifully crafted dolls' house, nearly as big as myself. On a relatively limited income, the parents were hugely generous at Christmas time, and we received stockings stuffed with small inexpensive items, then later a whole armchair of exciting and well-chosen gifts. Mum no doubt was over-compensating for her own impoverished childhood.

In spite of the goodwill and generosity, home life at this time was a cultural desert. There were a few shelves of books, mainly popular novels, but books did not feature as a big item in family life, though Mum did read to us. She was not fond of Beatrix Potter or Winnie the Pooh and I really only discovered these and other children's delights when I had my own sons. We had no television, a rarity then, though the radio was important. There was no interest in music or theatre to any serious degree, though we were once taken to *Madame Butterfly*, for which Mum tried to explain the plot beforehand. I thought it was a silly, pointless story and couldn't understand why it took so long in the telling. We were totally unprepared for the music and the venture was not a success. We watched *Giselle* on a neighbour's television and were utterly spellbound. It wasn't possible to appreciate to the full, in the absence of colour, the contrast between the real life of Act I and the realm of the spirits in Act II but our imaginations were fired by the portrayal of the mysterious other-world.

Jenny and I went to the village school which was rough and tough, and good for seeding democratic principles; or possibly for stamping them out for ever, I suppose, depending on the receptivity of the soil. We mingled well enough, though many of our friends at the camp looked down their noses as they went off to their private schools. At the end of the school year, if you had an unblemished attendance record you were awarded clogs or a pair of wellington boots. Clogs, which were worn commonly by both boys and girls, were heavy, ungainly footwear and made a nerve-jarring, scraping noise on stones and tarmac. I guess there was a class distinction between those who wore clogs and those who didn't.

The teacher of the first class was a coarse elderly woman, fond of losing her temper noisily and free with the flat of her hand. I was scared of her and retreated into myself, and consequently was very bad at the favourite activity which was to allow individuals to stand in front of the class and talk about 'What I did last night.' The natural extroverts clamoured to relate their improbable doings which were often wild and rude, most of which went completely unchecked. A not uncommon event in class was for a child to lose control and wet himself. If the unfortunate was a boy he would usually receive a wallop and be called a dirty pig; if it was a girl, especially a well-dressed one, she would be cosseted and allowed to dry off beside a radiator. I was grittily determined that this would never happen to me. I have had throughout life since then a recurring bad dream, that I needed to go to the toilet but could find nowhere a place of suitable design and privacy. I am half convinced that this nightmare had its origins in my early school days.

Luckily the teachers in the other classes were more enlightened.

Once I started to read I developed an insatiable appetite for which there was a shocking inadequacy of fare. I remember the tremendous excitement when words were suddenly decipherable and whole sentences made sense. I had to ration my reading in school because books were changed at predetermined intervals, by which time I could have read mine several times over. There was intense pleasure in reading and sometimes it was difficult to apply sufficient restraint not to devour a book all at once. At home I suspect our books were mainly Enid Blyton but perhaps the modern tendency to sneer at these and find them politically incorrect is overdone. We enjoyed her work and at such a young age pleasure in books is of the first importance. The particular book that has since been labelled racist, a story about a wicked, thieving golliwog, I read with as much emotion as one would derive from an adult tragedy but I don't think it had any other adverse effect. I was very proud to be given a book on nature and wildlife and remember its hard green covers and pencilled drawings to this day. Mum had a huge tome of anatomy, physiology and nursing which she let us borrow. This book, which had detailed illustrations and would even now be accurate enough in some respects, was a source of endless curiosity. Probably both these books influenced my choice of career.

When I now read biographies of people whose parents were especially artistic or cultured or intellectual I experience a pang of envy, for such homes must provide a garden of mental stimulation for children growing up in them. How well-read I might have been with a well-stocked library at my fingers' ends from an early age, how talented a musician given all the opportunities, how profound a thinker given a milieu of rational and controlled discussion! But we can all make these arguments, and such homes may not always get the emotional stability right and without that most other assets could be squandered. Our family life was warm, stable, interactive, demonstratively affectionate, and the desire to make us happy was abundantly evident. Again I am wallowing in old photographs as reminders; of picnics in the Derbyshire hills, en route for a holiday, sheltered against dry-stone walls in wild countryside, feasting on boiled eggs, cheese, tomatoes, cream crackers, cakes and fruit; or lazing in sundresses and sunhats amidst the golden stubble of a cornfield in high summer; on the beach at St Anne's, near Blackpool, where we would often be taken after a visit to the dentist, equipped with bulging picnic bags, rugs, buckets and spades; on a visit to Scotland when Dad's ancient

Austin broke down; or marching in brown and gold uniform with our Brownie pack in military order on some occasion, probably Baden-Powell's birthday, and Mum smartly leading her Rangers; or in later years, morris dancing in lavender and white with belled and ribboned sticks, like modern cheerleaders, in the annual village Rose Queen Parade. There are pictures of birthday parties with fashions changing each successive year. One picture in particular, when I and my generation were six, shows all the smiling mouths with at least one gap from a lost tooth; and all the girls with frizzy hair, the latest juvenile fashion achieved by means of pipe cleaners wound in the hair at night.

We expressed our love in the family very freely and I wonder if today's parents would behave in quite the same unreserved way, encumbered as they are with concerns about accusations of child abuse. My father sometimes caressed me in ways that today might be construed as over-intimate. To my mind these exchanges were of the utmost importance to my development, to my ability to relate to men in the future, for there was nothing to stop me saying, 'Hey, Dad, stop it,' and maybe retaliating with some innocent piece of play-aggression. One game he and I played which reduced everybody watching to helpless laughter was a form of parade-ground marching and square-bashing routine with my feet perched on his and my arms around his waist. We would march rhythmically to and fro to a background 'Left, right, left, right,' and occasional barked orders such as, 'Mark time!', 'About turn!' and so on. Attitudes to children have changed in other ways also, for there was still something of the Victorian formula that children should be seen and not heard, especially in company, and corporal punishment in schools of course was widely accepted. Looking back, children were not as cherished, as protected as now; they were thought to be pretty tough on the whole and able to cope with being tossed into life at the deep end.

I had two episodes of illness at this time which left vivid recollections. The first at the age of six was scarlet fever, still considered a dread disease from the way in which they treated me. I was whisked off by ambulance to hospital and from the time I left home and for the ensuing period of infectiousness -three weeks by their reckoning – I was segregated from my family. They visited of course and left messages and gifts but I was only allowed to see them once at a distance and wave from a window. I behaved in a stoical manner throughout but endured an inner despair which was probably not apparent to anyone. A child who is ill is expected to be dull and listless, and I was. The first night a bright and pretty nurse came to give me a pill which I found some difficulty in swallowing. Her line of jolly chat soon deteriorated into hectoring: 'If you don't take this you won't get home to Mummy and Daddy.' Then she concealed the pill in a spoon of jam but I was not fooled. The jam went down but the pill was delicately removed from my mouth. Nurse was furious and my misery became extreme. Heaven knows how we resolved this impasse but I suppose we did. As I improved I was allowed to get up and do things but I had no enthusiasm and got through things in a ritualistic way. I remember being told of the birth of Princess Anne (in 1950) during my hospital stay.

It came to an end, but then I developed a severe middle-ear infection with a perforated eardrum. Mum relates how the specialist was incredibly harsh to her and ranted about how my ears would be permanently damaged and I'd be stone deaf in a year or two – none of which proved to be accurate, fortunately. Two years later I had my tonsils out. Apart from the sore throat this was quite pleasant. I was put in an adult ward next to a young WRAF officer, who was very friendly and companionable, talking to me like a grown-up and smoothing out any difficulties or worries: like waking up on a blood-soaked pillow. How odd that I should remember her so vividly from such a brief encounter so long ago. Her kindness reverberates down the years and I hope she has had a good life. I think back now to my experience on the operating table and am aghast at the primitive conditions and thankful I survived them. The anaesthetic consisted of a white mask placed over my face which had little effect and I resolutely kept my eyes open lest they should think I was asleep prematurely. After a time someone grumblingly sprayed more liquid ether on the mask and irresistible languor supervened.

Like most children I enjoyed some aspects of being ill, usually after the malaise and uncomfortable bits had resolved themselves but while still receiving the extra cherishing and indulgence. Rules otherwise strictly enforced were relaxed and household activities revolved round one's own comfort and whim. After the scarlet fever episode I was given my first teddy bear and I was presented with the choice between a large pink and brown cuddly toy and a small exquisitely pretty green and pink bear. It was an agonising choice but I plumped for the big cuddly one. Maybe this suggests that tactile sensations appealed more than visual ones!

I began to have night terrors about this time which were strange and bizarre experiences. From time to time I have tried to describe them but no one else had ever had anything similar – until later in life I became aware that my younger son Peter was going through the same torment. I wondered if I was going mad and they were so unearthly that I didn't even try to tell Mum, like many things from this time on. They occurred in the prodrome of an illness and were probably associated with fever. It was as if my mind had been taken over by an external agent who repeated my thoughts mockingly in my head, accompanied by a kind of imperative rhythmic sound. I eventually developed the knack of sitting up and forcing myself to full wakefulness to dispel the sensation.

I was also visited by wonderful dreams about flying which I later learned are said to be an indication of sexual desire. Whether or not this is true, the dreams were deliciously exciting, though having to stay airborne required much concentration. Can you concentrate in a dream? I'm regretful that I no longer have these dreams. Vague erotic fantasies, undirected to any particular person, and centred on excretory function formed another intensely private experience.

In my progress through primary school I came across a teacher, Miss Day, with whom I developed a pleasant rapport. My friends, two Maureens and another Margaret, and I would stay after school to talk and sometimes we would be taken swimming. We were teacher's pets I suppose. Blonde, rosy-cheeked Maureen was my special chum and it was in her house that I saw my first piano. Maureen, lucky girl, was taking lessons and was supposed to practise for an hour every day, a source of conflict between her and her mother. I could not understand how she could be so blasé about being allowed to touch such a beautiful object. When I asked Mum if I could learn to play there was little enthusiasm and much lecturing about expense. I kept the pressure up although it would be another three or four years before I had my way. Meanwhile, whenever I was allowed near an instrument I would run my fingers up and down the keyboard to the discomfort of those within earshot.

Maureen and I acquired some glove puppets and entertained our close friends with little plays in the Punch-and-Judy style. Miss Day encouraged us to be a little more ambitious and to put on a play for the whole class, which we did. To my amazement we had the class roaring with appreciative laughter and, even more surprising, the noise attracted a wider audience from the next-door class, who crowded to the glass partition to enjoy the performance. There was a pleasurable power in all this.

Needlework loomed large in our curriculum and the first item everyone had to make was a dirndl skirt in check gingham. I loved needlework and, finishing mine in advance, looked round for something else to fill in the long hours devoted to sewing. Miss Day, being creative, helped me to piece together a red checked gingham rabbit, which was quite avant-garde in those days. Unbeknown to me she then entered it in a local art and craft show. The first thing I knew of this was receiving first prize in the children's class. The year was 1953, coronation year, and the award was a set of new-minted coins with the Queen's head on them, which I cherished for years before eventually spending them during some youthful financial crisis.

One day a stray cat arrived at school and adopted our class. The headmaster was angry and decreed that it had to be ejected but Miss Day was on our side and we sneaked the animal in again. He had an unusual dove-grey coat and we called him Charlie. A very self-assured cat, he picked his way around members of the class, staying for a minute or so, then moving on. To my utmost delight, when he got to my desk he gave a cursory greeting, then curled up proprietorially on my lap. At breaktime Miss Day said I must not move but have my milk and biscuits brought to the desk. Charlie only stirred enough to take a chunk out of the biscuit, then returned to sleep. And at the end of the day I carried him home, wondering what reception we'd get.

I was allowed to keep him.

A childhood full of varied interests and especially surrounded by caring well-intentioned adults conveys in retrospect a wonderful aura of protection. Maybe one spends one's adult life seeking that kind of security again. To be sure it is elusive. In Warton the feeling was reinforced to us camp-dwellers by the visible evidence of guards and pass systems at the entry gates, while we children were simply recognised and allowed to come and go. One unpleasant episode challenged the system and involved one of these self-same guards. Jenny told me furtively one day that this man would secrete himself in some cranny opposite the house and reveal his willie to her; she persuaded me to hang around and witness this spectacle. She was urgent in telling me to keep the secret, but she might as well have ordered the rain to stop falling. Of course I told Mum, and the full force of the law ground into action. Jenny and I were interviewed by policewomen, sensitively on the whole, and there followed a court case in which my parents acted as witnesses while Jenny and I sat in a dreary back room for endless hours. Probably the guard was punished, poor fellow, I have no doubt inappropriately. Jenny was furious with me and accused me of sending him to prison.

Fishing at such a distance of time in the lucky dip of memory can produce surprises. My delight in the countryside was not much indulged in this four-year period, though I do remember carpets of bluebells in woods and the thrill of the Ribble estuary viewed from a high point where we took part in some Brownie activity. The flat, soggy, brown-green terrain with its evil reputation for quicksands, gradually blending into the river which in turn merged into sea and sky, was a source of marvelling among ourselves.

Those years, still influenced by the austerity of the war, were not tainted by any expectation of unlimited acquisition and pleasures were remarkably simple. Mum once brought us each a purple colouring pencil – an unusual item then – and we were thrilled. Marbles were popular playthings which could be bought, but the best ones were acquired by bartering, and to my mind they were far too precious actually to play games with; I liked to admire the swirled and tortuous patterns of colour in the glass. One highly prized specimen had wriggles of bright gold in it, and I refused many advantageous offers for it. One annoying austerity was the rationing of sweets which persisted. For some reason the flat, square boiled sweets known as Spangles were exempt so we got very bored with these and although we did not realise it they paved the way for the extensive dental repair work which many of my generation had to suffer.

When I was nine or ten I discovered poetry, in the shape of R.L. Stevenson's *A Child's Garden of Verses*. I believe that the introduction to this lovely book came from singing some of the poems that are set to music such as 'The Cow' and 'Happy Thought'. It may be that these were presented by the excellent *Singing Together* programme broadcast on radio for schools and which were an introduction to traditional and folk songs, sea-shanties and carols. Stevenson's book was a joy and having learned some of the poems by heart I now find they still spring readily to mind, whereas things learned at a later date do not remain so ingrained. But besides being an introduction to poetry the verses did wonderful things in inspiring imagination. Though there is ample evidence there of Stevenson's privileged nineteenth-century upbringing (in the shape of references to nurse, cook, coach and horses, auntie's draped skirts) yet there is so much material, especially in the realms of the mind, that is shared by children of all ages and eras. 'My Bed is a Boat' embarked me on a fantasy of sailing away in my own craft every night. 'The Land of Counterpane' just sounds magic, and would be loved by any child confined by illness to bed and playing in solitude for many hours. 'North-West Passage' was another favourite for the exciting fearfulness of going from safety through peril to safety again. I rediscovered this book by chance association recently and rushed out to buy a copy, only to be enchanted all over again though with a number of new impressions as befits the passage of time. I smile at the innocent political incorrectness of 'Foreign Children':

> You have curious things to eat,
> I am fed on proper meat;
> You must dwell beyond the foam,
> But I am safe and live at home.

I am aware that in the content childhood portrayed, Nanny (or Nurse) looms much more important than Mamma, which would concern me if I were she. I find particularly entrancing those poems where the adult and child experience merge, as in 'Travel'.

In 1953 my father finally finished his RAF posting, and stressful were the discussions before it was decided that our new home would be in Somerset. My father planned to get a job in aero-engineering but meantime he and my mother bought a village shop in Chelynch on top of the Mendip Hills. At last we were going to become country children.

4

Cultural Conflicts

The preparations for the move to Somerset were exciting, as even we children were made to feel our increased consequence amongst our friends and teachers, because we were going away for ever. People were sad and showered us with gifts and messages. I felt no regret until late in the day of our travel, when with the dusk falling I became aware that I was not going back to all that was loved and familiar. Jenny and I having played, no doubt noisily and sometimes irritatingly, in the back of the car through the long drive, fell silent.

We had to stay a few weeks in lodgings in a farmhouse in a country lane with a childless couple called Mr and Mrs Kingston until our own house was available. Mrs Kingston later told us that the first thing she heard as we emerged from the car was Mum saying, 'Control yourself, Jennifer!' We were probably getting fractious. They made us welcome and comfortable in an unassuming way, showing us to the very large sitting room we were to use. There were two surprises, the first being the presence of a piano; Dad saw my saucer-sized eyes fixed on it and gently suggested I might not be allowed to play it. Indeed I noticed with resignation that it was locked. We were also amazed to find there was no electricity, but after dusk Mrs Kingston brought in oil-lamps, and patience would be required at a critical moment in the twilight when you could no longer pursue your playing or reading until the lamps arrived. But we loved the smell and the mysterious atmosphere created by the dark shadows which lurked at the room's edge and on the staircase. There were sympathetic echoes here from Stevenson's poems, especially 'The Lamplighter', and again 'North-West Passage':

> The shadow of the balusters, the shadow of the lamp,
> The shadow of the child that goes to bed –
> All the wicked shadows coming, tramp, tramp, tramp,
> With the black night overhead.

We also had to become accustomed to an outside toilet, but we did not immediately appreciate our luck in having a flush toilet. Most cottages in that part of the country were not connected to the main drainage system, and toilets had to be emptied manually into cesspits.

Jenny and I explored as soon as we could and I am ashamed to say did not immediately fall in love with our rural surroundings. The countryside is not at its visual best in November and there was an unpleasant smell of rotting cabbage from nearby fields. We were unused to wide open spaces and were perplexed at the stillness and lack of bustle. There were interesting new phenomena though, including a contraption in the garden for making cider. Mr Kingston said it was an adult-only drink but allowed us to taste its musty pungency all the same. He had a ponderous country drawl, and took twice as long to think about what he was going to say as to say it. He kept a cow, which of course had to be milked. The first time we went to watch this process the animal was being difficult, fidgeting and kicking the bucket. It took us a little time to realise that Mr Kingston was getting very red-faced and muttering incoherent suspicious-sounding words. We tactfully removed ourselves.

One delightful day when the rest of the family were out, leaving me in the house alone with Mrs Kingston, I asked shyly about the piano. She opened it up, sat down and played in a rough and ready manner. She had a collection of songs for family entertaining such as, 'Come into the Garden, Maud'. Then, even more delightful, she taught me to play with one hand, 'God save the Queen'. It was like learning to read all over again and I thought I was already destined to become a concert pianist. When the family came in Jenny was open-mouthed with admiration at my skill.

Mr Kingston was a bell-ringer at the church in Doulting which, we were told, had a very fine peal of bells as did many little churches in the south of England. He took us into the belfry to see the bells and we wondered at the size and might of them. He explained how they had to be 'rung up' before you could 'ring the changes': that is, the bells had to begin with the mouths and clappers facing upward. He explained in detail all about the intricacies of bell-ringing and though I didn't understand very much at all it sounded magical, especially when expounded in his West Country drawl. He also kept a set of hand-bells which belonged to the church. They covered just over a tonic scale and with five people holding one bell in each hand could encompass most simple songs and carols. Later, evenings spent visiting this household would usually involve getting out the bells and playing a few songs. The technique was simple enough and I adored this music-making. One Christmas, ladies of the village strolled from house to house playing carols on the bells. I was only allowed to collect money and was thoroughly disgusted as I was much better and more reliable than some of the ringers; but I was glad to be associated with the group which the villagers loved to hear. I sublimated by keeping an eye on the most forgetful of the ladies, who was the despair of the team, often quite oblivious that she'd missed her turn. It came to me with sudden insight that older people were not necessarily wiser or better or more imbued with desirable virtues than children, which my upbringing had, directly or indirectly, taught me to believe.

The next hurdle was school. Jenny went to the secondary modern in Shepton Mallet, having failed her eleven-plus when we were still in Lancashire. I was destined for Doulting village school, which was much smaller than the one at Warton, and on the whole I found I was well ahead of my schoolfellows. I made friends easily enough, in particular with another Margaret who shared my interest in nature. I was accustomed to rough-and-tumble but there was a small group of boys whose badness seemed a shade more sinister than any previous experience. It's difficult to define how I knew that: perhaps an aggressive attitude to the tiny children, a particular defiance of the teacher, a special surliness with authority. Near the school was an ancient well with reputed healing properties. We were not restricted to the playground at playtime but could visit this magic place where cold, clear, bubbling water emerged from the base of an ancient wall surrounding the old vicarage. It's probably pure chance that Doulting never became a famous spa like Bath. The school was visited by the vicar, Mr Tunstall, now and then, to give us a lesson on Scripture and matters religious and I immediately felt an affinity for him. Fairly undistinguished in manners, for he was shy and diffident, he had a powerful intellect and genuine enthusiasm for his calling, and was one of the few people I have known who lived according to his high principles. He seemed to have a genuine love and compassion for fellow men, an extraordinarily wicked sense of humour which would encompass their foibles while he respected their virtues, and absolutely no pretensions. He claimed me as an ally because he observed that I, like him, was left-handed: a sinister person. He became a valued friend both to the family and to myself, though that friendship was to have a rather bumpy start.

We moved into our house in Chelynch, of which the village shop was an integral part. Dad rapidly discovered that he was not well adapted to the required tactful handling of customers and Mum gradually took over the day-to-day running of the business. It was a considerable change of lifestyle for her, one with which she was not at all happy, though like many another mother she put up with it all for the sake of her children. We were regarded by the local people as interlopers who were not even country-bred and had no idea of country customs. I don't suppose they were ill-intentioned but they were suspicious of change and indulged in heavy-handed humour which could deteriorate into tormenting. One day a funeral procession was slowly passing through the village just at opening time. Mum had no idea of how much offence she caused by raising the shop blinds just as the cortège was passing, and only became aware of a general increase in the hostility and cold-shouldering. One Sunday when Jenny and I were playing in the woods with a friend we observed a group of boys stalking us; I recognised the delinquents from school with their leader Patrick. After preliminary taunts and jeers they became bold, trying to intimidate us with threats, and order us out of their way. Patrick threw a stone which hit Jenny, not badly, but she screamed hysterically and behaved as if mortally wounded. The boys took fright and ran off, shouting that I would pay for this on Monday.

I was miserable with foreboding and it required no great sensitivity on my parents' part to gauge there was trouble and to winkle out of me at least some account of what had happened. Dad, who had started working as an aero-engineer in Bristol, decided he would take time off work to come to school with me and sort things out. Other school-related miseries were unearthed at the same time, and it was clear that neither of us was ideally placed.

Dad walked with me to school next morning, working himself into the correct degree of sternness by being gruff and monosyllabic. On arrival he sent me inside and waited near the gate. I did not need to imagine what was happening, for I could hear his stentorian parade-ground voice bouncing off the walls, reducing Patrick to little shreds. Shortly afterwards our teacher, Mrs Doble, stared in amazement as Patrick crept, a quivering wreck with tear-stained face, into class. His mates muttered words of solidarity: 'What did old Whitmore say to you, Pat?' But I stood tall. I felt as if a ring of security had been created around me and knew that from then on I would not need to worry about being bullied. The confidence was liberating and my gratitude to my father was boundless. There is a feeling with me that that kind of support of child by parent, involving quelling others with a degree of aggression, has positive effects that go far beyond the immediate event.

After this little trouble my parents had to make some decision about our education. They hoped I would pass the eleven-plus the following year and get a grammar-school place; but realised that our immediate problems required more urgent solutions. And the answer came in the shape of a Roman Catholic convent in Shepton Mallet, whose fees were very low as nearly all the teachers were nuns.

When you rang at the imposing front door of this establishment, a sliding hatch clicked briskly open to reveal a stern-faced nun inspecting you – for horns and a tail? I wondered. Inside was another world: the sense of calm orderliness was awesome. Sanctity and holiness hung with the curtains. The school surrounded a beautiful garden and a field with cows which doubled up as a hockey pitch. The teaching nuns were humane, cheerful and almost wordly. They wore full-length, heavy, dark-blue gowns which suppressed all bodily curves, with white wimples and black veils; most impractical garments. A heavy-duty rosary hung from the waist. Yet it was no uncommon sight to see a nun running like a hare across the grounds with clanking key-chain and rosary, and they would join in games like rounders and hockey with keen enthusiasm or demonstrate country-dance steps with nimbly flying fleet. My teacher, Sister Marie Christine, had a Northumbrian accent, glasses, a plain round face and a roguish grin. She was by far the best teacher I had come across to date. Mrs Doble at Doulting had bitterly reproached me for being taken away from her, with dire warnings that I had forfeited any chance of the eleven-plus exam – that dreadful hurdle that obsessed everyone at the time. But I was behind Sister Christine's class in some things, notably French and history. She was appalled by my handwriting and set about training me to write a round legible hand, which I can do to this day if I try. We had access to as many books as we could read and there was stimulating debate about all varieties of topics. About half the class was Protestant but we were all expected to know the catechism – or at least encouraged to learn it.

Mr Tunstall was deeply shocked to learn from Mrs Doble that Jenny and I had been taken away from respectable Church of England schools and installed in a Catholic one. He arrived on our doorstep one evening after Jenny and I had gone to bed, to take Mum to task over this. Mum was defiant – and provoking.

'Their whole education will be slanted by the Roman religion.'

'And isn't it biased in Church of England schools?'

'Roman Catholicism is a very seductive and attractive religion. These young girls will be mesmerised by its glamour!'

Mum grew impatient. 'I think you're overreacting. Look, this is Margaret's school bag; see how harmless all this stuff is.'

She fished in my bag and drew out the catechism, which fell open at the day's appointed lesson. Mr Tunstall snatched it from her and read:

Q How are we in danger of losing our faith?
A We are in danger of losing our faith by reading bad books, going to non-Catholic schools, attending non-Catholic services.

He almost screamed in rage. 'Just see what you're exposing them to. What would you do if they became Catholic?'

Mum retorted, 'I'd turn Catholic too. At least that would keep the family together!'

At this, Mr Tunstall stalked out of the house and did not speak to any of us again for about a year.

He was absolutely right about the fascination and sensuous appeal of the trappings of Catholicism. The chapel at the convent was open to all of us at any time except when the sisters had services or singing practice. The drama of the mystical rituals with holy water and genuflections was not lost on my susceptible mind, nor the ornate decorations and statuary. Sister Christine worked away at our consciences. The Protestant children were never given the big sell on religion, but we were quietly and kindly made to feel slightly outside the group of chosen ones. The emphasis on regularly attending church services worked its way into my sense of duty. Why didn't we go to church? We used to go in Warton, though not often. I started to work on Mum with this question. Sunday after Sunday went by and I began to feel wicked because I didn't have the strength to say, 'Okay, I'll just go on my own.' But eventually I prevailed and we attended evensong at Doulting church. Mr Tunstall did not disguise his amazement. The Church of St Aldhelm was ancient, built of Bath stone and weathered to a dark grey, shaped in the form of a cross with a steeple and the fine peal of bells so dear to the heart of our friend Mr Kingston. One very fine and unusual feature was a brilliant copper-green malachite cross over the altar. We became regular churchgoers (Jenny, Mum and I, that is), joining the tiny band of the faithful who turned out to sit in the cold and quaver tunelessly through the hymns; but listening to the sermons was worth while, and it was here that I got my first lessons in social politics. The vicar regularly upset everyone with his uncompromising left-wing views.

I discovered that piano lessons were available at the convent and nagged Mum until she at length crossly presented the arguments against the proposal rather than just saying no. We could not afford a piano at home and had nowhere to install it. But a friend who lived near the school offered to let me practise there, and in holidays there was always the village pub. So at the age of ten I achieved one long-thwarted ambition and began learning to play.

I made friends with Susan – or Sue – who opened up a whole new way of thinking, and was my friend throughout the rest of my schooldays. She was a bit of a misfit in some ways, but one of the most intelligent people I've ever met. She read better and faster than me, she knew about theatre and drama, she had been playing the piano for several years, she was good with words and altogether clever. Sister Christine spoke to her almost as if she were an equal, not a pupil, and listened attentively to her opinions. Sister's great strength was that she would listen to us, which made her lessons a dialogue rather than a one-way flow of didactics, and consequently enriched them for her as well as for us, I think. This ability to receive may be better developed in someone leading a quiet contemplative life. Certainly the opposite is true.

I was surprised to find that in our playground games some of the singing rhymes and chants were quite similar to those we knew in Lancashire.

> Nebuchadnezzar the King of the Jews,
> Bought his wife a pair of shoes.
> When the shoes began to leak,
> Nebuchadnezzar began to speak.
> When the speaking had to stop,
> Nebuchadnezzar bought a shop.
> When the shop began to sell,

Nebuchadnezzar bought a bell.
When the bell began to ring,
Nebuchadnezzar began to sing
Doh, ray, me, fah, soh, lah, te, doh.
How dare you tread on my big toe!

I'm probably misremembering, but you get an idea of the rhythmic nonsense that was chanted as you played with two balls against a wall, with variations like throwing under a leg or behind your back. There were other chants for skipping, and one that was used in the game of blindfold with a circle of dancers.

The wind, the wind, the wind blows high
The rain comes scattering down the sky.
She is handsome, she is pretty,
She is the girl of the windy city.
She goes a-courting, one two, three,
Please can you tell me who she be!

I blossomed in this protected yet motivating atmosphere. I did some artwork that was considered good enough for exhibition, became our class representative, won the junior prize for a written account of the Queen's Commonwealth tour, and sailed with a high mark through the eleven-plus exam. I think Mum dreaded another change since Jenny and I were so settled and happy. But I had won a scholarship and lots of opportunities so, while Jenny stayed at the convent, Sue and I would travel together to Sunny Hill School, Bruton, starting September 1955.

5

The Gleam

I forever associate the colour green with Sunny Hill, for not only was it situated in the lushest of green, rolling West Country hills but our uniform was dark, practical and unglamorous bottle green: skirts, ties, jumpers, blazers, berets and macs were all in the same drab colour with biscuit-coloured blouses and socks. And I've forgotten a most important item: bottle-green knickers, which were not optional as we had to wear them with aertex shirts for gym.

Pupils came by two routes: half like myself through a scholarship, and we were mainly day pupils; the other half who were fee-paying were mainly boarders. There was something of a class distinction here which may have been partly responsible for the almost total failure of the two groups to mix. At this stage, once the boarders had got over their home-sickness they became obsessed by food, and when they realised my mother owned a shop I was besieged by requests for purchase of sweets and cakes. A friend, Gwenda, who knew the ropes better than me, warned me that this would be viewed as a heinous offence if discovered, so I promptly returned the money and withdrew from the business deal. This did not raise me in the collective boarding opinion and one girl, Virginia, in particular viewed me with undisguised contempt thereafter.

It was a taxing journey to school. I left home at 7.30 a.m., had a three-quarter-mile walk, then a short bus journey to Shepton Mallet where I caught a train to Bruton. This stopped at Evercreech where Sue boarded. The railway was part of the West Country line to Bournemouth and the trains were all steam-powered, which meant of course that they were extremely filthy, but romantic and historic. We arrived at school about 8.30 a.m. In reverse, the home train left at 4.30 p.m. with a very tight connection for the bus, which was missed not infrequently, then the walk. If I missed the bus I had to walk an extra two or three miles uphill.

The train journey was a lot of fun and we used the time to make strong bonds of friendship, to play games and even sometimes to get on with our prep. Certain toys such as yo-yos and fads such as knitting came in and out of fashion, but often we preferred more boisterous games such as mime and charades, or word games. Mum worried about my health and gave me a small bottle of Ribena to drink on the journey home. This was shared with all the other people in the carriage. Mum told me later that I was very prone to cough as a young girl and she had a deep unspoken anxiety about tuberculosis, which had been an untreatable scourge when she was nursing. I tested positive for tuberculin in my late teens, so she may have been right; but I must have recovered spontaneously.

We compared our prep on the morning journey, and no one had any compunction about cribbing. The teachers must have been resigned to the uniformity of work coming from the various train-travelling pupils. When exams approached the collective mood would swing from depression to hysteria, but humour and camaraderie would keep us sane.

We were not the only school to use the train: this facility was shared by grammar-school boys going to the unfortunately named Sexey's School. We were expressly forbidden to have anything to do with them, neither to speak to them nor share carriages with them. Miraculously we obeyed. The boys and girls just ignored each other. I'm not sure if our obedience verged on the pathological; I'm sure it wouldn't happen nowadays.

In wet, cold weather I was glad enough to get home. Our little cottage was very cosy, built of Bath stone with walls three feet thick, not a plane wall or right angle in the place, and very good at retaining warmth. There was an open fire with adjoining oven to toast my feet over as I dried out. But unfortunately this was the best way to get chilblains on toes and heels – inflammation resulting from cold injury which was both painful and intensely itchy. Almost no one suffers from these nowadays, with centrally heated houses. Mum always made a wholesome meal with dishes such as rabbit stew and dumplings, toad-in-the-hole, Lancashire hotpot, bubble and squeak, bread-and-butter pudding.

Then at six o'clock the homework – or prep – had to be tackled: one and a half hours (three subjects) on Mondays, Wednesdays, Fridays, and one hour (two subjects) on Tuesdays and Thursdays. But teachers were greedy and always seemed to think we had unlimited time, so often the work would take up most of the evening. Jenny and our red-haired friend, Sue (not the school friend), waited impatiently or left me to my own fate while they went off to the woods to play.

A year or two later we mounted a rebellion about the amount of prep and persuaded the teachers to allow us for a night or two to adhere strictly to the allotted time. They were appalled at how little we got done, called off the work-to-rule and went back to the old ways.

The school day started at 8.45 a.m. in our classrooms with the form mistress taking the register and quelling the general hubbub. At five to nine a holy hush was supposed to descend upon us all, so that we could get in the mood for praying. To this end a bell was rung; a nominated pupil, the school bell-ringer, would run through the corridors with her raucous, clanging instrument. The five to nine bell was an awesome thing and everyone obeyed it – if they knew it had been rung, because a terrible fate awaited those who disobeyed. No one did, except by accident.

We filed in silence into the hall where we sat by class cross-legged on the floor, the youngest folk at the front. The staff sat along the side of the hall on chairs and mostly kept silence too; we felt aggrieved if they indulged in chat. One of the senior girls came in to give out notices. We didn't have a single head girl but a triumvirate called the Big Three. I think this system was astonishing in its appreciation of democratic principles; an oasis of sense in an otherwise not very insightful system. After this task was completed any sinners would hold their breath with anxiety lest the question was posed, 'Has anyone been talking since the five to nine bell?' There was a maxim in the unwritten schoolgirl code that said you had to own up; offenders would stand up and had to remain standing until prayers began, looking and feeling dreadfully conspicuous. I only had to do this once, and this was some years later when I had established a reputation for being on the side of the angels. The prefect fixed me with an austere look and snapped, 'Well, have you any excuse?' My class teacher intervened and said, 'Yes, she was talking business with me. Sit down, Margaret!' I felt almost bereft of my moment of martyrdom.

While we waited for the headmistress, Miss Chappell, to appear, one of the music teachers played the piano. Each teacher had his or her own repertoire. Mr Leslic, whom we swooned over since he was the only presentable man within our daily encounters, played Schubert's

Impromptus and Rosamunde music, Schumann's Traumerei amongst others. As Miss Chappell stalked on to the stage we scrambled stiffly to our feet. We sang a hymn, had a reading, a few exhortations, and were then allowed to disperse. Usually the first lesson which was supposed to start at 9.20 didn't kick off until 9.35 or later, to the teachers' collective despair. But no one dared to take issue with Miss Chappell over this.

She was a highly formidable lady, very short so that most of us looked down to her, very round indeed with long grey hair which was worked into some complex plaited edifice on the back of her head. She had quite a pleasant, gentle face, a soft voice with beautiful enunciation – and a soul of steel. Everyone was in awe of her. She knew all there was to know about William Wordsworth and Church of England Christianity and not much about anything else. She knew little and cared less about sciences. She was totally out of touch with the modern world and its morals. How she managed to carry herself with such a queenly air I could never understand, as she was spherical: no bust, no waist, no hips, no neck either. Our library reflected her interest: whole bays with shelves of Wordsworth, other poets, approved literature; and only half a shelf of science books, all too archaic to be of any educational value and chosen mainly for historic merit. It was a trial of will and stamina as well as ingenuity to get qualifications to launch yourself into university to read a scientific subject. The teaching also in this area was uninspired, except for biology which was seen to be an acceptably feminine subject. Probably she failed to attract anyone of any dynamism to such a backwater.

The forces of competitiveness in education were allowed full play in those days and no one thought of streaming as unacceptable. For some reason, which I never understood, the first year in secondary school was Form III and I was in IIIA. There was an occasional switch of one or two girls at the interface of A and B but in general the streams stayed much the same for the next four years. This was undoubtedly unjust to some. One girl, Geraldine, who became one of the cleverest in the senior school, was not allowed out of the B stream till the lower fifth. She and her mother were told each year, 'Geraldine is not suited to an academic education.'

Our class teacher was young, pretty, newly married and otherwise quite unmemorable. She taught us French and after a few weeks we were expected to enact scenes in couples in front of the class to get us used to conversation. Gwenda, who was giggly and naïve, decided we would portray a honeymoon. Something in me felt uneasily that this might not be in the best taste but Gwenda's enthusiasm overrode my objections. Our minimal vocabulary did not rise to much more than the practicalities of a train journey, admiring yellow flowers from the window, observing that the sun was shining and that it wasn't raining. Possibly Gwenda had not yet learned the facts of life because she insisted on carrying the story through till bedtime – at which point our teacher intervened sharply with, 'Well, yes, I think we've had enough of that, don't you?' thus confirming my reservations. Still, I expect it gave her something to talk and laugh about in the staff room.

The staff room was a sanctuary to which no girl was ever allowed admittance. We got a glimpse of our teachers with their hair down if we had occasion to knock on the door on some errand. The air was thick with cigarette smoke, you got an impression of having just interrupted a highly unsuitable conversation or some frivolous activity, such as vaulting over the desks, and you were always made to feel an unwelcome intruder.

I knew the basic facts of life by this time, having bought myself an illustrated book on the human body. I wasn't anticipating any particular revelations, being familiar with Mum's nursing books, but there was an outline of male and female genital tracts and a brief description of the mechanics of sexual intercourse. We were having an informal teatime at home when I came upon this monumentally important piece of information. I don't think anyone else noticed my heightened tension as I digested the details. I had by now discovered that many things were best coped with by storing them in secret deep inside, a source of concern to Mum who felt I bottled things up and worried about them instead of letting her reassure and smooth my way. She probably would have taken a sly look at the book, I'm sure, to discover what I now knew. I don't recall ever discussing this, though she explained to me about my menstrual periods before I began secondary school. I don't think she found it especially easy to talk of intimate matters to me, and I certainly veered off the topic as soon as possible. Probably this reflected my own natural reserve rather than any short-coming in our mutual communication.

We were the recipients of the expected wide syllabus of school subjects accepted at the time. Of politics and current affairs we had not a single lesson though I have a vague recollection that Hansard was available in some side room off the library. But without any teaching input or exposure, no one's curiosity was aroused. Sports were vigorously encouraged and heroines were made of those girls who excelled. We played hockey and netball in winter, tennis and athletics in summer, gym throughout the year; occasionally running. Hockey was a nightmare. Though our grey shorts were ladylike and decorous, there was always a bare patch of knee and lower thigh exposed between these and the fawn socks, which would turn through a spectrum of blue, purple and livid magenta as we hopped around in the November chill. Running I quite enjoyed. We would be sent on a round tour of the country lanes and I found a satisfying capacity for endurance which enabled me to keep jogging up the frequent inclines and to be first back to the dubious comfort of the changing room. Showers were not available and the room – more like a cupboard – was cramped and smelly.

I was good at all academic subjects, especially English, and to my satisfaction I readily found myself at or near the top of the class in this and other subjects. Sue and I continued our friendly rivalry. I had been inspired by her fondness for theatre and acting and we naturally teamed up in English and activity classes to write and present small scenes. One such piece was called 'Everest Corn'. Our main character, a field mouse, set out to climb the largest ear of corn in the field, encountering a different adventure on each bract or segment of the plant. We loved nonsense poems, especially those of Edward Lear and Lewis Carroll, which we would dramatise. Naturally enough we encountered *Alice in Wonderland* which inspired all sorts of activities. We portrayed a scene from *Through the Looking-Glass* in which Tweedledum and Tweedledee offer to entertain Alice. Everything we said came out in chorus until we got furious with each other. The dialogue went like this:

'I'm going to—' (Stop and glare at each other)
'I'm going to sing—' (Stop and glare again)
(Gabbling) 'I'm going to sing you a song.'
(Furious with each other) 'No you're not, I am!'

The timing had to be immaculate. Unfortunately, I got carried away and gave Sue a resounding slap on the cheek. She turned beetroot and glared, and I ruined the scene by collapsing in giggles.

At some point in recent years I acquired a French copy of *Alice* and was amused to be reminded how much of it is a play on words, which renders the attempt to read it in French rather hollow – like missing the point of a joke and having to have it explained in the copious notes at the back.

At the end of term each girl had her marks in every subject averaged and assigned an overall mark. All these were read out in a mind-bendingly tedious gathering of the whole school called Long Prayers. No doubt this was supposed to spur us on to greater efforts. In my first term I had a B+ which was good enough; thereafter I had A− and never again dropped below that.

I had continued piano lessons and practised at lunchtime in one of the many available music rooms. During the holidays I slipped across the road to the village pub where I had the piano in the best room to myself. It was fairly typical of pub pianos but the landlady was kindness itself and always made sure it was tuned. I would play for hours but wasn't very systematic about scales and arpeggios, still less about sight-reading. My playing could be heard around the village and Mum would get sardonic comments from shoppers, such as, 'Bach for breakfast today!'

After a term I was transferred to one of the senior piano teachers, Miss Thorns, who had a reputation as a tyrant. At my first lesson I was scared of her; I had come straight from a craft lesson where we messed around with clay. Even after washing, the clay stuck in your nails and gave the hands an odd slippery texture, so it wasn't easy to play your best. For the first few lessons she was non-committal. Then one day I made too many stumbles for her exacting ear. She lost her temper and raged at me for wasting her time and mine; I was a 'naughty, lazy girl'. I was astounded, never having had such accusations thrown at me before, feeling physically the effects of fear constrict my throat, my stomach and elsewhere. Though afterwards we came to a better under-standing I do deplore this type of reaction. I was learning to play because I really wanted to, and this teacher nearly put me off altogether as she certainly put off others. She gave Sue a hard time also but Sue was deemed good enough to take her grade I piano exam around this time – much to my envy. I survived the temporarily stormy relationship, though for a while deeply dreaded the weekly lesson. It was two years before I actually began to get a little praise and encouragement.

We were now approaching the first Speech Day, when the whole school would be put on display. Miss Chappell liked to have her hair corrugated for the occasion. Everyone had to learn and be coached in the school song, 'The Gleam', which represented inspiration and which we were supposed to pursue relentlessly. The bouncing music was wholly inappropriate but Mr Leslie wrote a more ethereal version which must have caused him a good deal of heartache when he heard our rendering of it. My father, who was as much in awe of Miss Chappell as anyone else when he met her face to face, had nevertheless a healthy disrespect for her unworldly pietism, and amused himself with irreverent versions of the song. Only parents of girls being presented with awards actually sat in the hall, the rest being farmed out to other rooms and listening to the events by relay. It must have been excruciatingly boring, but after the first year I managed to have an award each year, which made Speech Day more tolerable for my long-suffering parents.

6

Fold, Fallow and Plough

Out of school, our lives were very free and we roamed the countryside for miles around without causing any anxiety for our safety. We had bicycles and no one dreamed of any danger from traffic. The country-side was pockmarked with quarries so there must have been lorries, but modest-sized and untroubled with urban time pressures. I loved to climb trees and get into inaccessible places and actually shed tears at the thought that one day I would no longer want to do this. One evening, red-haired Sue and I were climbing trees as dusk fell. We should have been heading home but Sue got stuck. Try as I might, I could not persuade or help her to extricate herself. Eventually I ran off to get some help, only to find two anxious mothers who rasped out in the roughness of relief after worry, 'Where the devil have you been?' Sue's mother dithered and debated, and wandered off to find a ladder. Mum looked at me, horrified. It was quite dark by now. 'Show me!' she said. We ran back into the gloomy woods, which I knew intimately. Mum had probably not climbed a tree since her childhood, if at all, but she shinned up that tree and organised Sue down it as if she were a trained firewoman.

The woods had mostly grown out of disused quarries so the ground was uneven and rocky which added to the potential as a playground. Two hillocks shaped approximately like ships we named the *Lou-Joy* and the *Jen-Mar* after our family's first names. An old, rusted and unsightly cylindrical oil-tank that had somehow been parked in the woods also kindled our imagination. We had been to see the film *Twenty Thousand Leagues under the Sea*, and as the tank lay longitudinally with a doughnut-shaped port at the top it answered all our needs as a submarine. Inside there were bars so we could swing ourselves in and clamber out easily enough.

We were familiar with wild animals and birds: rabbits, hares, foxes, voles, slow worms, even adders were common sights. There was plenty of evidence of badger activity. They were ferocious diggers and seemed to favour the clay soil at the margins of the woods. They must have lived in sizable colonies but we were never patient enough to see them as opposed to their workings. We were quite keen birdwatchers, though, lacking binoculars, the memories of birdsong are more deeply ingrained than the visual impact. The rumbling, cooing noise of pigeons was almost continuous and cuckoos arrived in mid-April. We would wake at sunrise sometimes to the most amazingly orchestrated dawn chorus. It was so ecstatic that I thought I'd dreamed it, until I gathered that Mum had heard it too. The cuckoo's call was in triplicate – 'Cuck-uck-oo' – followed by another bird's delicately musical trilling down the scale and other sequential components. And the sequence was repeated so it wasn't merely random. I do so wish I had been able to record it. The spooky, quavering, 'Whoo-oo-oo' of owls was also a familiar night sound.

One winter's evening when Jenny and I sat on either side of the fire doing our homework, a little grey mouse staggered out of a hole in the skirting board and crept to the hearth where he sat warming himself at the flickering flames. Jenny and I stared open-mouthed. We couldn't both be dreaming. After a few minutes he crept away again. He looked old and threadbare. Jenny found some cheese and put it near his hole. He came and sat with us for a few nights, then we saw no more of him, so I presume he had gone to a murine Valhalla. I'm glad he was well provided with warmth and food in his dotage.

The surrounding farms housed children with whom we made friends and which opened up further play areas. We tumbled and hid in the hay-bales, hunted for eggs, helped (or hindered) with the milking, rode the horses bareback between farmyard and field. There was a working heavy chestnut mare called Queenie and a riding pony called Choirboy. I loved the milking best. The cows were treated with rough affection by the farm-workers who knew them all by name. They had velvety coats and enormous eyelashes, wet noses, a warm smell and endless patience. The milking machine chugged its way rhythmically through the afternoon: Alfa-Laval, Alfa-Laval, Alfa-Laval, it seemed to say. We became accustomed to being covered with itchy insect bites which kept us awake at nights in spite of the calomine.

The radio was a much more important source of entertainment then than now and the programmes were more varied. One genre of which I am less aware since television took over was the radio play, which could be excellent entertainment. Infinitely more stimulating when your own mind had to supply the visual aspects, it could be enjoyed while doing some other manual activity such as darning, mending, painting or embroidery. Serials could be gripping also, most memorably the series *Journey into Space* and its sequels, *The Red Planet* and others. The half-hour this occupied – 7.30 on Tuesday, was it? – was sacrosanct. Jenny and I sat with our ears glued to the radio, wriggling and making eye contact at the tense and exciting parts. Jet, Lemmy, Doc and Mitch were the four main characters. 'That's a risk we've got to take!' was a grimly spoken, macho prelude to moments of high drama. One evening we had some unavoidable engagement but persuaded Dad to listen on our behalf and to report in detail our heroes' progress. He proved himself an adept and took detailed notes which he then conscientiously expounded. This was quite a feat as he had no previous exposure to the story; and so we were able to join in the discussions with our friends the next day.

The Church and religion were of increasing influence at this time, partly a legacy of the intense exposure at the convent, and partly because at our age religion had a natural appeal. Also Mum had deeply held convictions dating from early influences. Dad did not participate but was tolerant of our beliefs, though would tease us with irreverent remarks and pretence of ignorance followed by, 'I'm very good at RI, you know.' In truth he knew a lot about Church of England rituals as he had been a choirboy in his time in Frome. He would intone parodies of the psalms: 'Doulting is my washpot and over Cranmore will I cast out my shoe.' This was unfortunate as whenever we came to the original version in church, Jenny and I would be visited by uncontrollable giggles and would earn a reproachful look from Mrs Tunstall sitting in the pew in front.

Mr Tunstall, with his 'no-frills' attitude to his calling, would teach that the most important festival of the Church year was Easter which was central to the doctrine of Christianity. Christmas being such a secular festival was of much less significance, and even Harvest Festival had a lower profile. This was incomprehensible to most of his congregation in a farming district where harvest-time was the climax of the working year. Indeed the proof was evident at the service which was the only time of the year when the church was filled to bulging. To those of us who made up the congregation of ten or less at other times, the sight was awesome. An army of villagers invaded the church on the Saturday of Harvest weekend to receive and display the gifts of flowers, fruit, sheaves of corn and vegetables which came by the barrowload. They performed wonders of decoration till our rather ordinary church looked and smelled like a land flowing with milk and honey. The centrepiece was a huge harvest loaf which, shaped like a stylised sheaf of corn and covered with a shiny glaze, was totally inedible and mainly symbolic. The service itself was thrilling because so large a congregation raised a thunderous sound, almost drowning the organ, and all the hearty farmers threw their souls into:

> We plough the fields and scatter,
> The good seed on the ground

Probably they felt that they had to intercede as energetically as possible with the Lord on this their one visit to his house in the year, while seeking legitimate pardon for other times on account of the rigours of their calling.

The high spot of harvest-time, though, was the sale of goods on the following evening. Mum at first thought this was a terrible way to use the produce, and that it should have been given to the poor and to hospitals. Her perceptions had not quite caught up with the NHS and the welfare state, we told her. Instead there was an auction sale in the school and a rollicking occasion it was, with funds going to support the church. Villagers went along to buy good stuff at low prices, to have a happy sociable time, to take part in this custom and perhaps a few went to give more than they received. We children developed our own little custom, which was to bid for some of the juiciest carrots, then to chomp away at them through the evening. The auctioneer was slick and witty according to tradition, but not too ruthless, though some of the items went at prices way above their value. Indeed, some of the wealthier people used this as a discreet way of making donations. The harvest loaf was the last item to be sold, and traditionally was a means of extracting a lot of cash from various willing pockets. No one really wanted it, so folk would bid against each other until it was knocked down to one of them. He would say, 'Oi don't want un. Put un up again!' So the process was repeated, usually several times. When bids began to flag it was usually knocked down to some youngster who bore it away with pride.

Social occasions like these were among the best things about rural village life, which brought everyone of all ages and classes together. The Women's Institute or other bodies would occasionally hold barn dances (the English equivalent of the Scottish ceilidh) which produced similar communal jollity. Inevitably, though, there were also quarrels, feuds, spiteful gossip and faction-fighting. Many people (women especially) would preface a bit of venom with 'I'd do anyone a good turn, but ...'. Mr Tunstall must have heard this piece of insincerity enough times, and one Sunday he preached a sermon about the parable of the sower, with the text, 'Some fell on stony ground.' He railed against a religion of good turns, intending to convey the notion that rectitude should inform all one's actions, and spurious deeds when convenient were not enough. But this philosophy was not within the grasp of most of his listeners. With unbelievable lack of tact he alluded to certain church workers going grimly about their tasks with no real philanthropy. There was a significant atmosphere of rebellion among the faithful few emerging into the autumn twilight. Jenny murmured in my ear, 'I could hear the seed bouncing off Mrs B ...' The vicar's popularity ratings plunged down a few further degrees.

Discussions about our confirmation began to be heard. Jenny was deemed to be the right age but I was a little young. Mum thought I was ready and voiced this opinion to the vicar, who snorted and said, 'You make her sound like a piece of toast!' Still, we were accepted and so cycled to the vicarage every week for our confirmation classes, about which I remember little. I suspect at this time I was in danger of becoming a little prig. I decided to read the Bible from end to end and set about reading a chapter every morning and every night.

For our confirmation we wore white dresses and veils and looked pure and saintly. The ceremony took place in Frome which gave my Aunt Mary, who lived there still in her maidenly state, a chance to take over the arrangements. She gave us gold crosses and chains for the occasion and expected us to wear them for the ceremony. But Mr Tunstall, who held us in considerable thrall, had said, 'No embellishments!' so we thanked Aunt Mary nicely but explained that we couldn't put them on. She was deeply hurt, and showed it. Mum interceded tactfully and we fortunately, imbued with an unusual spirit of accommodation, agreed to wear the crosses. There were many priestly persons at the church, all decked out in varying degrees of clerical finery, but only our vicar had a simple cassock, surplice and hood.

I think he was blissfully unaware of the resentment he aroused with his intransigent teaching, and referred to all his parishioners as his friends. There was another sermon a few years later which created an even greater furore, and this time he even upset our mother! This was concerned with the third commandment about remembering the sabbath day and keeping it holy. He interpreted this as not working for a profit on a Sunday. At the time our shop opened on Sundays as it had as long as anyone could remember. Mum's conscience was seared, as was that of many people. Also, she took it very personally. She rehearsed all the arguments she could think of as to why he was wrong. 'When he goes on holiday who does he think makes his bed and cooks his meals?' she raged. But her protests did not quell her mental discomfort and a few weeks later she announced the shop would close all day Sunday in future. I welcomed this as at long last she would get a whole day off. She had become rather a slave to the shop, knowing well that any changes were resented and tended to drive customers elsewhere. She could hardly be prevailed upon to take time off for holidays and so Dad would take Jenny and me away to the seaside for a few days, when he would often unwind and be as irresponsible and adventurous as we were. I worried over this extreme form of self-denial on my mother's part. We would try to tease her out of it, calling her an early Christian martyr, but to no avail.

7

Pangs of Pubescence

Memory at major external changes in a life seems to be sensitised to receive, and at periods of consistency may be less receptive. The next years, in which those changes that took place were mainly internal, tend to fuse in my mind. Doubtless advancing puberty made me introverted. In later life when we visited the New Forest at Easter, I made friends with a young girl in her early teens whom I only saw once a year. Of course she grew and changed in the times between visits but in the gap between thirteen and fourteen she was transformed from child to woman and was unrecognisable physically and mentally. This metamorphosis from child to adult is much more dramatic in girls than boys, and, looking back at my own generation, made a big change in our interpersonal relationships and perceptions of each other.

At twelve I moved into lower IVA and felt like an animal in a social group feels when it is no longer at the bottom of the pecking order. The new girls in their crisp uniforms looked at us with our well-worn air and confident friendships as if we were light-years ahead of them. This year brought the start of a new subject, Latin, which I found very satisfying with its almost mechanical construction and unbendable rules. Our teacher, Miss Brierly, looked rather strict and frightening but was a very sweet-natured lady, though eccentric. She was immensely tall and thin, giving her a disproportion amounting almost to deformity. I developed a distinct bond with her, partly because I was well-behaved and good at the subject; but there was something else as well. I became aware of something peculiar about myself which I had noticed before but dismissed as coincidence. I occasionally had strong premonitions that turned out to be true. These were usually about trivial and relatively unimportant events, nothing momentous or significant, and I could not understand why I should get portents about these. But in Miss Brierly's class – and this sounds bizarre, I know – they came with extraordinary regularity and accuracy. We would be going through exercises in our books, with the teacher picking out girls at random to translate or answer questions; and I always knew when she was going to ask me, with a peculiar clarity. This gave me a few seconds' grace to prepare the answer. There must have been some subliminal message. It wasn't visual, because I had my nose in my book. Was it the sequence of people she picked out? I don't think so because I got these feelings right from the start. Did I by some body language catch her eye? I don't think that's likely either. But it was a fascinating phenomenon – and useful, and I've certainly had powerful and accurate forebodings since then, including one about a serious car accident.

Another subject that had to be tackled was the approaching menarche and aspects of reproduction. We all knew what was coming when we were herded into the biology lab for a forty-minute film and factual account. It was badly done, though the topic could not fail to arouse and stimulate. The black and white film was hopelessly ancient and stilted, and a male voice made the commentary. There was an allusion to the tendency to premenstrual mood swings and we were exhorted to avoid dramatising and face the world with a smile! A touch of the womb-linked hysteria theory showing itself. Thereafter a favourite question amongst cronies was, 'Have you started yet?' We were all longing for the first period, but thereafter the inconvenience and minor discomforts gave us ample reason to grumble about 'the curse'.

Mum had dropped some packets in my lap one evening, with belt and pad enclosed, and told me to keep them in my school bag. In fact this important event took place one day during the holidays. Getting ready to go on a day trip, I couldn't find some vital item and quite uncharacteristically lost my temper. I still remember the uncontrollable surge of irritation. Mum resolved the problem and made no comment. That evening as I undressed I found the bloodstains for the first time. And so I became a woman at twelve and a half. Mum smiled and pointed out the significance of my crossness in the morning. Ever since then when visited by an unexplained excess of irascibility, I pause and think what day of the month it is. If you know there is this specific reason for bad temper, which with me only lasts for the preceding twenty-four hours, you can avoid aggravating circumstances and confrontations.

Another more visible change was breast development, and the first girl in the class to wear a bra was a heroine indeed. Sue was well developed and got teased for not wearing a bra; she said, 'I haven't got anything to put into one,' which was not true. I was skinny and did not have much shape, but oh! the psychological trauma I went through before I got that highly symbolic garment. You felt particularly sensitive when changing for gym. Eventually when out shopping I steered Mum into the department store and over to the lingerie counter, when she finally tumbled to my need. I remember my first bra: a tiny confection of embroidered cotton costing two shillings and sixpence. There was no Marks and Spencer's wide-ranging choice of garments then, at least not in Frome.

A period was not deemed a suitable excuse for being let off gym, and though I loved this activity normally, found it distasteful and unpleasant to have to scramble over bars and ropes feeling vulnerably exposed in the dreadful green knickers. After a year or two most of us found better ways of dealing with our periods with considerable liberation, and by this time I sorted out my own personal affairs without reference to Mum; it was good to be in control. One or two of my friends did make a big thing of period times – lying on the floor clutching the lower abdomen, ostentatiously taking aspirin, even being absent from school. I despised this behaviour and expect I showed it, being a stoic at heart.

Round about this time a major domestic upheaval occurred as my father became seriously ill. He developed severe abdominal pain while at work and was speedily taken to hospital. At this time Dad lived in digs in Bristol on weekdays and came home at weekends, having found commuting unacceptable, so having sold his car he took the bus on Sunday night and came back to us on Friday evening. In this day and age of long-distance commuting it sounds crazy, I know, that a mere twenty miles should so disrupt a man's domestic comfort, but so it was. When he was ill Mum was in great difficulties, being at such a distance and with no transport. She was told by phone that he had an intestinal obstruction and thought the worst, that he had cancer. She shut the shop and went to his bedside, travelling by bus. Dad had had an emergency operation and fortunately there was no serious disease, only adhesions. They were both shaken, though, and still thinking he was going to die. Dad told us later that when he came round from the anaesthetic there was a group of white-surpliced choirboys singing a hymn around the bed of the patient opposite, who was a clergyman. His immediate thought was that he had died and gone to heaven. He was sadly sentimental with Mum, iterating all the things he'd meant to do and hadn't.

At home Jenny and I were able to cope. The news quickly spread around the villages and adjacent neighbourhoods, and on the whole people were accommodating about the shop shutting. No one offered to drive her to Bristol though. However on the second day I had a phone call from the vicar.

'What bus do you expect your mother to catch from Bristol?' he enquired abruptly. I told him and he rang off. He drove to Shepton to collect her, thus cutting short the journey by half an hour. She was touched: not just that he had done it, but that it had occurred to him to do it.

Dad made a good recovery but soon afterwards developed a duodenal ulcer which required the standard treatment of the time: some weeks' complete rest and a bland diet. I recall our doctor visiting and saying to him, 'You've got another twenty years or so to trot around this globe.' I was deeply shocked. My father was in his mid-forties, did not have a life-threatening illness, and did not need to be reminded so brutally of his mortality.

Neither of these events should have left any residual physical deficit but my father never seemed to recover fully, and always was careful with himself thereafter. I think this was psychosomatic. He was rather an indolent man and it quite suited him on occasions to have an incontrovertible excuse for not doing things.

The following academic year, aged thirteen, in upper IVA, I was form captain for a term, which was surprisingly demanding. This position was achieved by a popularity vote, the school philosophy embracing the principles of democracy under certain constrained circumstances. The form captains sat on the school council with the prefects, the Big Three, Miss Chappell and a few senior teachers. I suppose we discussed trivial things like not running in corridors and keeping silent in the changing rooms. Through the term, work was frequently brushed aside for special sessions of a cultural nature: illustrated lectures on art or travel, concerts by professional soloists – pianists, violinists, flautists – and even visits by university drama groups. These were extremely well done and added a significant dimension to our cultural lives. The teachers used to seethe with irritation because there was enough difficulty getting through syllabi as it was. Some visiting drama groups would put on a straight Shakespearean play, but others were more interactive, showing how actors were trained, taking large groups of us and moulding us into crowd scenes such as in *Julius*

Caesar. On one occasion when I was fairly senior we were looking forward to a lovely programme of piano music and as I settled myself with pleasant anticipation near the back, a pert child arrived and told me Miss Chappell wished me to go and turn the pages for the soloist. This was the most awful responsibility and my afternoon's enjoyment was demolished.

Bruton was quite a centre of culture, probably influenced by the presence of three large schools, which besides Sunny Hill and Sexey's included a prestigious boys' public school called King's School. Through the winter there was a series of concerts with visiting top-class musicians, including the harpist Osian Ellis. The name stood out because once, having heard him on radio, my philistine father made mockery of the effeminate name. Mum and I were impatient to see the owner of the name, who turned out to be imbued with all-masculine charms. He was an excellent musician too.

The 'Opera for All' group visited regularly and I enjoyed the first of many performances of *La Bohème* on the Sunny Hill stage. Mum had been weeping quietly through the last act and I steered her out by a discreet route so that no one would see her red eyes.

My own musical career was flourishing as I prepared for the grade II piano exam. The piano lesson was no longer dreaded, rather it was the high spot of the week, and as I became more proficient and worked for various goals, I often had two lessons per week at no extra cost. Despite my earlier ambivalence, I now developed a schoolgirl crush on my teacher Miss Thorns. Crushes or cracks as they were oddly termed were common and widely accepted. Sometimes a younger girl hero-worshipped an older girl rather than a teacher. At exam time, 'Who's your crack?' was a common question amongst the juniors and it was thought odd not to have one. If you dared, you asked your crack for a mascot for the exams, usually a little toy which you sat on the desk for good luck. Gwenda once lost her mascot and went through agonies of misery and mortification before owning up and being forgiven. There was never any physical association; we just gazed, calf-eyed, from afar. My crush on Miss Thorns persisted for two or three years and was quite as painful and bewildering as any subsequent experience of being in love. Though one must assume this is the female counterpart of homosexuality in boys' schools, as I have said, it was totally innocent. There is, I believe, a graduated line between homo- and hetero-sexuality and though most people will be at or near one

57

extreme, not a few have varying proportions of both tendencies. Analysing myself, I hope dispassionately, I would say I am ninety-nine per cent heterosexual. This particular emotional upheaval in my early teens I would regard as a developmental phase (rather like the human foetus in utero goes through a fish-like phase with gill-like structures). But it did seem to be unusually strong and enduring and I am aware that at least one teacher was aware and was concerned, though nothing was ever said.

At this stage, however, my inner turmoil produced nothing but good as it made me even more devoted to my piano practice and determined to do great things. In March 1958 I took the grade II exam. There was always quite a bustle and ceremony associated with music exams: silence was imposed, the music teachers all wore smart clothes and made a fuss of the candidates. In short we were made to feel like little prima donnas for a day, and I for one revelled in the atmosphere. It was surprising that we were able to perform at all given the inco-ordination which nervousness produces. To my astonishment I passed with distinction (the highest grade) and still have the assessment form and certificate to prove it.

Sue's interests were diverting more towards elocution than music and to my disappointment she gave up piano at this time to concentrate on her more gifted area. We read a comedy play in our English class which we were encouraged to perform for one of the Speech Day entertainments. It was called *The Doubtful Misfortunes of Li Sing*. The plot centred on the thwarted attempt at suicide of a Chinese couple fallen on hard times. The language was quaint and polysyllabic and full of quasi-Confucian philosophy. The opening line remains with me: 'It is obvious to the meanest intellect . . .' Li Sing and his wife are having a slanging match. They are actually quarrelling about the best way to put an end to their troubles and Li Sing rejects his wife's violent proposals in favour of her preparing a feast with all their remaining provender, and putting poison in it. As they sit down to their last supper, a notorious bandit, Hung Hi, is sighted. Li Sing's wife suggests that they should submit to his depredations since they are to die anyway. Li Sing, who is clearly a coward as well as a male chauvinist, demolishes this proposal with horror, arguing that Hung Hi will hack them to pieces, 'And then shall we be rejected at the gates of paradise, for the gods do not accept instalments!' This line brought a gratifying laugh from the audience.

The couple hide, Hung Hi and his gang barge in and consume the feast, then die in vocal and theatrical contortions of agony.

We were at the age when verbosity and obscurity seemed terribly clever. Nevertheless it was good for our diction, I'm sure, and wonderful for dressing up and making up. One or two artistic teachers had a field day, with scant attention to the realities of destitution and affliction, for in the guise of Mrs Li Sing I was transformed into a seductive and languorous creature with upswept hair, whom my father sitting in the front row totally failed to recognise. Our little group made a sufficient impression for us to be earmarked for future theatricals in the senior school.

The following academic year would see the start of our O-level courses and our two academic streams were to be diverted into three directions, termed S, A and D for science, arts and domestic science. I had a briefly held romantic notion that I would go into the arts stream because I dreamed rather fancifully of an international career in music or something equally improbable. I was summoned to the presence of Miss Chappell, no less, and told very firmly (and quite rightly as it turned out) that I would keep my options open and go into the S stream. It was fairly clear that S, A and D were codes for graduated academic ability.

8

Metamorphosis

For the next two years, as befitted our 'S' suffix, our classroom was the science laboratory. There was a new addition to our number, Geraldine, who rapidly gave notice that having come from the B stream she was to be a contender for the brightest and most diligent in the class.

A change came about with my relationships amongst my classmates which was troubling, which had been developing slowly before the summer holidays of 1958 but which only became noticeable at the start of the lower fifth year. I was no longer popular; indeed I was treated distinctly coolly by a number in the class. All my life previously friendships had come easily, I had been readily accepted into social groups even through the frequent changes of school, and had never suffered loneliness or neglect. But suddenly now things were different. Sue and Geraldine were to a lesser extent marginalised within the class. I'm not sure even now I fully understand the shifting currents that made these changes, but it was at least partly to do with the three of us being 'goodie-goodies', the hard workers, the conformists, whereas at fourteen everyone else was more interested in the outside world, a life of films, dancing and pop music, and rebellion against authority. We were, I suppose, letting our peer group down by siding with the establishment. At this time, Elvis was the chief pop icon and the film *Psycho* the height of thrilling and forbidden entertainment.

To make matters worse for me, Sue had formed a new alliance with Valerie, a rather serious girl whom I didn't know very well. Sue being an only child was often isolated and needed a companion for her home life, which vacancy had been filled by Val, so naturally the friendship continued into school life. Sue and Val shared topics of conversation to which I had no natural entry and though we formed a trio I began to feel increasingly isolated. Geraldine was a new friend but I found her a little dull, interested in her work and her career but not much else. Another girl, Penny, with whom I had shared some interests, secrets and gossip, now treated me with frank dislike. All this was exceedingly bewildering. With the increasing pressure of work, luckily there was not much time to brood or become seriously unhappy. I responded by turning inwards and becoming more reserved. Small-group teaching provided opportunities for new alliances including those with teachers. I had taken on ten subjects to study for O-level which was rather a serious overloading. German and music were two new subjects, in which we found ourselves in small, select groups. Mrs Mullins, a comfortable Dutch lady who taught us German, was more like a granny than a teacher. She was full of warmth and smiles and a sense of fun. She contended that only the British and the Dutch shared a truly subtle sense of humour; certainly not the Germans. The demands of our timetable meant that some German classes were held after school, following which we were given steaming cups of cocoa and doorstep slabs of bread and marge, lest we expire on the way home.

For music there were only four of us to share the attentions of Mr Leslie, and, quite apart from the novelty of a male teacher, the subject was a delightful one. Every aspect appealed. The mysteries of harmony and counterpoint were captured by arithmetic formulae which regularly produced melodious results. This was the foundation of composition, we learned, and even the towering figures such as Bach and Beethoven had been constrained to submit to its discipline. The history of music was full of romance and personal interest, and some raciness too. And best of all, some lessons were devoted to listening to music, often with the score to follow. I felt that fathomless mysteries were being unravelled before my eyes. The solid pleasures of these forays into uncharted country made up for a great deal of personal difficulties. Also the social tensions seemed to be less in evidence in small groups, as if only produced by herd antipathy.

Mr Leslie, who was mild-mannered, courteous and shy, endured merciless ragging and teasing in his large singing classes, full of buxom, nubile wenches whose only interest was to spark off sexual tensions. He was ridiculously innocent and would have us sing carols with such lines as, 'A breastful of milk ...' which provoked excesses of crude mirth.

Biology, another new subject, was attended by everyone in the year, and being essentially factual consisted almost entirely of dictation and copying diagrams. I found I could switch off mentally while taking reams of notes and being oblivious of the contents. But it was during this class that a departure from the routine caused me to reach a momentous decision.

A film entitled *Red River of Life* was obtained for our instruction, dealing with the circulation of the blood in humans, and the function of the red cells in carrying blood gases. Being American, it was extremely well presented but had an unfortunately pious overlay, in which we were constantly reminded of the originator of the miracles we were observing. The fervour became almost comical when the tricky feat of gaseous exchange in the lungs was compared to 'inscribing the Lord's Prayer on the head of a pin while being shot from a cannon'! In spite of the hyperbole the factual content was gripping, and at home that evening as we sat over supper relating our day's happenings, it dawned on me that medicine was the subject I most wanted to pursue. As I shared this revelation with the family, Mum said quietly, 'Good. That's settled then.' Just how much, if at all, this mini-exposure of the film influenced my specialty choice of haematology I don't know. I really don't.

I became aware of problems with my eyesight, related probably to growth. Jenny had glasses by now to correct short-sight. I knew I needed them but didn't confess the problems I was having in seeing the blackboard. I wasn't vain at this time – indeed I was oblivious of my appearance – but somehow dreaded the fussing and tutting of adults over a physical shortcoming. At last it dawned on me that if I didn't do something my school work would suffer. So then I became even more of a blue-stocking with a studious pair of specs. I allowed the dentist to make me a brace to correct my crooked front teeth, and wore it religiously for a year, after which I discarded it, aware that nothing would ever straighten my teeth. I compromised with the dentist who suggested that when I was reading or working at a desk I should press lightly on my front teeth, a habit which I have to this day. And still the teeth are crooked.

I passed grade III piano exam with merit and entered the memory class of the prestigious Mid-Somerset Musical Competitions in Bath. I played a piece called 'Flood-Time' by Thiman, which was wonderfully evocative of heaving sea and crashing waves, and won a first-class certificate, only a handful of marks behind the winner. Sue, meanwhile, was doing even greater things with her elocution. She landed a quite large part in the school production of Jean Anouilh's *The Lark* which was an ambitious undertaking. I had a small part but, as we were the privileged young ones in a senior activity, was happy to be a part of the venture.

Bristol University held an annual German poetry-speaking competition for schools and Mrs Mullins decided Sue should have a go. I must confess to feeling a little miffed at not being allowed to enter. However, two or three of us went along to support Sue, travelling in Mrs Mullins's car, and to our great delight Sue won one of the honours – I think it was second. Since competitors came from all round the West Country, we were really proud.

The following summer, 1959, a trip to Germany was planned to visit our sister school in Leer, Ostfriesland. I pressured Mum to let me go, more, I think, because I felt I ought to seize the opportunity than because I really wanted to go. My father gave me a stern talking-to, because it was an expensive undertaking, saying I couldn't expect this every year, and I was to look upon this as a 'once in a lifetime event'. If he only knew! But life was still austere compared with today.

We were away for three weeks. Each of us stayed with a German family, including a girl of our own age which occupied us for the first week. In the middle week the entire group travelled by train through Köln and Bonn to the Mosel valley where we stayed in youth hostels. This was magical. German youth hostels were strictly run, almost military, but were immaculately clean and organised. After travelling all day and walking through steep vineyards to the first hostel in Brodenbach we were so hungry and thirsty that the humble fare tasted like nectar. I drank huge mugs of tea, whose flavour suggested it had been brewed with hay, with no milk and sugar. Hearty hiking songs were played over the intercom not only at seven in the morning to wake us up, but also at ten thirty at night to make sure we didn't go to sleep too soon! We did a lot of hill-walking, taking the most spartan fare in our packed lunches: dry black bread and sliced sausage. When opportunity offered we would ditch this and nip into town for *Pflaumenkuchen mit Sahne*: plum tart and cream. We also stayed in Berkastel and Trier – all names that are now more familiar to me on account of their wines.

During the third week we accompanied our German friends to their school. I was asked to read to a class to demonstrate my impeccable English accent, and read from Steinbeck's *The Red Pony*; fortunately I didn't get to the end which is far too moving to read aloud. Naturally I read it from cover to cover at a later date. At fifteen I was extremely

thin which worried the family I stayed with. They were all huge eaters
and very sturdily built as a result. Their three-course lunch would be
followed with massive helpings of a huge circular cake – a fresh one
each day. Then at teatime a large platter of dry bread would be brought
in; no butter or jam. It was so dry that I could hardly manage one
piece, but everyone else stashed away at least half a dozen. I was going
through a rather anti-social phase and all the photographs I took have
no people in them at all. But I was fond of Irmgard with whom I
stayed, and we arranged that she would come to me the following year.
Although there were moments of homesickness, especially during the
first week and when the family were chattering away in German so
fast that I lost touch, it was an influential experience. Prior to this,
although I knew about the war, it seemed to be lost in the mists of
antiquity and I was quite moved to discover that people wanted to talk
about it, to touch on the dreadful things that happened and to claim
ignorance of them. Irmgard used to refer to 'the other Germany'
which I later connected up with Walter's disappearance. She was much
more concerned about the fate of gypsies – *Ziguener* – under Nazism
than Jews. Her own father, who was a teacher, had suffered some
religious discrimination in Bavaria some years earlier when, as
a Lutheran, he had refused to become a Catholic to advance his
career.

Major changes were happening at home. Jenny at sixteen had left
school after doing her O-levels. At that time the convent had no sixth
form, though had she wanted, her education could have been extended
elsewhere. But she decided to become a nurse and was accepted at the
Bristol Eye Hospital to do her ophthalmic training; they took girls at
this astoundingly young age for two years, after which they usually
went on to the Bristol Royal Infirmary to do general nursing. For
these two years Jenny became very distant and treated me like a kid
sister who was beneath her notice.

However I acquired a new companion at home as we adopted a
Welsh collie dog called Billy from one of the farms. He needed a good
deal of exercise which was not in the least a sacrifice. His boundless
energy meant that Mum had to take him out too, which was beneficial
as it got her away from the thrall of home and shop, and she also began
to discover the hidden secrets of the countryside. In his puppydom he
was very destructive and an unrepentant thief. When the family were
out together walking he would circle round us and herd us together,

obeying the dictates of his breeding. He was also a ferocious guard-dog.

One day when Dad and Billy were sauntering through the woods, which Billy probably thought of as his own property, they espied a young man walking ahead of them. Billy launched himself in pursuit, a black and white frenzy of barking, growling aggression. The young man turned slowly, quite unperturbed. The dog's headlong charge came to an abrupt, skidding halt. Silence fell. He stepped slowly back, his belly on the ground, his eyes fixed on the man's face. Dad caught up, apologising as he hastily put the leash on. The gypsy smiled and said, 'I can deal with the likes of he!' My father was highly impressed with the mysterious authority he displayed and Billy's instant recognition of it.

My father showed a particular characteristic on this occasion which I had noted and admired many times, and that was his natural courtesy, which was extended to everyone, no matter what their condition in life. This appears to sit oddly with his staunch conservatism, which was better demonstrated by his exaggerated respect for those he deemed his social superiors. His politeness was an attractive quality that I tried to emulate, and it is a mystery to me how I later came to marry a man in whom it was totally lacking. But I anticipate.

At fifteen we faced our O-level year. Sue, Geraldine and I all had ten subjects to contend with, which worried our teachers. One day Miss Haskell, our much respected maths teacher (who was universally known as 'Hack'), called us to her and proposed that the three of us should take our maths O-level that winter, before Christmas, to get it out of the way. We were stunned. She was confident of our ability to get through comfortably, and in any case there was nothing to lose. The three of us wandered away to discuss the bombshell. Geraldine shrugged. 'I can cope with it. Seems like a good idea,' she said with brief, bland confidence, and left us. Sue and I gazed at each other with trepidation, fellow-feeling and all sorts of other complex emotions. Some of our old, close amity returned with this bond between us.

In the event, we all passed, myself with an especially high mark. At the end-of-term session in Long Prayers, Sue, Geraldine and I always shared the top grade and as Miss Chappell read this out our peer group would chant, 'A-minus average: Geraldine M., Susan S. and Margaret Whitmore!' No wonder we were unpopular.

The rest of that academic year passed in a haze of hard work, in spite of dropping maths. My nine remaining subjects were English language, English literature, French, German, Latin, physics, chemistry, biology and music. I still remember some of the books for English: *Pride and Prejudice* for one, which I've since read innumerable times, including once in French, and adored Fitzwilliam Darcy long before Colin Firth portrayed him so sensually. We had a book of prose extracts which was an excellent way of introducing us to an array of literature. The first section had extracts from the books dealing with the First World War by Blunden, Sassoon and Graves, which not only led to the avid consumption of these entire books, but others and also poetry by these authors.

Musical developments this year were grade V piano which I passed with distinction and grade V theory of music. Miss Thorns left at the end of this year, which caused me much sorrow, which did not however have any legitimate outlet; except that then as now I found much relief in pouring out my feelings on to paper. Heaven knows where those ramblings are now; I hope they have been destroyed.

As our exams drew near we released tension in all sorts of strange ways. Sue and I got our heads together to make up a comical poem about our classmates. They were segregated, as always, into boarders and day girls.

> It may be thought that the boarders are 'crude',
> But they meditate deeply – on Kings' boys, and food!
>
> There's Virginia B, with scientist's brain.
> Would you like Marmite? – or dichloro-diphenyl-trichloro-
>   ethane?
>
> The life of a day girl is all milk and honey;
> That's if you think – getting up on a cold frosty morning in time
>   to catch train or bus, remember satchel, gym gear, hockey
>   stick, violin, indoor shoes, books, dinner money, and finally
>   remembering it's Saturday – is funny!
>
> Who's sensible, helpful and quiet, please guess.
> Could this be Ann B? Of course it could. Yes!
>
> Who's witty, intelligent, graceful and clever?
> Could this be Caroline J? No, never!

Most other verses I've forgotten The final one went:

> That was the cream, now we come to the dregs.
> Susan S. – Margaret W. – the form's two square eggs!

The poem was received in the spirit in which it was written, I'm happy to say.

Soon, in the height of the English summer, the exams were upon us. The atmosphere of tension and imposed silence pervaded the entire school, as we were aware from previous years when not directly involved. The hall was used to accommodate us all with sufficient space between desks so that no one could copy. It was not uncommon to have four three-hour papers on different subjects in the space of two days. From a number of sources I have become aware that the strain thus imposed could not be tolerated by people beyond a certain age – probably mid-thirties – without major mental breakdown, and one wonders if any assessment has ever been made of the effects on young folk. Probably not.

And then there was no let-up, because the next batch of papers required preparation. But at last it was all over and the sense of relief was like basking in balmy sunlight. I recall reading a novel in bed at the end of exam time, drinking a mug of hot chocolate and being aware in that moment of time of perfect contentment.

9

Sacred and Secular

In first-year sixth form, at sixteen, I began at last to rebel; at least two years after everyone else had got it out of their systems and were beginning to think seriously about A-level courses and careers. However I did not mean to throw away everything to the wind but fully intended to have some fun, and to my parents' alarm I began to go to the occasional party and dance. I thought ballroom dancing, which was popular then, would be a good social asset and went along to classes with a group of good-time friends who had left school and were earning money. I also started learning to play the church organ, so another evening had to be put aside to practise. It occurs to me that these two activities represent the obverse sides of my nature, both equally essential: one an intensely solitary activity, struggling to acquire an elusive skill; the other sociable, joyous, physical, mindless. Mum had to ask permission of the vicar for me to practise the organ in church and much to our amused surprise he agreed – provided we paid for the electricity. Shortly after, the organist became incapacitated through illness, so the job of playing in services fell to me and another lady of the village. When Mum, with a defiant air, handed over the first electricity payment, Mr Tunstall said, 'I feel very guilty about this,' but he still took it. Dad said sourly, 'I expect he wept all the way to the bank!' But later he waived the payment.

One Saturday afternoon in late autumn I cycled to the church to practise for next day's service. The church was never locked, but the electricity had to be switched on in the vestry and the organ key collected. It was quite a fine pipe organ, very old but recently renovated to a high standard. I liked to be tucked away in the organ loft with the two consoles, the great and the swell, at my disposal, the immense seat to provide access to the pedals and the array of stops on either side with interesting names like 'hautboy', 'vox humana', 'trumpet', 'gamba'. A series of mirrors enabled the organist to see choir and minister.

On this particular day I played longer than intended and when the

organ and its lights were switched off found myself in pitch darkness.
The key had to be returned to the vestry and the mains switched off.
I was not unduly perturbed and felt my way to the vestry in the western
arm of the cross-shaped church. The darkness was absolute, with not
a shape or outline visible. Then by feeling the pew heads I passed, as I
thought, down the main aisle towards the door which was halfway
down the 'foot' of the cross. I gauged the distance before turning right
to the door, but came smack up against a stone wall where no stone
wall had any right to be! All presence of mind deserted me; primeval
fears and superstitions flooded in. I have seldom known such a moment
of terror and complete disorientation! Very fortunately at that moment
a car passed along the road nearby, and the headlights momentarily
illuminated the interior; long enough for me to perceive I had mis-
takenly fumbled my way along the eastern arm of the cross. With all
haste I scuttled out of the church while the memory of the light was
still with me.

Playing for church services was nerve-racking at first, even with our
small uncritical community, because I felt compelled to achieve a
certain standard. Then I had to acquire some music that was suitable
for voluntaries before and after service, and, clearly, playing most weeks
demanded a certain breadth of repertoire. Luckily I discovered a
shop in Frome which sold albums of voluntaries which were not too
complex. There was Corelli's Christmas music, Mozart's 'Ave Verum',
Handel's Water music, themes from oratorios such as Mendelssohn's
Elijah ('Oh Rest in the Lord') and his choral work, 'Oh for the Wings
of a Dove', Bach's chorales such as 'Jesu, Joy of Man's Desiring', and
cantata theme, 'Humble us by thy Goodness'. A favourite which almost
became my theme tune was from Stainer's Crucifixion: 'God so Loved
the World'; its sustained notes and harmonies seemed so beautifully
adapted for the organ. Then I branched out into opera themes such as
Pilgrims' Chorus from Wagner's *Tannhauser*, whose muscular sound
also came over well, and the theme from the first movement of Dvořák's
New World Symphony where I used lavish amounts of swell. I also
played occasional spirituals. But becoming too secular was not
approved, as when I distracted Mrs Tunstall with 'Sweet and Low'; and
Gluck's 'What is Life to me without Thee' was thought not to strike
quite the right note. It was a wonderful time of discovery, and even
though I have long since ceased to have any belief in Christianity or
other organised religion I still retain an adoration for all sorts of sacred

music, and indeed for the atmosphere in old churches.

When I played a voluntary at the end of morning service, Jenny and a friend, Diana, would come tumbling into the organ loft and slide along the seat beside me, causing immense distraction. I have always needed to have my mind one hundred per cent on the music, but felt it would be churlish to object. On festival days such as Easter when many more than the usual half-dozen communicants attended I would play softly as the queues came and went, and at eight o'clock communion on Christmas Day I played carols one after another. Mr Tunstall liked to hear 'It Came upon the Midnight Clear' which he deemed the greatest of all carols because of its theme of peace.

> And man, at war with man, hears not
> The words of peace they bring;
> Oh hush the noise, ye men of strife,
> And hear the angels sing.

His least favourite carol was 'Once in Royal David's City' for its last verse which seriously ruffled his socialist feathers:

> Not in that poor lonely stable,
> With the oxen standing by,
> We shall see Him, but in heaven,
> Set at God's right hand on high,
> When, like stars, His children crowned
> All in white shall wait around.

He referred to this once, from the pulpit, as 'unspeakable vulgarity'.

At school for the end-of-term carol service I teamed up with Sheila to play a two-piano duet, a Fantasia on Christmas carols. We were lucky enough to have two grand pianos in the hall. Music-making in company doubles the pleasure and I often wished I had learned an orchestral instrument.

There were so many extra-curricular activities this year that it was wonderful that we got any work done at all. There was a performance of *Alice in Wonderland* in which Sue was the White Queen and I played the Red Queen. The backdrop was magnificent, portraying a chessboard stretching out to the horizon. We competed for the McGibbon Cup for French and English verse speaking, which was an annual event for senior girls. Predictably, Sue won it easily; indeed I think she won it twice, and thereafter was asked to drop out and let lesser mortals have a chance. Her diction and debating skills won our school honours in inter-school debating when her style was described as 'mellifluous', and at the Mid-Somerset Competition, when she was first in the extempore public-speaking class. As her topic was 'A victim of fashion', she was able to use her school uniform to good effect.

The question of sixth-form dances raised the collective blood pressure. The dance was dear to the heart of the boarders, many of whom had secret dalliances with Kings' boys; the day girls had their own social lives, so were less concerned. In 1960 the fashion in shoes was for stiletto heels, which had to be covered with plastic caps lest the hall floor should be damaged. Having learned how to dance I looked forward to the occasion with confidence. At that time, in our circumstances, it was not possible to be a stylish dresser, but by serendipity I had acquired a white sheath dress in bouclé material which fitted like a glove and which was definitely flattering. The important thing was not to be a wallflower. Early on I was asked to dance by a nondescript young man with whom I rapidly became bored. He was clearly determined to stick like glue the whole evening. There were many young men sitting round the edge of the dance floor, looking uneasy and unmotivated. I had a brainwave. I said to my partner, 'You fellows seem to be outnumbered. I don't know many Kings' boys. Why don't you introduce me to some of your friends?' He looked nonplussed, but could not refuse, so introductions were made and I acquired an entourage of about six young men who supplied entertainment and partners for the evening.

The following day, Sue, who had not attended, eyed me speculatively and said, 'I gather you had a good time.' The result of this event was that my stock was considerably raised amongst those girls whose main aim in life was a manhunt. I think we were all maturing a bit anyway, and my relative outcast status for the past two years was resolving itself.

Musical milestones were grade VI theory and piano and for the latter I only got an ordinary pass. With the new teacher I had only indifferent rapport, but also found the standard after grade V ascended pretty steeply. By now I was reconciled to the fact that I was definitely not going to be the brightest star in the firmament of world-class pianists. It was a source of regret.

I had become very specialist now, studying only physics, chemistry and biology in preparation for A- and S-levels; and some maths in order to do additional maths O-level (my eleventh) that year. I had also kept on a German session, reading literature with Mrs Mullins for an hour a week. At lunchtime a small dining room was set aside as a 'French room', where you conversed in French over the mince and carrots and stodge. Virginia, Sheila and I became permanent fixtures here, supposedly encouraging the young things to lose their inhibitions about speaking a foreign tongue.

The Bristol University German poetry competition was on the horizon and I said I'd like to do it. Mrs Mullins dithered a little, but agreed, rather reluctantly. She pondered over a few rather lightweight verses, but I wanted a strong subject. The one I chose was 'Wiegenlied' (or cradle-song) by Bertolt Brecht some of which I still remember:

> Mein Sohn, was immer auch aus dir werde,
> Sie stehn mit Knüppeln bereit schon jetzt.
> Denn für dich, mein Sohn, ist auf dieser Erde,
> Nur der Schuttablagerungsplatz da, und der ist besetzt.
>
> Mein Sohn, laß es dir von deiner Mutter sagen:
> Auf dich wartet ein Leben, schlimmer als die Pest.

It was a passionate, deeply sincere poem in which a mother mourns the wicked state of the world into which her son has been born, warns him of the traps, the endurances, and desperately wonders how to save him from its evils. Sue and Virginia came with me as support. I was meeting my parents after the event, to go and see a Gilbert and Sullivan production. Mrs Mullins mentioned the special tea laid on for winners and their teachers, and I reacted by saying, 'Oh dear, that will cut things a bit fine.' Virginia raised her eyebrows, saying, 'She thinks she's going to win!' Sue burst out laughing, saying, 'I love you for that!' I blushed furiously, because I knew I was going to win. There were two heats, so we had to recite twice, and apparently I gave a much better performance at the second attempt. Sue said my eyes blazed with fervour. And yes, I did win; it was a wonderful moment and I still treasure the two tomes of literature I received as a prize; and which I clutched to my person all through the performance of *The Gondoliers*.

My sister had fallen in love with Reg, a self-employed mineralogist who was fourteen years older than herself. He was to her, I suppose, a rather romantic figure, a loner with a mysterious craft. He was a regular in the shop and would leave French and German business letters for me to translate. Jenny had heard his voice and registered his dry humour long before she met him. They had a whirlwind romance, which was also rather stormy, and became engaged. Jenny was treated with disapproval by her tutors, as she was supposed to complete her ophthalmic training and move on to general nursing. Mum was distracted, not sure that this was the right relationship, that the age gap was too great, wondering if this was simply a means of escaping the challenge of the daunting Bristol Royal Infirmary. Plans for marriage moved forward inexorably through the highs and lows, culminating in a December wedding just after her eighteenth birthday. I was the only bridesmaid, dressed in a long gown of red velvet, trying to lighten the occasion by laughing at the camera while the bride and groom looked solemn and dignified.

Then my maiden Aunt Mary, now in her mid-fifties, amazed us all by announcing her engagement to her cousin Maurice – he whose battleship had escorted Mum to South Africa in 1941. This was the third marriage between the Whitmores and the McCabes, so it's as well they were beyond procreating. At the wedding, which was unusually harmonious, we met distant cousins previously only existing in family lore. The photographs show my parents still looking young and handsome and full of life, and as I write it dawns on me that they were younger than I am now! Time and memory can play strange tricks.

In second-year sixth, at seventeen, life became serious again. I put in some applications to London hospital medical schools, having been advised to do this early. To my chagrin, they were all turned down flatly before I had even taken my A-levels. What were they looking for? No one could have a better set of O-levels, to say nothing of extra-curricular activities. I assumed that it was the wrong school, the wrong connections, the lack of medical background. My plan was to stay in third-year sixth to do zoology (necessary for medicine) and also take Oxford and Cambridge entrance exams.

There was an immense amount of factual knowledge to be assimilated in the three science subjects, and as always it was a race against time to get through the new material while keeping a nodding acquaintance with the old. I'm not sure where my pattern of working went wrong but I became aware as the exams approached that I was struggling to master the facts of all the topics. And the more stressed I became, the less efficient was the assimilation process. The day before my chemistry inorganic paper I learned some new material, hoping to have it fresh in mind. And the topic came up. But to my horror I could not recall anything of what I had crammed the previous day! There was a choice, but I had to change my plan and lost time and confidence.

I passed all my subjects but the grades were not brilliant. This was my first academic reverse. Probably things had been too easy before. But it taught me a lot about planning well ahead and I've never had quite the same frightening experience again.

Other imperatives asserted themselves that summer, and I began to go to Saturday night dances with a friend, Diana, who was a working girl with her own car. I was asked to dance by a young blond man with friendly eyes, who looked like every mother's idea of 'a nice boy'. This was Edward who, when I asked his age, looked ashamed and said, 'I'm an old man – I'm twenty four!' I smiled secretly to myself. At seventeen it seemed wonderfully sophisticated to have a partner of that age. We stayed together the whole evening and exchanged phone numbers. He escorted me politely to the car and gave me a chaste kiss on the cheek – to Diana's amusement. I liked his old-fashioned chivalry.

So this was my first serious boyfriend and the relationship lasted well over a year, in the course of which I discovered for the first time the delights of an established partner with whom to share confidences, secrets, ideas, trust, letters, amicable silences, frenetic activities. We went to parties in which maybe half the evening would be spent chatting and flirting with other people, but with the confidence that we would end the evening together and everyone else would be elbowed aside. Edward was a product of the public-school system (Kings, Taunton), and his sister was at Sunny Hill. His family was prototype middle class, and he found mine a little off-beat and hard to classify. My father took me to Sennen in Cornwall for a few days after the exams (Mum minding the shop as always), and Edward came down for an afternoon and stayed for dinner. My father left us on the beach together and wandered off, clearly feeling rejected and sorry for himself. I joined Edward's family for a caravanning holiday, learned to play respectable tennis, spent many weekends with him either at his house or ours. In winter we skated or tobogganed, or took trips to Bournemouth where we would skate (ice or roller), go to a tea-dance, take in a show. Mum began to question my wish to go to university, saying, 'Wouldn't it be nice to settle into a job nearby, and save up to get married?' But I had no intention of settling down with Edward.

He was a delightful person, but not profound or clever (he had several attempts at his chartered accountancy exams), and though I was having wonderful fun, knew that my feelings were not seriously engaged. And much more importantly, I wanted to go places, have a future, be a person.

In the winter of 1962 Sue and I both took Oxford and Cambridge entrance exams. There was no experience or know-how at Sunny Hill so we got on with it ourselves with no coaching. I was called up for interviews and practicals to both universities, and felt daunted by the well-dressed, well-connected people I met. One girl in particular, who looked as if she had just stepped out of the pages of *Vogue*, dropped her dressing case which opened to reveal toiletries and feminine articles of the most exquisite and expensive taste. 'I'm from Roedean,' she said as we helped her gather her things; we hardly needed to be told.

I achieved the standard for admission, which was a sop to my ego, but didn't get a place owing to the intense competition. I later learned that Lady Margaret Hall in Oxford, which was my first choice, only took one medical student per annum. Not surprisingly I began to despair of a medical-school place. The next step was to apply through the newly installed UCCA computer system, putting Edinburgh as my first choice. The weeks slipped by. I was so accustomed to volumes of windowed, brown-envelope correspondence that I lifted the letter from the mantelpiece without thinking, talking volubly to Mum and Jenny, who was home for the day, and in an advanced state of pregnancy. My chatter came to an abrupt halt as I read those long-deferred words: 'Dear Madam, We are happy to offer you ...' I dropped the envelope and screamed, 'Mum! I got a place, I got a place, I got a place,' grammar and decorum deserting me simultaneously.

So my school days were effectively at an end, but I stayed on to tie off a few ends.

Way back in my middle-school years when I had fallen in love with music and all connected with it, I had formed an ambition to get to grade VIII piano exam. I just had enough time, but only if the determination remained at full strength. The previous year I had struggled through grade VII with only a few marks to spare, so expecting to encompass grade VIII in a year was hazardous; particularly as there were so many other channels into which enthusiasm could be dispersed. I was aware that my heart was not as much committed as it should be, but could not bear to forgo a chance at the exam. I entered the Beethoven Sonata class at the Mid-Somerset Competitions, playing the second movement of the seventh sonata, the *largo e mesto*. I knew the piece from O-level days, and modelled my playing on Solomon's recording. The piece is a compelling testimony to sorrow and despair, and demands expressive playing but not too much technical expertise. To everyone's surprise, not least my own, I came second with a mark of eighty-four per cent. Possibly this lulled me into a sense of false security over the exam; but of this, more later.

Another reason for staying on to take zoology and improve my chemistry grade was to compete for a chance to get a direct entry into second-year medicine, which was possible for an English student at a Scottish school. The six-year course would then be reduced to five.

Earlier in the year Sue had been head-hunted by King's School drama group, who were presenting the play *Sergeant Musgrave's Dance* by John Arden; a female was wanted to play the part of a trollop. This was thought to be beyond the capacity of the younger boys. Sue had had a wonderful time and we all turned out to watch the performance. The subject of the play met with great disfavour among the parents and even Sue was hardly convincing as a soldier's moll. Just as well perhaps.

Ben, the drama teacher, wanted to put on Jean Anouilh's *Antigone* with Sue in the lead part. He enquired of her if there was anyone suitable, with some drama experience and not too many other commitments, to play Ismène. Sue asked me the same question. I said promptly, 'How about me?'

Thus it came about that on many afternoons we would walk down to Bruton to join the drama class. Ben was different from our teachers, who always maintained a thin social barrier between them and us. He treated us as equals, and we were expected to call him Ben. He was decidedly attractive too, with brown curly hair, a gymnastic physique, blue eyes and the merest hint of a divergent squint. His nickname at the school was 'the curly-headed darling'. He had a rattle-trap of a van, in which he drove me and Sue home after rehearsals, during which we learned that he was a recent graduate from Oxford, had a fiancée and left-wing views. How were these reconciled with his job at a public school? we asked. 'They aren't,' he replied honestly. 'The parents are utterly ghastly. The boys are decent human beings. I would like to think I can do something to keep them that way, so they don't turn into replicas of their parents.'

Rehearsals progressed. In our cloistered ambience at Sunny Hill our innocence was given a high premium and sex was treated as a no-go area. No one was fooled by this, but appetites could be ungoverned when the restraints were removed. So when Ben said to one of the actors (Antigone's lover), 'Imagine you're necking with a girl in the back of a car,' Sue and I tried to look unsurprised but probably failed.

We enjoyed being the centre of male attention. The cast were a year or two younger than ourselves, but they were charming and fun, and we were easily flattered. As soon as we arrived, one or other would begin to whistle, 'All things bright and beautiful . . .'

For the journey home, Sue was dropped first, and I became aware of enjoying having Ben's company to myself rather more than I should. Indeed, I was very attracted.

One evening over supper, Mum said drily, 'You've got stars in your eyes.'

'I know.'

'But he's got a fiancée.'

'I know that too. Don't worry, Mum. I shan't make an idiot of myself.'

But I knew, as one does, that it wasn't wholly one-sided. Ben was attentive to both Sue and me, and after lengthy rehearsals would take us to a pub for steak and chips. One day Val had joined us at rehearsal as she and Sue were going off somewhere together.

Ben appeared from the hall to take me home. 'Hello, love,' he said, rather warmly.

A frisson went round us all.

Sue said, rather sharply, 'How's your fiancée these days, Ben?'

'I haven't got a fiancée,' he replied. 'Not any more.'

Sue and Val took the hint and ran off to their waiting car. Ben and I went to the pub.

The dress rehearsals and performances came in a whirl of excitement and activity, and the play was well received. 'So much more suitable than that *Sergeant* thing,' twittered the parents. Miss Chappell and all our supporters were impressed, and she gave us quite a eulogy from the platform in Prayers. She had met Ben of course (otherwise we wouldn't be allowed under his tutelage), and actually became a little flirtatious in his company.

After the last performance I thought, Is that it? Is it over? I went home with Mum and her friends in the car and she handed me a cigarette, knowing I was feeling emotional.

A day or two later, Ben rang. 'I'm going to Oxford today. Do you want to come?'

And so our affair began, and I was really crazily, head-over-heels, unconditionally, wildly in love for the first time. Some people never experience this feeling. Truly and profoundly did Tennyson say, ''Tis better to have loved and lost than never to have loved at all.'

The first thing I had to do was to give Edward his marching orders. I did this by phone and he got little warning. I told him the truth. I felt badly, but one cannot dissemble under these circumstances.

The attitude of my school-friends veered between admiration and envy. I was beyond caring. Once, rather rashly, we attended a concert at Kings, to hear a string quartet. One of Ben's senior colleagues said to him later, 'That was a nice girl you were with. Very nice, very pretty. Who is she?'

Ben replied, 'She's at Sunny Hill.'

The colleague looked affronted and withdrew.

I went to the sports day at Kings, and while Ben performed some necessary duties was escorted by my friends from the drama group. All this was heady stuff to an erstwhile prim schoolgirl.

I planned to have a last shot at the French and English verse-speaking cup, and with Sue out of the running thought I might win. Miss Chappell announced one morning that she had asked Mr Ben B——— to judge the competition; a gasp went round the senior school.

Sue took me to task over this. 'You must withdraw!' she said vehemently. 'You ought to win, and of course you won't if he judges it. He would never have the brass neck to put you first!'

But I was brazen and refused to back out. I went along trying to look demure in my school uniform and recited my Shakespearean sonnet and French poem, trying not to catch Ben's eye. Then he was invited to Prayers to make the assessment and announce the winner. Well, I won, and got a huge ovation. He said later in defence of himself that it was pretty obvious really.

The last event of term was the grade VIII piano exam. I guess I knew it would be a disaster, and it was. I thought I might have scraped through, and dismissed it from my mind. It was Ben who broke the news that I'd failed, as he had been talking to Miss Chappell about some matter when she had just got the results. I suppose it was good for me not to have everything my own way, but this particular thing was intensely mortifying. Ben said, 'There's more to life than passing exams, love.'

Our form teacher was devastated that I hadn't confided in her about Ben, and disapproving too. The general view seemed to be that I would not now be going to university. It was odd how the prospect of marriage seemed to override all else.

10

And so to Bed

With the unfounded confidence of youth we said cursory goodbyes to friends as if we were going to see them again in a few weeks' time. Most of them I've not seen since, but with many I have maintained a yearly contact. Shortly after leaving Sunny Hill I passed my nineteenth birthday and had a feeling that my departure was long overdue. I was longing for pastures new. I had received a booklist and applied for a place in hall at Edinburgh; too late, the few places were taken, so I applied for digs. Then there was nothing to do but wait, and October seemed a long way off.

I thought Ben might disappear to some much-to-be-resented home for the holidays, but discovered he was a waif with no fixed abode. He had a couple of functional rooms at the school and was planning to move into a flat in the town. He had parents somewhere but did not feel bound to visit them; indeed it was clear there were some tensions there. At twenty-six, he was rather defiantly independent. This was extended to his relationship with me as he hated to commit himself to a date, but preferred to act on impulse. We would take off in his van to Bristol to some avant-garde film, or to an al fresco musical or theatrical performance. The school swimming pool was available on hot days for lazy hours or brief bursts of activity.

Love-making with Ben was heading towards new dimensions altogether. Edward and I had been equally innocent at the start of our relationship, and we had embarked on a happy journey of mutual discovery. Ben's student days, by contrast, had been as sexually liberated as one might expect, and he clearly expected that I would sleep with him, as the euphemism expresses it. There was no pressure from him, just an affectionate acceptance that I would naturally follow my instincts – and his. It occurs to me only now, thinking back, what effective psychology he used. The start of our affair as I've described it was very exciting. As Mum said, 'It's like a romantic novel. Who would believe it?' And the teacher–pupil relationship was risqué. So what better plan could he follow than letting me get just a little bored? He collected me one day (before the end of Kings' term), probably after leaving me alone for a few days. He took me back to his rooms, then settled down at his desk to work. I had no book with me, so picked up one of his history tomes: very dusty and heavy-going, difficult to concentrate on. Soon I was at his side, distracting him, winding my arms round his neck ... On that occasion we were interrupted soon after by a senior boy knocking at the door with some request. But Ben was patient, the formula was repeated; and of course I succumbed. At nineteen I was probably two years behind the average in this, as with my rebellion against authority.

Our relationship changed subtly and pleasantly and I became more nearly part of his everyday life. I helped to find his flat and accompanied him to auction sales for some basic furnishings. At one of these sales I saw an old upright piano – rather out of tune. 'Do you want it?' asked Ben. He paid ten shillings for it. We spent time in the flat, had friends round for a meal (a rather inexpert stew). Then he would be seized by an impulse and take off in the van, disappearing for a week.

As the summer wore on, having no immediate goals or pressures, time hung rather heavily. Ben planned to visit the Edinburgh Festival Fringe and indulge in some concentrated culture, living rather rough as far as I could gather. I didn't accompany him. With an empty two or three weeks and a feeling of profound ennui I found myself a job as a waitress in a down-market café-restaurant in Frome.

My fellow waitresses were a rather frumpy girl in her twenties and an older married woman whose husband was in jail for fiddling his national insurance. We got on amicably and I listened in fascination to their stories. I didn't talk much about myself. The work was unbelievably hard, physically demanding and taxing on the memory – we weren't supposed to write orders down – and generally unthanked. But it was a huge relief to have something to do and I felt I was seeing life in the raw; also making a few extra pennies to equip myself for student life.

Mum had for some years been preparing for my departure. Money was always a little tight. She smoked heavily then, cigarettes that were sold with tokens to save and use for buying goods. This was the means by which she acquired my leather briefcase and set of towels, I'm ashamed to say.

One day at the café as I was scurrying to and fro with afternoon teas, lo and behold, there was Ben sitting in state at a table. I think he was glad to see me occupied; like many men at all ages he resisted being tied down.

As the time drew near for my departure to Scotland he seemed to withdraw a little. Finally I taxed him with this, recognising that it was not his style to make the most of the time before I left, but also indicating that going to the opposite extreme was rather hard. He acknowledged this. One of his failings was a tendency to do the opposite of what was accepted or expected, just to rebel against convention. How silly, I said; you still end up being manipulated by externals.

He didn't exactly resent my going, but was really envious. His advice was to be sure and do things I would be very ashamed of. He predicted of himself, not wholly seriously, that he would degenerate through a series of relationships with young things until he was thirty and over the hump.

'Will you marry me then, love?'

'I'll think about it, Ben.'

Humbly: 'Thank you, love.'

Mr Tunstall gave me a book called *Christian Sex Ethics*. The dear man had taken the trouble to go to a Church bookshop in Bristol and select a suitable moral guide. I was deeply touched, although was already a lost cause. Mrs Tunstall gave me a book of modern verse. Interestingly, I still have this with her inscription in it, but have long since lost the sex ethics book, though I dutifully read it.

Ben drove me to Bristol to catch my train to Edinburgh, and because of the early departure I spent the previous night at his flat. As we struggled downstairs in the early morning with my luggage, the landlady's small girl appeared in the doorway. This was to have repercussions. We arranged to correspond, and waved farewell at Templemeads station, as my train slid away to the north.

My carriage was full. A young blond man of about my own age made a point of sitting next to me. We began to converse; his name was Barry and yes, he was going to Edinburgh University too, a fresher like myself. He had got his place at the very last moment. We talked for the greater part of the journey.

The first term, indeed the first week, were so full of wonderful things, of new experiences and hosts of new friends, that I could write an entire book on this brief spell alone. I felt completely at home in Edinburgh from the start. In my digs were four other girls, all freshers: Jean, from Inverness, who was my room-mate, Morag, Nancy and Athlene who all came from Kirkcaldy High School, along with numbers of their peer group. I contrasted this ease of access to university with the struggle at Sunny Hill to get even a single entrant, my first exposure to the advantages of the Scottish educational system. Our landlady, Mrs Murray, was a tough businesswoman, who luckily saw her way to being very tolerant with us. We had keys and total freedom to come and go.

Freshers Week was a concerted effort to introduce us to as much of university life and people as possible. We gathered in huge lecture halls to witness personality parades from the highest to the lowest, the most prominent to the most obscure. How is it that freshers adopt student-style behaviour as if it is instinctive? There was plenty of audience participation with drumming of feet on the floor in approval, and good-natured heckling. We received vast amounts of coloured paper giving information vital to our survival. We queued to matriculate and have vaccinations. One of my early visits was to the Faculty of Medicine office where I discovered to my elation that I was to go directly into second year; straight into anatomy, with human dissection and other relevant subjects. And best of all we enjoyed the social programme.

I had expected to enjoy a full social life, an intellectual and cultural life, and even to do some work. The initial emphasis was definitely on fun and frivolity, and making bonds of friendship. On the first evening there was a dance for which I wore a slinky and probably *démodé* gold lamé dress. I was commandeered by Barry for a large part of the evening. My girl friends were full of admiration. 'Who's the nice male? Where did you find him?' But no one was short of partners and there were many amiable people from the Kirkcaldy circuit. I discovered to my amazement that there was a strong commitment to Scottish nationalism amongst them, Morag being a particular enthusiast. This was totally outwith my experience, but since it was adopted by such intelligent and friendly people I felt I should keep an open and receptive mind. Barry blotted his copybook later that week by referring to the Nats as 'Scottish Nits'. This intolerance was unacceptable and most especially ungracious in an English student occupying a student place in Scotland; so he was dropped forthwith.

The debate in Freshers Week was usually on a topic that attracted interest; this time it was 'This House Believes in Free Love'. The Union debating hall was filled to the galleries and all the extrovert and articulate personalities took to the platform or raised sardonic points of information from the floor. It was hilarious and lively and I felt joyously that this was what student life should be all about.

Another night, after various engagements, Morag appeared in a state of sparkly-eyed enthusiasm. She had discovered that a café, the Bothy, on George IV Bridge, was hosting a folk group, the Corries, that evening. Always willing to extend my education but not quite sure why there was such collective delight, I joined the group. I was even more mystified when we were expected to part with four shillings and sixpence for a cup of coffee. That covers the floor show, they explained. And it was worth it. My folk-singing experience was confined to 'Singing Together' in primary school, but in 1963 it was very much part of the nationalistic resurgent culture, and I paid homage to the plangent, earthy, comic and tragic moods of the music with as much ardour as anyone.

Many of our nights' activities ended up in a flat in Fountainbridge, temporary lodgings of Stewart, George and Melvyn. The place was invariably crowded with people, which was just as well because viewed empty and by daylight it was as filthy and depressing as any student pad you've ever seen. One evening as I sat on a sagging sofa surrounded by male suitors I conferred my attentions on George, a first-year medic, with whom I subsequently kept company before realising what a terrible faux pas I had committed. He was Athlene's steady boyfriend. I believe I was his final fling before they settled into a long-term relationship. Anyway, he drifted back to her, and there were no hard feelings among us.

The last dance of Freshers Week, before we had to begin taking life a little more seriously, was in the Union, which I may say was for men only, with all its privileges. Many of my new friends from Kirkcaldy were gathered in the bar, notably Stewart who was in an advanced state of inebriation and fired with vocal nationalistic fervour. He was red-haired, already balding and sported a ragged beard, a deep voice and a big ego. He raised his glass; 'Rot the English!' he roared. Then, leering at me he murmured, 'But we don't mean you, my dear,' putting his arm around my waist and getting more affectionate with each glass. I went out with him a few times, gradually realising that he too was the considered property of at least two other girls.

I decided to avoid forming a relationship of any seriousness at first. For one thing there were so many fish in the sea, and I had dates with eighteen different fellows in my first term alone. For a second there was Ben at home who wrote every week that first term. For a third, like most girls who have a complete change of lifestyle, my periods ceased altogether for two months, inevitably raising worries about pregnancy. I thought, how sickening it would be to enter on this wonderful life and have to cut it short because of impending mother-hood. But nature sorted itself out eventually and I heaved a sigh of relief.

Meaning to live life to the full I collected a handful of society membership cards. I longed to keep up with my dramatic activities and be able to dazzle Ben with a colourful account of my triumphs. Dramsoc was a cliquish group and difficult to penetrate. I joined, went to an evening meeting or two, auditioned for a part, but I got nowhere so didn't persist. When everyone else was so welcoming, why bother? I thought. Joining the musical society choir, I attended rehearsals for *Carmina Burana*: almost unknown in those days long before Classic FM. Needing some healthy outdoor activity I presented myself at the Union Canal on Wednesday afternoons to learn how to row. In one of his letters Ben was very rude about this. 'I am sufficiently reactionary to believe that the only sportive posture young ladies should adopt is flat on their backs!' he wrote. This energetic attempt did not survive too far into the windy Edinburgh winter; or maybe it just withered under Ben's scorn. I was eventually enticed into joining the Nationalist Club. It did not consider itself exclusively Scottish nationalist; I was warmly welcomed, as was everyone of any nationality. The interest was enough. One of the most delightful things about university life was that you felt part of a group – often several groups. It is terribly important to belong.

Back at the digs the phone went incessantly and as often as not it was for me. Mrs Murray grumbled, 'I think she's given her phone number to every boy in the varsity.' One Saturday afternoon I was expecting a special counselling visit from a senior student to explore any problems I might have and to give helpful advice. When the girl arrived, I patiently heard her rehearse her piece, anxious to reassure her and hustle her out of the door. But she was determined to give me the works, and listed all the problems that could arise and how I should deal with them (usually religious solutions). This must have given her some personal satisfaction; it left me feeling depressed.

The rectorial elections fell in our first term. We elected James Robertson Justice, who acted Sir Lancelot Spratt in the *Doctor* films, amidst the mayhem of mock flour and water battles in the Old Quad, and then torchlight processions up the Royal Mile to the castle, where the crowd, which was getting disorderly and euphoric, were met with soldiers with fixed bayonets. I remember it well, being right at the front of the procession.

Most of my friends were non-medical at this stage, and drifted off to an easy life with maybe a couple of teaching sessions a day. My day started at nine o'clock with a physiology lecture, then two hours of human dissection, then an anatomy lecture at twelve. At two o'clock came another lecture, usually biochemistry, then two hours of practicals. We approached the dissecting room with a degree of nervousness, most of us never having seen a dead person before. The room was longer than a hospital ward, with two rows of tables along each side, each supporting a grey naked body reeking of formalin. We started our depredations on the upper limb, three persons on each side. Senior students worked on the head and neck and sometimes lower limb as well, though not usually all together. The delicacies were observed: the few women in the class worked on female bodies and student sexes were not mixed. Not officially at least. The dissecting room was very sociable and assignations were often made here. Years later, my mother told me she wanted to donate her body to an anatomy department after death. I tried to dissuade her, asking how she liked the idea of two young things leaning their elbows on her bosom as they made eyes at each other. Her response was characteristic: 'I can't think of anything I'd like better.' We were taken away in small groups for tutorials, again with sexes segregated. Most of the male tutors were trainee surgeons and quite human, but the two females were terrifying white-coated figures, strict and spinsterish. No first-name informality here, it was: 'Miss Whitmore, would you care to explain ...' with exaggerated politeness and a degree of sarcasm if the explanation did not come up to scratch.

In physiology and biochemistry practicals, requiring live bodies, we had no other recourse than to use ourselves. We learned to syringe

First portrait, Pretoria 1944

Dad and two-year-old Jenny in
the garden, Pretoria

Mum with her daughters outside
the rondavel, Pretoria

In ascending order; me, Clive, Jenny at Topcliffe

German prisoners of war make up a band
for the New Year party, Topcliffe 1947

The family enjoys the
RAF Christmas Party,
Warton 1950

Brownies and Guides, Warton 1952. Mum first on the right, back row.
Front row, from left, Maureen, me. Last two on the right are the other
Margaret and Maureen

At sixteen I'd
given up on the
tooth brace

The Red Queen (me)
introduces the dinner
to Alice, whilst the
White Queen (Sue)
looks on. Sunny Hill,
1960

In the bear's cage at Edinburgh Zoo.
Edinburgh Students Chanties' week, 1966

Three's a crowd. Morag, Rod and me, Sennen Cove 1964

Graduation Day 1968. Me, Barbara, Anne

The world's at our feet! 15 September 1969

Ebullient
bath-time.
Chris, 1973

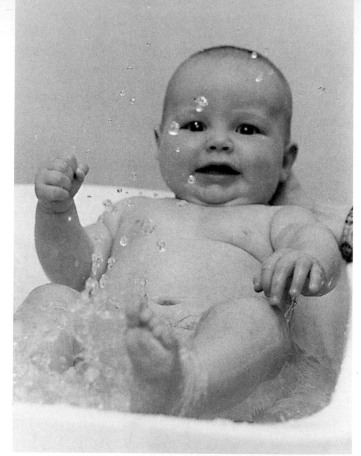

BELOW Big Peter
and wee Peter,
Buckland,
Cotswolds 1975

BELOW RIGHT
Chris at three
months with his
proud mother,
Kirkcudbright
1973

blood from each other, manipulate it in centrifuge tubes, on slides, under microscopes. No one thought of blood as dangerous then and no safety measures were taken. We experimented with measuring temperature, pulse, respiratory rates, urinary output after doing things like running up three flights of stairs or drinking a pint of water. Some poor unfortunates were persuaded to have naso-gastric tubes inserted via their nostrils to measure gastric juice. We did delicate operations on frogs' gastrocnemius muscles, discovering the effect of chemical mediators and showing the effects by a stylus drawing lines on a smoked drum. My partner, Barbara, wore a mohair sweater which rubbed the smoke off the drum, thus obliterating our afternoon's careful measurements. Our most adventurous experiment made use of Archimedes' principle, involving weighing objects in air and water. Our intention was to work out how much fat by weight there was in the persons of the average male and female medical student. We stripped off, donning swimsuits, and weighed ourselves in a special tank, completely immersed; and also on an ordinary set of scales. There were various assumptions made and complicated calculations. If I remember the results correctly, the fattest, most beer-gutted male was ten per cent; the slenderest, most anorexic female was eighteen per cent. Maybe some of the assumptions were erroneous. I was twenty-five per cent.

One of Ben's early letters informed me that he had been given notice to quit his flat, the result of the landlady's daughter seeing me descend the stairs at six in the morning ('Dirty-minded little bitch'). I was horror-struck, still sensitive about losing my virtue and being the subject of gossip. I was touched by the regularity of his letters which as term moved on became more liberally spattered with expletives. He said of himself that he got progressively more small-minded and bad-tempered. As we also got busier with end-of-term exams looming I was late with a reply – and received a sad and importunate note enquiring if I had met with any dire disaster, which notion I hastened to dispel.

One of my classmates, Colin (another red-haired, bearded person. Is there a theme here?), who was hugely popular and fun-loving, kept teasing me to come and watch Yogi-Bear at Holland House hall of residence after classes. So one day I turned up, much to his amusement. We went out together that night, though we should have been swotting for an exam. For the first time in my life I got definitely drunk, and probably did some of those things destined to make me ashamed of myself. So they probably would, if I could have remembered them. The next morning I felt so ill I couldn't even drink my tea and returned to bed. Another morning's studying lost! Colin turned up on the doorstep to apologise for getting me so drunk, and charmed Mrs Murray with his gallantry.

I travelled home at Christmas by overnight train via London with a gang of male friends, including one Martin, with whom I'd had a few dates. I was aware that my dig-mates had some mischief afoot and oblique references were made to 'Plan X'. They turned up in force to see us off and showered us with confetti on the platform and in the carriage. I later found Martin's pyjamas in my case.

It was delicious to go to the peace and tranquillity of home and revel in relaxation and the atmosphere of Christmas, plus of course dazzling everyone with my tales of student life. My services were still required at the church organ. I saw a lot of Ben, but kept him at arm's length as seemed appropriate to me, but inevitably the relationship cooled from then.

II

Celtic Twilight

To Mum's sorrow I did not stay long at home, as I was enticed back to Scotland with promises of a traditional Hogmanay. In the excitement of travelling north on 31 December I did not eat much, which was poor preparation for the evening's events. I was to stay with Athlene and her family in Kirkcaldy and thrilled to the experience of crossing the magnificent Forth Railway Bridge for the first time. The road bridge was nearing completion then, with just a small gap left in the middle.

The party was every bit as wild as predicted. Neat whisky was the only drink available. People got emotional and introspective as midnight passed, then veered towards euphoria as first-footers joined the throng. One moment I was sitting cosily on Stewart's lap, the next I was being carried up to bed, where I found myself the next morning, still fully dressed and with a head like the inside of a *bodhrán*. But I had not disgraced myself as comprehensively as many others. Still, even the smell of whisky made me nauseous after this and I didn't touch it again for years.

The next new event was a rugby international at Murrayfield. The enthusiasm again indicated this was not to be missed, but this time I failed to see the attraction. Standing for hours in a crush of humanity in the freezing cold with a bursting bladder, seeing little and understanding less, was not an experience I wanted to repeat. And I never have.

Early in the winter term came the Burns Supper season and the Nat Club looked forward to a big event with Hamish Henderson, the folk music expert, as main speaker. There was always difficulty in finding someone who would reply for the lasses, so I agreed to do it. This was rash as the only Burns I had ever read was 'To a Mouse'. I laced my speech with, as I thought, apt quotations, but judging from the blank expressions had clearly selected lines that nobody knew. Stewart recited 'Tam O'Shanter' which, to my then uninitiated ears, was like listening to a foreign language; since then I have heard it many times and know it well.

Colin and I established a pleasant relationship, which, however, we agreed need not exclude other friendships. He was universally popular and if there was a nucleus of jokes and laughter in the dissecting room, he was usually at the centre of it. One of my female colleagues took me aside with a serious air and asked if I knew that Colin had another girlfriend. I laughed and explained our agreement. She looked disappointed (perhaps I'm being catty) and said, 'I didn't want you to be hurt.'

Colin and I went to a ball at the Assembly Rooms. Balls were quite numerous in the university year and dress formal. Late in the evening I was asked to dance by Sandy, a huge fellow, one of the Kirkcaldy contingent, and somehow got so engrossed with conversation and dancing that more than an hour had passed. I became aware of a grim-faced, smouldering Colin bearing down upon us. There was a little clipped conversation, some posturing and jutting of chins, and I allowed myself to be borne away by Colin. On the way home I got a lecture on the courtesies of our give-and-take arrangement. 'In my time,' he emphasised, '*my* time, you don't go off with anyone else, right?' I humbly agreed I had behaved badly.

I fancied myself in love with Sandy and had a brief, intense affair with him. But he was a man's man; his world was full of rugby, Covenanter's group, Bell's bar, mountaineering and other essentially male pursuits, so it did not last. The following winter he was tragically killed by an avalanche while walking in the Scottish hills.

Morag and Nancy moved out of the digs into a flat somewhere in Leith. Their landlord kept open house in the flat below theirs, or so it seemed judging by the number of sailors who visited there and the number of scantily clad women one met on the stairs. There were many jokes about their house of ill-repute and I wrote home saying, 'Morag and Nancy have moved in with a ponce!' Unfortunately I forgot I had written in these raw and undefined terms. Shortly afterwards I moved into a bed-sit beside them, and wrote, 'I am now living with Morag and Nancy.' I had some explaining to do.

We all threw ourselves whole-heartedly into Charities Week. One activity was to go round the pubs with a collecting tin, and this was my first exposure to the functional, spit-and-sawdust, men-only places which were still the norm in the city centre. No woman would dream of going for any other reason. And it was like trying to extract money from a stone. I got weary of being told, 'Charity begins at home.' Another time I was told, 'If ye hadnae had a zip up the front of yer jeans, I might hae gi'en ye something.' Mid-line zips for women had just come into fashion. Charities Café was a huge all-night affair with continuous entertainment, bar and light refreshments. Female students volunteered to be waitresses, which was a popular occupation as you did as much or as little work as you pleased, and it was an excellent way of meeting people, making friends, getting dates. The only time I ever managed to go up Arthur's Seat on May morning to wash my face in the dew at dawn was when I went directly there from the café.

I made special friends with Mac that summer, a left-wing nationalist from Tain, ex-editor of *Student* magazine, who could never make up his mind whether to present himself as a romantic or a cynic. I think the romanticism was inherited, the cynicism acquired. He would make frequent reference to 'When the revolution comes ...' especially in debates when someone was getting carried away with his own rhetoric. He was volatile, verging on the violent when under the influence of drink, but had the sweetest and most pliant nature underneath the mood swings. He had a huge network of friends and always knew at weekends where the parties were, which we would gatecrash unashamedly and usually get a welcome. There was a thrilling sense of degeneracy in wandering home from parties with the dawn and the early chirruping of birds. I had no professional exams that year, so escaped retribution. Mac had a deep reverence for Scottish culture and liked to inhabit Milne's Bar where contemporary poets met. One day when we were there, relaxing and sipping our pints, I observed an older man sitting on a bar stool, eyeing my legs which were clad in tartan-patterned tights. As we left, Mac murmured reverently, 'I hope you realise how honoured you are. Your legs have been admired by Norman MacCaig.'

For our first long vacation in the summer of 1964, Morag and I took a job at Sennen Cove in Cornwall, where I had previously stayed on holiday, working as waitresses in the hotel on top of the cliff. We worked long hours but had time off in the afternoon to enjoy the beach, and late evenings to enjoy the night life. The folk revival here also was vigorous and with the help of Morag's guitar we provided a Scottish flavour. The summer would have been perfect but for an obnoxious head waiter, whose conversations were laced with 'As we say in rep . . .' and who affectedly called everyone 'Darling'. He seemed to acquire an extraordinary hold over the lady owner, taking over financial control and throwing his weight about like a manager. He created an altercation with a mixed-race family staying at the hotel, referring to them in derogatory terms; thereafter, on discovering that the father of the family held a prestigious job in the BBC, he became placatory and unctuous.

I felt this was a bad scene and decided to leave. Morag came soon after and stayed with me. Mum said, rather disapprovingly, 'When you've got a proper job you won't be able to walk out when you don't like someone.' But we were free as birds and enjoying it. We took off to Liverpool to stay with some people we'd met at the hotel, then we returned north and camped for a week on the banks of Loch Earn. And finally we joined the Nats for a week at Strathtummel Youth Hostel for a so-called 'Summer School'. Morag and I swam in Loch Tummel in mid-September, mainly, I think, for bravado. It was as cold as mountain melt-water. Morag, Stevie, Stewart and I remained an extra day to climb Schiehallion. Resting in contented achievement at the peak, Morag said, 'What wouldn't I give for a pint in the Captain's right now?' The Celtic glow vanished. We headed down the slopes for the car, and some three hours later reached the Captain's Bar.

In the middle of third-year medicine in those days came the dreaded, most difficult and influential second MB, ChB exam: the so-called 'Second Prof'. Many more people were chucked out here than at finals, for the simple reason that by the time we reached finals we were rather an expensive investment. It was now essential to buckle to, and keep the mind on the work. I renewed my relationship with Mac, probably having a steadying influence on him too. Gone was my butterfly existence of the previous year. I had moved, with Morag, Nancy, Jean and another Kirkcaldy girl, Anne, to a two-floored flat in Inverleith Terrace, opposite the Botanical Gardens, where we troubled the neighbours for three years. The rooms were huge, high-ceilinged, designed for gracious living. It was ideal for parties of which we had a number. For heating there was a two-barred electric fire in the sitting room and nothing else. It must have been well insulated as we didn't feel like the cast from La Bohème.

Here in my narrative is another point worthy of emphasis. For here, October 1964, I first set eyes on Robin who, in spite of only being a first-year student, was a person of some reknown, having been a distinguished debater on the Edinburgh school circuit. A meeting was held in the Union debating hall, to set up a European society, and all interested people might go. A committee was elected, among them Robin, notable for his flaming red hair and scholarly aspect. I remember nothing else about this society and presume it didn't flourish.

Submitting again to the yoke of discipline still gave some time for party-going and I kept my membership of the musical society choir, performing at various times, Handel's *Israel in Egypt*, Mozart's Requiem, Verdi's Requiem, all in the Usher Hall. Also I kept up with the Nationalist Club, whose club rooms, dusty and dingy, were a gathering place for social contact in the daytime, coffee-drinking and even sometimes for studying.

At Christmas I was offered a lift home which I accepted gladly enough. The vehicle, when it arrived, was a van with no seats in the back – just the metal floor – and no heating. There were three others sharing the expenses of the trip. The two driving participants shared the front between them, so I spent the entire four hundred-mile journey in the extreme discomfort of the back. Further, the weather was bitterly cold; freezing fog all the way. The only way to cope was to endure. We arrived at my home after midnight, everyone cold and miserable, so I had no recourse but to invite them in to make themselves as comfortable as possible in our sitting room, trying to persuade Billy not to eat them. After making cups of tea I retired thankfully to bed. My mother woke me in good humour next morning with the dry remark, 'It's easy to see you're home!' The guys were being given a hearty breakfast and entertaining Dad with exaggerated accounts of our journey.

I soon found out that all was not well. A family crisis had erupted, of the sort that leads to misunderstandings and interpersonal strife. Mum tried to break things tactfully and it was difficult to read between the lines and make out what had actually gone wrong. In my distress I wrote and told Mac, who was spending his holiday mussel-picking in Tan. He wrote back, quite voluminously, trying to make sense of things and offer what consolation he could. He also sent a Shakespearean sonnet: 'Thy love is better than high birth to me ...' He reminded me that not even Anne Hathaway had a report on a freshers' debate dedicated to her! With his mixture of support, comedy and romance he certainly cheered me immensely. I had apparently adjured him to 'be sensible about drink at New Year, as you're just as irresponsible as I am about it'.

I stayed home for New Year to cheer the parents up a little.

About the next term I will say little; it followed a pattern I knew only too well. Work, work and more work. The only variation was where you did the studying. I moved around the various reading rooms and developed a pattern of reading till 4 a.m., then sleeping till midday. It was a fairly solitary existence, apart from seeing Mac regularly.

Then it was over, and all my friends were safely through. The thirty or so women in the class of 140 were always grouped at the top end of the list; that is, we had to work harder and be cleverer to compete with the men. It has changed somewhat since then.

Then tensions arose between me and Mac and we had furious rows; really strange because I've never actively quarrelled with anyone before or since. We split up and it was Colin who consoled me, and who remained a good friend through all the university years. I had discovered that the more intensely you loved, the more turbulent the relationship tended to be. And yet I had never up to this time found anyone to whom I wanted to commit myself for life, even when most disorientated by love. To what extent does anyone find this? Most people pair off, so presumably some compromising goes on.

My twenty-first birthday fell in the holidays and after a merry party of friends and neighbours I set off for my planned holiday job: farm work in a Concordia camp in Lincolnshire. This was an unmitigated disaster. The living quarters were an old prisoner-of-war camp with canvas, bug-ridden beds, primitive buildings and a tower which still housed a rusting machine-gun. The food was almost inedibly disgusting. We pair four pounds ten shillings a week for this, which had to be recovered before we actually made any surplus. At three and sevenpence ha'penny an hour, piece rates, and regular stoppages if the weather was inclement, we were almost bound to be out of pocket. Still, I'm glad I did this, for it gave me an insight into real physical labour. There were foremen to see we really did our full complement of hours. My first job was sugar-beet singling and weeding. Women were always put on to this task because they were more careful. The plants were tough to extract and at the end of eight hours my hands were so stiff I could hardly hold a toothbrush. It was back-breaking too, and after a while I found it easier to crawl up the rows on all fours, in spite of the mud and rain.

On the day of my actual birthday I did eight hours of potato-picking! Which was considerably easier than the sugar-beet work. We also picked raspberries.

I went to the pub one night with a crowd of camp-dwellers. The barman viewed us with suspicion, picked on me and said accusingly, 'You're not old enough to be in here!' I drew myself up and said haughtily, 'I am twenty-one actually!' He forbore to ask the others, which was just as well, as they were all under age.

The only other incident of note was that I narrowly escaped being raped by an Italian worker, who later wrote me a profusely apologetic note.

I returned home and got a couple of catering jobs, earning money the hard way still, but at least with the creature comforts of home. I had made friends with a farming couple, Margaret and Ed, and their trainee farming manager, Blair. Margaret was an enthusiastic maker of wine out of all sorts of improbable ingredients, one of our favourites being wheat and grapefruit wine. After sampling a few we would go and swim naked in their outdoor swimming pool. Ed took photos of us; I sincerely hope they have not survived the years.

At the end of the vacation the Nats held a Crofters' Aid Scheme in Skye, the idea being that we would help the crofters with ditch-digging and farm work. Over a few weeks people came and went, living in a large house made available to us. It was thoroughly enjoyable and we worked hard, though were probably not as useful as we thought. The crofters would do anything to distract us from our tasks, inviting us in for 'a wee stroopach' – a cup of tea – invariably accompanied by a huge spread of buns, cakes and cookies. As one of our number was a divinity student we walked four miles to the kirk – the Free Presbyterian Church of Scotland – to hear a characteristic fire and brimstone sermon, which fulfilled all our expectations. The minister said he'd cut his address short since we'd walked so far in the rain, and spoke for forty-five minutes!

Fourth-year medicine was a big landmark as we began our clinical studies, being attached in small groups to teaching units in the Edinburgh hospitals. I felt quite inhibited at first about approaching patients, asking intrusive questions and expecting to be allowed to examine them, when at the time I had so little to offer back. I soon came to realise that many patients enjoyed this contact, some out of sheer goodwill, others because most people like to talk about themselves, and students had plenty of time to listen. But I also noticed that a number of male colleagues had considerable confidence from the start, as if they were stepping into a role; possibly they came from medical families. This was the era of the omnipotent consultant, and some undoubtedly abused their power. A girl in my group, very pretty with blonde hair and china-blue eyes, when stuck for an answer to a question, put every ounce of charm into, 'I'm afraid I don't know.' The consultant took her apart, demolished her, called her immature – and all in front of us and the patient.

Another time in an orthopaedic ward round we followed the professor as part of his vast ego-propping entourage. Here students were beneath contempt so were relatively safe. He stopped by a bedside which had a protective cage over the patient's leg. He turned to us and launched into an exposition on something or other, emphasising each point by thumping his hand down on the cage. The patient winced each time, clearly in pain. No one, not ward sister, senior or junior doctors, physiotherapists or students, dared to tell him. The senior registrar tried to steady the cage with his hand.

One learned more from observing this incident than anything the professor was saying.

In surgical units the big excitement was being allowed to assist in theatre. Operating theatres are worlds apart, and you need to know the drill if you are not to make a complete ass of yourself; in particular what is sterile and what is not, and how to handle either. On 'waiting days', or emergency receiving days, we were expected to hang around, see patients come in hot off the street, follow them through investigations, preparation and to theatre if needed; and to assist with simple things like appendices.

Meanwhile, the Nat Club was gearing up for the mock election, won almost invariably by the Conservative Club; an interesting point this. The composition of students at a Scottish university ought to reflect the population if there is no class bias, and one would have hoped for a voting pattern more closely reflecting that of the nation. It didn't happen. Labour was usually a poor third. Under Melvyn's presidency the Nat Club had put together some practical proposals, including my extremely naïve and uninformed health policy. In student terms we made a formidable showing, and were sufficiently convincing to win. My friends went berserk with joy. I never claimed to support a separate Scotland so my pleasure was more moderate.

Robin would undoubtedly have spoken at this debate though I don't remember his contribution.

My political sympathies were unsophisticated but unequivocally left wing. My parents both declared themselves to be Tories, but this owed more to brainwashing by the newspapers they read – and in my father's case, his middle-class and service background – than any profound ideological commitment. My mother had a deep-rooted hatred and fear of communism, the emotional content of which precluded rational discussion. Reg, Jenny's husband, had once unwisely admitted to communist sympathy and this created a rift that was never wholly overcome. For my part, I had a young person's sense of fairness, felt that accidents of birth or income should not determine one's role and fate in life, that the best health service and educational opportunities should be available to all and that it was the government's job to set the scene for this to happen. I recognised that there would always be a layer of non-achievers (for a whole spectrum of reasons) and that society had a duty to provide a safety net for these to ensure a decent standard of living for all people and most especially for children. For a time I was a pacifist, though never joined CND.

Once, while I was still at school, a friend Sheila had been given a telling-off by the janitor and her pride was severely wounded. She fumed that he had no right to speak to her like that, he was barely literate (which was true: he inscribed 'FISKS' on a dustpan belonging to the physics lab), and that 'The working classes should be kept in their places!' I was astounded, never having heard such a blatantly classist statement before, certainly not from my Tory-voting parents. At the first general election at which I was eligible to vote (1966) I supported Labour, to my mother's dismay. In spite of having a lot of sympathy then with the Scottish nationalists I never joined the SNP and would never have voted for them.

Debates could on occasions be rather dull. Students took themselves terribly seriously and frankly the most lively debates emerged with the more frivolous motions, such as 'Women should be kept pregnant, barefoot and in the kitchen'. I showed enough interest to be asked to represent the Nat Club on the university debates committee and accepted eagerly as there were many associated perks: mainly dining with invited guests and partying with them afterwards. Evening dress was worn on such occasions by the committee.

On my first such formal session, after dinner I joined my friends near the back of the hall. They were dressed in the usual scruffy student gear, contrasting with my clinging blue evening gown and ornate hair-do. I became aware of Robin, who was also on the debates committee, with stern expression, stalking down the aisle towards me. He asked curtly if I would go and relieve Clare at the clerks' bench. I had no idea what the clerks were supposed to do, but wouldn't have dreamed of admitting it. I swished up the length of the hall to the platform and took Clare's place. Robin told me later he had turned and followed my progress with admiring eyes.

Another well-kent figure on the debating scene at the time was James Douglas-Hamilton, who was a little more mature than the rest of us, having already taken a degree at Oxford. I will say this of James, that few people cut a finer or more elegant figure in a kilt. Most folk avoided this garment since it was adopted so possessively by the nationalists. James, like many aristocrats, was hyper-courteous. Sometimes when wandering around university precincts I would hear the sound of running feet and James would arrive by my side saying, 'H-h-h-h-h-hello, Margaret!' then seem absolutely stuck for words. So it was over to me to observe the banalities for the required amount of time, after which we would go our separate ways. But he was a capable debater and took part in team competitions. At the committee meeting when decisions were required for *Observer* Mace or *Scotsman* competitions, Stewart and James were teamed together. For simplicity, Malcolm Rifkind, who was the president, referred to them as the two Hamiltons. Stewart visibly swelled with pride at each mention, glancing at me and other impressionable women to see how we reacted to this linkage with his aristocratic namesake.

Women were allowed into the Union at certain times, notably Saturday lunchtime – if invited by a man. I frequently availed myself of this privilege as the food was better than at other student catering establishments. I remember seeing Robin saunter into lunch with his girlfriend, Susan, who had long red hair, well colour-coded to his. He always looked sombre; but much worse, he stalked ahead of Susan, arrogantly looking forward and expecting her to trot after him. I murmured to my companion, 'If that was my boyfriend I'd change his ways in no time!' I may as well record here that I never did, in spite of remonstrance, and that unless I reminded him he treated me in exactly the same way.

In the shake-up of committee office-bearers in summer 1966, Robin was to become secretary and I agreed to become publicity convener, taking over from him. We needed to confer a few times and he invited himself round to my flat for a discussion. I made him a cup of instant Nescafé, served in a plain mug with no frills, and remember to this day his expression of distaste as he peered dubiously into its depths.

I continued to have a succession of boyfriends; as soon as one liaison ended someone else was waiting in the wings. Sometimes I ended the relationship, sometimes he did. I was fully awake to the deep need in me to have such a partner, but there arose a dilemma when I found I was relying on someone with whom I did not feel an adequate affinity. In the summer I went out with Donald who was president of the Conservative Club – not a natural liaison for me! But I was fond of him, probably because he reminded me a little of Edward, and also of my father. The day before the vacation was to separate us for three months, he said, 'Don't you think we've been seeing too much of each other?' Of all the crass ways to end a relationship! I said tartly, 'Well, don't worry. Tomorrow will take care of that!'

About this time, a cult French film called *Le Bonheur* was much talked of, in glowing extravagant terms. Someone called it a symphony, the epitome of happiness and so on. I saw it. Beautifully filmed, with beautiful people, it certainly was, but I found the theme disturbing, and also the uncritical reaction. It dealt with a young couple with children, a perfect family. Then the man falls in love with another woman, whom he wants as well as his wife. His wife does not see things his way and commits suicide. The man marries the other woman and the family goes on being as perfect as before.

I think the eulogies were all made by men of my acquaintance, and it's interesting how blithely they all ignored the wife's perspective.

I travelled to Ballymoney in Northern Ireland to do a compulsory six-week residency period in a hospital there. I loved the country and its naturally friendly people, as well as enjoying superb medical experience, taking some minor clinics and stitching up lacerations, assisting at my first Caesarean section. I watched an Orange parade, and with a degree of perplexity observed the enthusiasm of the Protestant community for England winning the football World Cup. I was made aware of the religious discrimination in terms of employment, as few if any posts of any responsibility were held by Catholics. While I was in Northern

Ireland the voice of the Reverend Ian Paisley and other discontented Protestants began to be heard. It was clear even to me that trouble was brewing. We visited the golden empty beaches of Donegal, the Giant's Causeway, swam at Ballycastle where the water was colder than a Highland loch, and admired the colourful fuchsia hedgerows.

Then Morag and I took our bicycles by the ferry to France and travelled around Normandy and Brittany, staying in youth hostels. We had the least possible amount of gear, only what could be packed in saddlebags. French hostels were primitive in the extreme compared with German ones. We subsisted on bread, marge, potatoes, onions, mushrooms, chocolate, wine and coffee. We literally had to fight off the men, who clearly thought we were fair game. After two weeks I failed to recognise myself in a mirror. I thought it was a gypsy.

I had to write to Robin about some debates matter and did so, sitting on my bunk at Dinan. I had just the least inkling of what was about to happen.

12

My Intellectual Lover

Robin and I were both involved in our separate spheres in Freshers Week, and our paths crossed on a number of occasions. I can't remember the precise moment when I became aware that we were (metaphorically) circling round each other like a pair of courting blue-footed boobies. On the Wednesday of that week the Nats held a ceilidh, a wild and physical affair that was not Robin's natural milieu at all – but there he was, staying close to my elbow most of the evening. Conversation wasn't so easy, but then the loud music precluded any deep discussion.

Matters came to a head quite quickly: on Friday 7 October to be precise, which we always regarded as our real anniversary thereafter. The occasion was the freshers' debate, the motion 'That the world owes less to Marx and Lenin than to Marks and Spencer', and the guest speaker was Edward Taylor, MP. No, my memory isn't clinging to these details, I still have my committee card for that year! We had had a discussion about the topic in committee and Malcolm Rifkind, who struck me as being serious and a little straitlaced, thought freshers deserved something a little more sophisticated than the usual free-love debate. It was not an evening-dress occasion as I wore a camel-coloured suit. Afterwards we gathered with the guest and some bottles of whisky and beer in the Union committee room to be convivial. Later, as the party broke up, Robin asked to see me home. He lived at Bangholm Terrace, in the same direction as my flat, so we shared a taxi. We fell into a very pleasant embrace and the taxi was instructed to drive on to his flat.

With inhibitions released, Robin surprised me by being a warm, talkative and witty companion. The flat was a surprise: there was a better standard of decoration and furnishing than usual, and I learned it belonged to his father, bought for Robin's use while at university. There were noticeable feminine touches by his mother, like ornaments and lacy light-shades. So he went off to make coffee and I couldn't help thinking of the reaction when I last made some for him.

The coffee was brought in on a tray, in delicate china cups and saucers – and with a tray-cloth! And it was made with warm milk! I'm afraid I teased him about all of those things. Parental influence was almost palpable. Conversation was easy, so free and so natural, with mirth instead of his usual gravity.

When you touch a person it can completely change your perception of him. Messages are imparted and received well below cerebral level. My sensorium went into overdrive that night, accepting and welcoming my alter ego. But now I shall ask my reader to withdraw discreetly from the room, and turn the light off, please. These moments can never be honestly revisited without changing them, and should remain sacrosanct.

At Freshers' Fair the next day I was involved in Nat Club publicity and enrolling. The hall was vibrating with people as we dashed about, conducting our various bits of business. I stopped at the Labour stall quite early on and had a pleasant chat with Robin who was welcoming and at ease. We made eye contact, smiling at the memory of the previous night. Some hours later as I passed by again I turned to flash a smile in his direction, and got a distinctly – not frosty – but cool reception. He was talking to handsome, well-connected Lindsay Mackie. I wrapped up my smile and went about my business, thinking that I was out of my social depth here.

The day was an exhausting one after a hectic week, and as we packed up, Morag and I agreed to have a quiet Chinese meal, go home and retire early for once. We entered the restaurant in Forrest Road that was one of our usual haunts – and there to my embarrassment was Robin, holding court among his Labour Club friends, clearly having a working supper. We greeted each other affably enough, but I very firmly took a table some distance away. He is convinced, probably to this day, that I was purposefully following him around.

Lindsay clearly didn't waylay him for too long as we came together soon after this, and I was persuaded to stay the night at his flat. He gave me a pyjama top to wear. His bed was a double one as his parents came to stay fairly often. We became engrossed with each other, oblivious to the world and its events, spending most of each day in bed, getting up in the evening to go and find some sustenance. My French tan provoked much admiring comment. My impression of him previously had been of a cold, aloof individual, but now I was charmed by his affectionate warmth. In a few days, he said, 'I'm falling in love with you, Margaret.' Then later, 'I want you to have my baby.' And then, 'Will you marry me?' – after only two weeks. I replied, 'I'll think about it,' but he looked so crestfallen I added, 'Yes of course I will.' One thing that impressed me very much was that with him I could be entirely my true self. I did not need to hide anything, or pretend, or cover up, for I was confident he would love me for exactly what I was. The empathy between us was astonishing. Sometimes after a companionable silence we would start speaking together and say exactly the same thing. I felt I had come home at last.

A remark I made about this time went into family lore. Talking, presumably responding to a question about his appearance, I said, 'You're not classically handsome, but by no means ugly.' A man's appearance was never especially influential with me, though I did not like obese men and preferred to look upon an elegant and graceful form; which, it must be said, Robin did not have. But he had interesting green eyes and a fair complexion. He had the beard when I came to know him, the result apparently of a decadent party lasting two or three days. His mother hated the beard and tried to bribe him to shave it off, but I was uneasy about this, never having really known him without it. In the early years he let it grow very bushy, secretly modelling himself on the likeness of George Bernard Shaw.

I did not enquire about his previous girlfriend Susan, assuming that they had parted; but they had not exactly done so. One day as I hastened to the bank, my mind occupied on inner thoughts, my attention was caught by a young woman looking at me with a super-cilious air. She had long red hair and a beautiful white coney coat. I just caught a glimpse of her before she was past me and as I turned to look at her retreating back, struck by her expression, I saw she was arm-in-arm with a companion. It looked just like Robin.

We met for supper in Willie's café. I had almost forgotten the lunchtime incident. Suddenly I said, 'I saw your double today.'

He looked at me sheepishly. 'It was me,' he said.

I was stunned. Indeed I burst into tears. He was profuse with words of apology, of appeasement; 'I can explain,' he protested. An unfortunate man sitting next to us bolted his spaghetti and hastily left. Robin really was shamefaced. He had met Susan to give her some things she had left at the flat. I thought it strange that she should hang on to his arm so possessively under the circumstances. But I let it pass, and forgave him.

Compared with every other man I'd ever known Robin was impressively well informed and intellectually mature. He knew this and had learned that he could make himself a dominant figure in any group he joined. There was an ebullient confidence directly resulting from this intelligence which I greatly admired. At this stage he did not feel unduly challenged or forced to compete and had not yet become battle-scarred. He had read most of Dickens before the age of ten; contrast this with myself, who read *David Copperfield*, my first Dickens, at the age of twelve. When I asked his age and found he was only twenty, I was momentarily dumbstruck: eighteen months younger than me! It didn't feel like that, not then.

As a student I had almost completely dropped the habit of reading for pleasure except for an occasional lightweight novel. Robin was reading English literature and had quite a library of good books in paperback. He began to guide my reading, suggesting things to try. I'd never read Scott, so now devoured *Guy Mannering, Redgauntlet*. He handed me books by Grahame Greene, Waugh, Fielding, Thackeray; and best of all, Anthony Trollope. His own career plan had been to get his MA and proceed to divinity college. Even by the time I met him, politics had taken the place of religion. He was conscientious to the point of being obsessional with his course work, or indeed any work he took on, and this could be a problem as he was totally undistractable. He would become distant, lost, inaccessible, the shutters interposed between me and him. It said a lot for his concentration, but was disconcerting. It also meant that he could be quite ruthless in avoiding things that got in the way. I used to say to him that if he'd been a dustbin man he still would have worked harder than anyone else.

Although, as I have said, he was intellectually mature, I was to find out gradually that his emotional development lagged behind, and he had an exaggerated need to be loved and praised. But how can you perceive this when you are yourself in love? Also he lacked the qualities required to make friends easily. At university it was impossible not to have friends unless you were a complete recluse. But at other times of his life he has been a loner, able to charm those of immediate consequence to him, but ruthlessly ignoring the rest and making a few enemies in the process. Some people liked to associate with him because his intelligence and dominance had a certain magnetism; this was one feature that attracted me. He affected a languid disdain for sporty and manual activities which could extend to people practising them and cause offence. He was intensely, primitively competitive. I realised early on that it was a good thing we were not in the same profession and that few of our leisure activities coincided, for to compete successfully against him would probably earn his unyielding enmity.

Sometimes we had to emerge from our love-nest for lesser activities such as work, debates and even social functions. Few people had been aware of our mutual magnetism, and there were some amusing double-takes from friends such as Raymond Fraser when we were first seen walking arm-in-arm. We both took part in heats for the *Scotsman* debating competition, mine in Dundee, his in Glasgow. We arranged a lift for me to Glasgow so we wouldn't have to spend the night apart.

My debating skills, if I had any, were not of the cut-and-thrust variety and I lacked confidence in political topics. On one occasion Robin demolished my speech publicly and mercilessly, making me wonder if I was out of favour, but no, afterwards I was greeted as affectionately as ever. I perceived that 'out there', in his world, when on display, you gave no quarter to anyone.

His self-regard was easily punctured and his reaction to such a challenge was protracted and troublesome. At a time when I was trying to interest him in music I had got tickets for the Usher Hall to hear Menuhin play Beethoven's Violin Concerto. We also had invitations to a party later, so the evening promised well. I came to the Union, where he was involved in a management committee meeting, to collect him. He emerged visibly bristling and stalked past me with barely a greeting. My mood plummeted from delighted anticipation to horror. What had gone wrong? I hurried after the hunched figure.

'Have I done something to upset you?'

'No, not you.'

After some time I ascertained that David, the president of the Union, had disagreed with him over something, possibly had even reprimanded him. Robin could not bear to be demolished. His crusty mood lasted the whole evening and ruined it. I could not concentrate on the concert and he did not lighten up at the party.

But this was unusual in those days, though gave a foretaste of the future; in similar situations, I learned to cut myself off from him, retire into myself until such times as he came back to normal.

My rather colourful love-life contrasted spectacularly with his as he had really only had one girlfriend, Susan. They had first made love when she was a schoolgirl. It worried me that he had had so little opportunity to sow his wild oats, and I felt there was a distinct risk that he would seek to do it later, particularly as he, competitive in this as in virtually everything, also felt at a disadvantage.

One other contrast between us was his relative dependence on his parents. He could not altogether avoid this as, whereas I had an almost full grant, his parents had to supply most of his spending money. But I would have found it stifling to live in a flat owned and organised by my parents, down to the cutlery and crockery, the furnishings and even the cleaning lady. I loved my parents and my home very much indeed, liked to return there, was grateful for their continued support; but I needed to feel a measure of independence. Because his parents kept him a little short of ready cash he began to borrow from me. By the end of term he owed me nine pounds, a goodly sum them. My upbringing had taught me neither to borrow nor lend, so this troubled me, especially as I found out that he also owed Susan some money. But he paid it all back eventually.

Robin spoke a lot of his father Peter, held him in high esteem and clearly identified with him. One of a family of four brothers, sons of a miner, Peter was selected as the one to be educated on account of his ability. He got his university degree on a shoestring, living extremely humbly, and then paid back debts to his family. He worked in ICI during the war, then took a drop in salary to become a teacher, his vocation. He had worked in Aberdeen, then moved to the Royal High School in Edinburgh, bringing the family. Robin had been bitterly resentful of the move, as it took him away from his friends and achievements. After this, Peter took up the post of Rector of Kirk-cudbright Academy just about the time Robin went to university. Peter was an elder of the Presbyterian Church, a pillar of moral rectitude – but not uncomfortably so.

I met his mother quite soon. I had to move back into my own flat of course while his parents visited. Robin came in the family car with his mum to collect me and, to my surprise, made no attempt to introduce us. I slid into the back of the car, waited for the formalities … but nothing happened. Silence. Robin started the engine and moved off. Mrs Cook said, 'Quite a nice day, isn't it?' I firmly squashed the desire to burst out laughing.

At Christmas we corresponded during the three or four weeks apart. I still have his letters. In some the style is pompous, self-consciously constructed with a view to impress. Then suddenly he would become natural, and the style improved accordingly. In one he quotes the following lines from Milton. Lest any feminists rise in murderous rage, he did have his tongue in his cheek (Robin, not Milton).

> Therefore God's universal law
> Gave to the man despotic power
> Over his female in due awe,
> Nor from that right to part an hour
> Smile she or lour.

He continued to send me books of edifying merit to keep up the newly acquired habit of reading. To make sure I did not forget him he also sent a little wooden figure with a mop of scarlet hair, which I then kept on my dressing table throughout our long partnership. Over the years the hair has faded to a pinky grey.

In a letter written on 2 January 1967, he outlined his New Year's resolution to be conscientious with work, moderate with drink and thrifty with money.

For most of that year's academic work I had to contend with numerous tiny subjects like social medicine, ENT, ophthalmology. We had a professional exam in each subject after the course had finished. By this time most of us had become rather blasé about attending lectures. It so happened that venereal disease lectures were all at nine o'clock, so I got to very few of them, probably only those coinciding with the days the cleaning lady came, when I would have to remove myself and my belongings early. The exam loomed ever closer, and obviously no one was going to lend me their notes. When it was only two days away I bought a paperback edition on the subject from Thin's, and spent the weekend reading it, cuddled up to Robin in bed as usual. Then on Monday I took the exam – and won the class medal! It was almost always won by a woman, and was the only one I ever won. My father was to say in exasperation, 'Why couldn't you win something we could boast about?' Nevertheless, it is a very fine medal, a heavy, solid, fist-sized disc with 'Margaret Whitmore, Venereal Diseases, 1967' inscribed around the circumference.

Robin was deeply troubled that medical expertise of such an order could come from reading a paperback from Thin's. Actually he didn't relish my profession, having much greater respect for mental and artistic skills than manual and scientific ones; though in good medicine there is a great deal of all these qualities. He reviewed the specialist options open to me and fixed on psychiatry as being suitably refined. He would under no circumstances allow himself to be treated as a guinea-pig and I was never allowed to lay a professional hand on him. He showed a strong affinity for the orderliness of urban living, and it was only gradually that I later introduced him to country life and slowly reduced his disgust with, almost fear of, good healthy muck. He had a particular aversion for dogs, associating them with the ordure they produced.

I was invited to stay the weekend with the parents in Kirkcudbright. Wandering up and down Lockerbie station, waiting to be collected, I came face to face with a tall, slim, smiling man with features similar to Robin's minus the beard. We contemplated each other for a moment. Again there were no introductions, but I warmed to Peter immediately and we became very good friends. This was the first of many delightful weekends in the beautiful countryside in the south-west and along the Solway coast; it was our rural retreat and we were thoroughly spoiled. There was a nice piano in the sitting room. Who plays? I asked. No one. Ina (Mrs Cook) boasted they'd bought it for one pound in an auction sale; simply, it seemed, because in her circle it was the done thing to own a piano.

When we went out walking, Robin did not want to leave the footpath and cross a field. 'Why not?' I asked. 'Those are cows over there. Quite harmless.'

'There might be a bull among them.'

But we went anyway. Then suddenly behind us came a panting noise and the sound of pounding hoofs. Well, paws, I should say, but he had taken to his heels before realising we were being pursued by a terrier. He got no end of teasing about this.

We decided it would be prudent for me to go on the contraceptive pill (he didn't want me to have his baby quite yet) and I discussed this with my doctor at the student health clinic. Attitudes were more conservative then, but as we were in a steady relationship – I said we were engaged which was half true – the prescription was made. Shortly after this the furore over the demands by Edinburgh students for free access to the pill blew up in the press, giving Malcolm Muggeridge his chance to be pious from the pulpit. It was all nonsensical; no prescribing practices were going to be changed by a student demonstration. About this time I got an attack of honeymoon cystitis and felt sorry for myself for a few days. Robin treated me with tenderness and consideration even when I was cross and irritable. He liked me to show my vulnerable side.

One of the more colourful characters who was regularly invited to debates was John P. Mackintosh, Labour member for East Lothian, who had a well-deserved reputation as a lecher. Once in the course of conversation at the après-debate party somebody mentioned engineers. Robin looked disdainful. 'Oh, engineers!' he exclaimed. 'They work with their hands!'

John looked at me rakishly, murmuring, 'Doesn't he work well with his hands?' and coarsely ran his hands from my shoulders over breasts, belly and thighs.

I uttered a scream and leaped back in disgust, expecting Robin to make some defensive or protesting action. But he didn't: he couldn't risk offending an MP.

Nicky Fairbairn was equally regular as a guest – and equally lecherous – but his style was more discreet. He would disappear with a female committee member for several days. No, not with me. I never liked either handsome or overtly libidinous men.

George Foulkes was another debating, Labour-supporting acquaintance of the time. I had once let George take me home from a party; rather ill-advisedly under the circumstances. We went back to his flat where he passed out stone cold on his bed. Realising he was unrousable I left and found a taxi to take me home.

Martin O'Neill and George Robertson, both now Labour MPs, were also of our generation, though members of other student bodies, whom we met on SALSO (Scottish Association of Labour Student Organisations) business. Robin was president of this group. On one of these trips, John Keay (now an Oxford don) said to me, 'You didn't say much today.'

'I didn't feel I had much to contribute.'

'It didn't stop anyone else,' he drily observed.

For the last year and a quarter of my course we entered 'Final Phase' which was more intensely clinical and involved protracted hours and even the chance to do locums. We had a meagre two weeks' holiday during which Robin drove down to visit my family. We then motored back via Stratford-upon-Avon and the Lake District, passing as a married couple.

Back in Edinburgh we resumed our co-habitation, though my official residence was in a small flat with Morag in Bruntsfield. Morag had begun work as a teacher and was not happy. It can't have helped that her flatmate was so much of an absentee.

But the course of our true love was to experience a few rough patches. Robin asked me to absent myself from his flat for a night for some transparently lame reason. I knew something was amiss and felt miserably depressed. The next day, returning to his flat on my own, I found two coffee cups on the draining board. It was not my style to throw a hysterical scene and I cannot for the life of me remember how this situation got itself resolved. He had succumbed to the charms, or perhaps the concentrated attentions, of a classmate, Maureen. It didn't last long. Perhaps he was tentatively trying himself out, seeing if he could cope with two women. Ah, those wild oats I had worried about!

The next rough patch was much more destabilising and this time it was my fault. My clinical attachment was in the children's ward at Leith Hospital. We were treated generously there and given a deliciously sustaining three-course lunch free of charge each day. This unusual financial support enabled me to splash out and buy my first set of contact lenses. But I digress. On the surgical side was an Australian registrar, Jack, who was free and frank with his attentions; so much so that at first he irritated and embarrassed me. But he persisted and I suppose I was stupid enough to be flattered. My next clinical attachment was a residential one, at Chalmers' Hostel attached to the Simpson Maternity Pavilion. We had to deliver a certain number of babies and be available at all hours to do so. Needless to say the period in residency was sociable and highly enjoyable. It also provided a chance for Jack to visit and for me to go out with him. When my classmates saw this, many eyebrows were raised. 'Why is everyone being unfaithful?' Jan asked, perplexed. I was not the only one.

I still can't explain this infatuation. There was no feeling of a deep or lasting attachment, or anything other than a wild exciting fling. There was something mad, bad and dangerous about Jack, which stirred me. He was undoubtedly all sorts of things that Robin was not, and lacked all those solid qualities which made me feel Robin was my life's partner. I'm afraid I have no excuse, or reason, for this aberration which can only be explained by a flaw in my character.

After a few weeks of this double life I felt that I had to give Robin up; I argued, how can I really love him if I behave like this? Also, finals for both of us were on the horizon, so a catastrophic split had better be made sooner rather than later. And I was disgracefully cowardly in my method of telling: I left him a letter in his flat, explaining everything. To be honest, his obsession with his work was so absolute that I wondered if he would react at all, or if he would put it aside and carry on reading. Maybe this was just sophisticating on my part. In fact he came to me immediately and we had a highly emotional scene, with floods of tears on my part. But I made him understand that I really wanted to finish with him.

Some of my friends predicted I'd go back to him. My affair with Jack ran its short course and faded out. Robin and I didn't see each other for a few weeks, while we each in our different ways coped with finals: he in his solitude, myself in jocose company. Our class came together for the first time in a year and in between the hours of hard study were times of lively partying. The reading room was comfortable, rubbing shoulders with friends, comparing notes, smoking. In my corner were long-standing friends – Colin, John, Anne, Barbara, Frances, Hugh, Arthur, Sandy, Dave – to name only a few. In those sociable weeks I dated any number of my class, but became aware that though collectively they were wonderful fun, singly they did not entice me. I was certainly not remotely drawn to a love relationship with any of them. Almost I felt that biologically and subconsciously I had committed myself to Robin and my inner self would not accept anyone else. At the same time I recognised that there was a sombre, cold, inhospitable side to his nature which could potentially act as a barrier between me and other friends.

I was old enough to know that life consists of compromises, and when he eventually phoned after his finals to say he'd got a 2–1 and would I go out and celebrate with him, of course I accepted. We dined at the Handsel and began to meet regularly but at first without making any strong commitments. At this point, my career could have taken a complete turnabout, as I was offered a part as an extra in the filming of *The Prime of Miss Jean Brodie* in Henderson Row! But I couldn't fit it in as after my graduation I left immediately for Kirkcaldy where I had a locum job in the children's ward for a few weeks at the Victoria Hospital, in order to make enough money for a holiday. Our definitive house jobs began in October and April. Robin came frequently to visit but deep within me lingered a niggling doubt. He described me at this time as hard and difficult to melt.

He was certainly doing his best to woo me. Having borrowed his father's car, he was persuaded to give me some driving lessons. I had a provisional licence. We had some delightful trips to the Highlands. Once while motoring down the single-track road beside Loch Tay we came face to face with another car whose driver was oblivious of the passing place just behind her. Gesticulating brought no result, so Robin leaped out to go and explain. Unfortunately he forgot that the top button of his trousers was undone; he'd loosened it for comfort's sake. To his dismay his trousers descended round his ankles. The woman needed no further encouragement, but backed hastily away.

Another time we found ourselves near Gleneagles Hotel. This was way beyond our means and we certainly were not suitably dressed. But he was keen to impress me and so we stopped for lunch. As we walked up the drive an imposing man, a colonel type with a cut-glass accent, hailed us.

'I say there. We can't move this car. Can you lend a hand?'

Robin was furious, though he could hardly refuse. He wanted to play the grand gentleman and he was being made to feel like a skivvie. This typified his deep-seated sense of insecurity. Any of my confident medical friends would have leaped with alacrity and a laugh to the rescue, with words of bonhomie, afterwards enjoying a hearty lunch all the more.

On my day off from my second locum at Bruntsfield Hospital, Robin and I motored down to the Borders with a picnic lunch which he had prepared himself. The roads were quiet, so I took over the wheel, somewhere near Greenlaw in Berwick. Not knowing the road and being an inexperienced driver I didn't see the hidden crossroad until the car crossed our path – by which time it was too late. We collided with a monumental bang, the two cars deflected and I hit a signpost, demolishing it. There was glass and crumpled metal every- where. We leaped out to check that the family in the other car was not seriously hurt, and found that the mum had a bleeding head; I attended to her. Her husband said gloomily, 'That's the end of your afternoon out, kids.' Police appeared, or were summoned, by which time Robin had told me to say that he'd been the driver. This was not to protect me but because he wasn't sure about the terms of the insurance.

His parents took the news with remarkable equanimity: 'Just as long as you two are all right.' There was much corresponding in the Cook household and he was charged with careless driving. His mother may have suspected the truth but I'm sure Peter didn't. For us the event was deeply significant. I was so aghast at the mayhem and destruction resulting from my irresponsibility that I went into meltdown and became insecure and dependent ... for a day or two at least. But in this time I had again agreed to marry him and we planned our formal engagement soon afterwards.

After a holiday with Morag in Vienna and Salzburg I travelled home to Somerset to spend a few days with my parents before starting my life's work. While there I had a letter from Robin. A very important letter indeed.

In it he poured out over five pages his continued bitterness and indignation about the way I had treated him at the time of my infidelity. How stray associations would open old wounds; how well I had deceived him, and how he wondered if he could ever trust me again. He contrasted my love for him with my infatuation for the other; enlarged on my selfish indifference to his near collapse as his finals approached. He wrote of how I must have planned to betray and humiliate him and of how shallow my grief at parting must really have been. The pain for him had been profound and with my renewed affection the anguish had not subsided. Indeed he thought very seriously of making a break and starting with someone new and innocent. With real insight he declared he wanted to make me suffer and though he had fantasies of revenge on Jack, it was really me he wanted to punish. In spite of this, he reiterated that he loved me to distraction and wanted us to survive.

I was horrified at the intensity of his smouldering resentment and wrote back in haste. Now I can only read his side of the correspondence of course, but we tried hard to lay bare our souls and find sense in what happened. He was angry that I hadn't humbled myself or begged to be taken back. With a further flash of insight he admitted that pride accounted for much of his present suffering, as well as for my unbending attitude. I realised I would have to eat humble pie or the resentment would smoulder on. The last letter from him before we were due to meet was full of pure affection.

After this, for many years, he would have recurring nightmares that

I had left him again. I would then need to spend time and effort reassuring and comforting him.

I was deeply shocked and moved when I read this correspondence again recently. I could not help pondering whether the desire to punish me had stayed with him through all the intervening years.

13

Learning to Take the Reins

For the next year, which was highly influential for my personal development, my relationship with Robin of necessity took second place, and
he was both tolerant and supportive. No one who has not been a house
officer can appreciate what extreme demands are made of those young
persons. Nowadays there is a radical change in attitude, recognising
that even first-year doctors are not automatons with no private lives.
But in my day we were exploited to a degree that was little short
of scandalous. We were full of youthful illusions, committed, keen,
compassionate – and tough.

In October 1968 I was house physician on the professional unit at
the City Hospital, and very honoured to be working with Professor
Crofton who had done much of the pioneering work in the modern
treatment of tuberculosis. I had worked here as a student and knew
some of the personalities. My senior colleagues all needed handling to
some degree. I was aware of a huge disparity between what I was –
immensely ignorant and lacking in experience – and what was expected
or required: total commitment, extreme responsibility and capacity to
cope in all circumstances.

I fell into a degree of disfavour almost immediately by getting
engaged. When the professor heard it he grunted and looked displeased,
muttering that he hoped my dedication to the job would not suffer. I
was told that if my impending engagement had been known about
previously, I would not have been appointed. Robin and I had hardly
a bean between us and bought a twenty pound sapphire ring. Remembering his finances I suspect I paid half.

My fellow houseman, Tom, and I covered the unit (two chest wards,
male and female, and two TB wards) round the clock. Outwith
ordinary working hours one or other of us was always available, on
site, as often as not in the wards. Essentially you had alternate nights
and weekends off. Thus after a weekend off, during the next seven

days the only free time you had was Tuesday and Thursday evening and night.

When I had just done a weekend on call, Robin and I would look forward to Monday evening. He rang and asked, 'Where do you want to eat?' I would almost burst into tears and say, 'Don't ask me to make another decision!' We would have a meal somewhere, then go and sit in a pub. After my first drink I was so exhausted and sleepy I would have to be taken home to bed. Robin still had his flat but it was due to be sold. He was still a student, a post-graduate, doing a PhD on some obscure aspect of Dickens, about which he was ambivalent. Having a strong social conscience he compared my new life with his, and was dissatisfied with himself.

Sometimes I found it almost more stressful to be off duty than on. You tried to finish in reasonable time, but it was difficult; sometimes it was easier knowing that you were on call so the evening could be used to finish up routine work. Patients, especially motherly types, expressed horror at our hours. 'Do you never go off duty?' they asked. 'Do you never have time to yourself? Go out and enjoy yourself?' One of my predecessors deliberately grew his hair long until his chief objected, when he was politely informed that hours of duty genuinely did not allow time out for a haircut. I would find that my mind continued to work around the job even as I went off for my bus into town. And then I would remember some vital task I'd forgotten. The imagination would run mad, thinking of all the awful consequences: that Mrs Brown would go into intractable respiratory failure because I'd forgotten to change her medication, for instance. So as soon as I could, I'd dive for a phone (no mobiles then) and contact my co-resident, who was usually disgruntled at being disturbed at his supper, and hand over the (by now) trivial-sounding message.

One day I admitted a lady who was a deaf-mute. She could lip-read but most communication needed to be written down. Her problem was heart failure, and after due assessment, the valve disorder mitral stenosis was diagnosed. She needed to be considered for surgery, and I requested the cardiac surgeon Mr McCormack to come and advise. He liked nothing better than to diminish a junior – especially female – doctor. He asked for my stethoscope. My heart sank, as an ear-piece had recently cracked and I had effected temporary repairs with some tape. When he saw this he looked at me contemptuously, dangling the offending article in front of my nose.

'Oh, doctor!' he said wearily. 'Oh-h-h-h, doctor!'

I forbore to say, like my colleague with the long hair, that all would be rectified in due course whenever I had a moment away from duty. He examined the patient briefly, tossed my stethoscope back at me and said he would operate. I was surprised at this decision as she was fairly old and frail. 'Nonsense!' he said and stalked off.

I had a chat with the lady by means of pencil and paper. She had a sweet and patient nature. Perhaps deaf people are protected from the over-brisk pace of life as we know it, and don't get so scarified by stress. I was conscious, as I also became later in dealing with children and horses, that I had to check and slow up in order to communicate with her and it always left me feeling better.

'Im glad Im to have wee oporation,' she scrawled on the paper.

I'm telling this story as she was one of the many patients from whom I learned a disproportionately enormous lesson in those early months. My registrar organised her medical treatment in order to get her heart failure under control, and herself in a fit state for surgery. She was on a large range of pills, but she improved. The registrar then reduced her treatment and vanished for a few days. I was aware that she was slipping back but couldn't find the registrar and didn't have enough confidence to effect changes. Then, without warning, the surgeons sent for her and she was transferred. All hell broke loose, as they realised she was in no fit state for surgery.

A more senior doctor on our unit, who had been summoned peremptorily by the surgeons to sort things out, came fuming into the duty room and laid into me verbally for the mismanagement of the patient. 'What were you and Dick thinking about?' he raged. 'It makes us all look such incompetent idiots!' And much more of the kind. Housemen are dogsbodies and one of their chief roles is as a receptacle for everyone's fury and wounded pride. As it was, I retired to my room in grief and shame, thinking that my career was at an end before it had begun.

The world did not come to an end though, and I made up my mind to be scrupulous in checking any patient in future, especially before discharge or transfer, and having the courage of my convictions.

These principles were soon put to the test. A lady patient with a mysterious lung disease was to have a diagnostic lung biopsy using a relatively new technique which carried a risk of collapse of the lung as an after-effect. My ward work kept me busy until nine at night, when

I remembered that I still had to give her a check over. She looked surprised that I'd come to disturb her so late. When I listened to her chest, with whose musical sounds of varying pitches I had become familiar, I discovered that things had changed. The sounds had shifted, had changed in pitch and quality, some had gone altogether. So then I had to get in the radiographer and organise a portable chest X-ray. There is an inbuilt resistance to doing these things at such a time, which you must have sufficient authority to overcome. Nurses don't like the routine to be disturbed. But it all happened, and after about an hour the radiographer appeared with the film.

'Looks nasty to me,' she commented and walked away.

I put the film on the lighted box and felt a constriction in my solar plexus. It had indeed changed. She had a pneumo-thorax: a collapsed lung on the left side. Now the biopsy had been planned for the right side, so if I hadn't checked and she'd then got another collapse . . .

I phoned the registrar on call, Chris, and explained.

'Have you put in an underwater seal drain before?' he asked.

'No,' I said firmly.

'Well, I'll do this one, you can watch and then you can do the next one.'

'Fine.'

So he came in speedily and stood, hands on hips, looking at the X-ray, comparing it with the previous one.

'The good Lord was with you tonight,' he said briefly. This was all the praise I received, but I say this without rancour, for my inner sense of satisfaction was reward enough. He put in the drain and the biopsy was deferred.

Robin got into the habit of joining me at the Residency dinner as it was the only time he could be sure of seeing me. This required quite a change of attitude on his part as he was naturally very squeamish. At table our talk was nearly all shop; we had little else to talk about, but in general it was light-hearted. Many doctors indulge in black humour which is an effective safety valve. One evening Robin stayed latish, then I was needed on the ward. The City was an old fever hospital and was built on the chalet principle with acres of green space between buildings. I came back to my room, only to find Robin in a contorted position with his foot in the washbasin.

'What the devil are you doing here?' I asked, not very welcoming. It seemed he had found the gates locked and tried to climb over the formidable spiked fence. One of the spikes had penetrated his shoe and his foot was bleeding freely. There was nothing for it but to plaster him up and let him stay the night, sharing my narrow bed.

I despatched him the next day with instructions to get an anti-tetanus jab. He told me later that a little group of domestics had peered after him curiously as he limped along the corridor, then stood gazing out of the windows to check him off the premises. That's my reputation ruined yet again, I thought. But after this he stayed quite frequently, and was no more a nine-days' wonder. I relied on him heavily for vital supplies such as toiletries including tampons and other personal items. As Christmas approached I mentioned that this would be the first year I would not have a stocking. To my utter delight, he produced one for me on Christmas morning, full of delightful feminine scents, cosmetics, lacy hankies, chocolates and other delectables. Thereafter we always made one for each other, often wildly extravagant; he was generous and very good at selecting presents, rather unusual for a man I think.

Social aspects of sickness, cause and effect, were evident on this unit. The incidence of TB was diminishing considerably, and the majority of the patients were middle-aged or elderly men from hostels for the homeless: the down-and-outs of the city. But there were others too, including two young women in their early twenties, like an operatic scene from the nineteenth century; the Mimi syndrome as the professor called it.

One hectic afternoon Sister called me peremptorily from my duties. An elderly lady had been admitted, and arrived clutching several carrier bags stuffed to capacity with pound notes. It all added up to several hundred pounds which had been carefully saved from her pension and put aside for a rainy day. This unfortunate soul was severely mal-nourished and poorly clad and came in to us for reasons of self-neglect.

The pace of life on the surgical wards was quite different. On waiting days there was continuous frantic activity, with a strong probability that you'd work twice round the clock without any rest and even sometimes without adequate sustenance. For the rest of the week things eased up a little. Sometimes you had to receive emergencies at the weekends as well, which meant losing your precious fortnightly off-duty. Many hours were spent in theatre doing nothing mentally demanding, mostly holding retractors. I regularly dropped off to sleep while assisting, living as one did in a perpetual state of tiredness. Generally I coped as long as I'd had a minimum of two hours' sleep.

Our first waiting day was reasonably busy with fourteen admissions. My first was a young woman with what looked superficially like appendicitis. But she had an odd history of menstrual irregularities, so I stuck my neck out and diagnosed a tubal pregnancy.

'Rubbish!' said the registrar. 'It's appendicitis. Go and tell her so.'

The next patient definitely had appendicitis. I thought it had perforated.

'Nothing of the kind,' said the registrar. 'Perfectly straightforward.'

At operation, the first patient had a tubal pregnancy and the second had a perforated appendix. Everyone was very good-humoured about this; I was told not to get big-headed, as it was the well-known phenomenon of beginner's luck. Still, I felt good.

The following evening in the ward as I escorted one of the consultants round, I was accosted angrily by a young man, the husband of the lady with the tubal pregnancy. He wanted to know why I had misdiagnosed it and why I hadn't been there the previous night when he'd tried to insist on seeing me. I floundered around, attempting to explain in a way that would alleviate his fears and anger. The consultant stood by without comment. Life was definitely unfair at the bottom of the ladder.

I shared all these experiences with Robin. He was by now considering jettisoning his PhD, though was deterred for a while as his father would be upset, having himself longed to do a doctorate.

What little attention I had to spare for external happenings was caught by the arrival on the political scene of Bernadette Devlin, elected as an MP from Mid-Ulster at a by-election in April 1969. As a rebel, left-wing republican she was naturally a figure of some interest, provoking a comparison with Joan of Arc, and I felt a good measure of sympathy for her and her views. Robin did not agree and demolished her opinions on housing and employment as naïve and simplistic. A suspicion of jealousy occurred to me, which I suppressed; but maybe I was right.

I needed to think seriously about my career development during my surgical house jobs, as otherwise I'd be unemployed in six months' time. Robin and I planned to marry in mid-September but he could not make up his mind what to do, although by now he was certain he was going to give up his PhD. He looked for a job desultorily. He would not grasp that I needed to know where in the country we would be. Jobs were easy to come by but you couldn't leave things till the last minute.

Although at the time I was the only one earning money, we both assumed that his decision would come first and I would follow, which was a standard attitude in these pre-feminist days. He applied for a job as a manager of some sort in a big company in Isleworth, Middlesex. He was accepted. As luck would have it there was advertised a trainee rotating laboratory post in the Middlesex Hospital, and as I was thinking of haematology or pathology as a career, this was ideal. I applied, was interviewed, and got myself a registrar's job. This was rapid promotion and I was delighted. While in London for my interview I queued for ages to get our student tickets for our honeymoon.

Robin wasn't sure he wanted the Middlesex job; then he decided after all he didn't want it. Maybe he would teach for a while and look around. He got a job at Bo'ness Academy, following in Tam Dalyell's footsteps. So then I had to write to Middlesex and explain my position, and withdraw my acceptance. This dithering is severely frowned upon in medical circles and can affect job prospects. My guardian angel continued to hover, however, and I applied for and got a senior house officer post in haematology at the Western General Hospital in Edinburgh. My boss looked perplexed as he said, 'I thought I'd given you a reference already. How many jobs do you want?'

There were other problems causing me much vexation. Our honeymoon was planned in Innsbruck and Stresa; not at all an extravagant holiday as there was a limit of fifty pounds per head allowance for holidays then. It sounds a ridiculous sum now. My passport was slow in coming and eventually I was told that having been born outside the country, and my father also, I had no claim to British citizenship and could not get a British passport. On previous trips abroad I had taken out a one-year passport. By the time I had got this decision there was less than a month to go. I resolved the difficulty by applying for a South African passport, to Robin's disgust, and received it by return of post.

The next problem, which I could not persuade him to address, was where we should live. Two weeks before our wedding, on one of my rare evenings off, I found at the edge of the Meadows in central Edinburgh a delightful one-bedroomed flat, well furnished, all the arrangements ideal, and I was so relieved that we had somewhere to lay our heads. I had a feeling that Robin might be a bit negative, and was not mistaken. It hadn't got a view.

'Okay,' I said. 'You go find us a flat with a view then.'
But of course he didn't and so we moved in.

We were married on 15 September 1969. It's a strange thing but we hardly ever remembered our wedding anniversaries though his mother religiously sent us a greeting. My parents were now living in a flat in Redland, Bristol and we were to be wed in St Alban's Church, Westbury Park. It was not a huge wedding as, apart from anything else, they could not have afforded that. Robin's mum sent out vast numbers of invitations, to my mother's concern, while assuring us that these people wouldn't be able to come but would send presents.

The day before the wedding I said farewell to Robin for the last time before the ceremony; but there was a crowd of family and friends milling around, so I was perhaps a little cursory. Afterwards Jenny was cross; she said, 'He gave you such a wonderful loving look, and you weren't even paying attention!'

On the big day, Robin, Eddie, the best man, and another friend Raymond all went to confer with the verger.

'Which one of you gentlemen's the bridegroom?' he asked in his slow West Country brogue, looking at Raymond who had on a gorgeous waistcoat and bow tie.

'It's him!' acknowledged Robin.

'No – him!' said Raymond, indicating Eddie. And so on. The poor man stepped back, bewildered. Then he beamed. 'Now come on. I know one of you's the bridegroom.'

I wore a traditional white dress and veil, Jenny was matron of honour, in glowing gold, with her two boys as pages with gold sashes and bow ties.

Eddie was a conscientious organiser, meticulous in detail, and I later learned he was driven mad by my parents' laid-back attitude. To them it was a day to enjoy, not one to get obsessional about. There was a fair degree of friction between the families and their adherents but happily I was unaware of this. The reception was held at a hotel overlooking the gorge and the suspension bridge. The speeches were excellent. Raymond, who had been asked to propose a toast to the parents, outlined his dilemma: 'I could not speak about them with authority, and I could not speak about Robin and Margaret with propriety!'

I went away in a white trouser suit with black velvet flowered jacket, which I had somehow found time to make myself. I made Robin a matching waistcoat. He adored brilliantly coloured flowery or paisley-patterned waistcoats and ties. We travelled to London on the train, when he famously produced his briefcase and asked me to remain silent so he could get some work done; political work this, nothing to do with his PhD which he'd by now abandoned. At Luton we were stranded by fog for some hours, but eventually took off for Munich from where we travelled to Innsbruck for a week, then the Italian lakes.

Following hot on the heels of the tour was the Labour Party conference held in Brighton that year, and whither Robin made his way from London, leaving me to travel back to Edinburgh alone. My family thought this was dreadful and said so. But I didn't mind. It was in keeping with my notion of emancipation, which applied equally to both of us. It did occur to me, however, that I had the whole of October to get through before pay-day, and next to no money to survive on till then. By a stroke of extreme good fortune, on the mat when I arrived home was a tax rebate of fifty pounds, so I survived the month in a state of solvency.

Haematology, the subject that was to become my career, and that I now embraced as a senior house officer, is a hybrid subject composed of laboratory and clinical aspects. There was a steep learning curve, and a need to prepare for an array of post-graduate exams, so it was back to book-learning again. Robin took up his new teaching post at Bo'ness Academy, which he found intensely demanding and tiring at first, but soon began to rise to the challenge and to enjoy it. In this he was his father's son. The timing of my working day was different from his as I didn't finish till six or later, so he had time to waste before our evening meal. I prepared his packed lunch to take to work, did all the shopping, cooking, washing, ironing, so I suppose I wasn't really emancipated at all.

His pupils included a number of unruly types and though he had set out with all sorts of high ideals, like not using the belt, he found that in the climate of the time this just did not work. With self-loathing he did use the strap once – and got instant respect, and did not have to use it again. He introduced his kids to courtroom activities, and found the scene surprisingly familiar to them. Not surprising at all, he discovered, as many of them were on probation for some offence or other and knew all about the inside of law courts. Altogether he enjoyed his teaching experience very much and would have continued in the profession, he said, had the prestige of the job been higher.

He was meanwhile active in the local Labour Party, aiming at a career in politics, and these activities quickly took over most of his evenings. At some point around this time he was adopted as Labour Party candidate for the seat of Edinburgh North. In no time, it seemed to me, I was seeing less of him even than when I was a resident. One night I felt particularly fed up and took myself off for a long soulful walk around the Edinburgh streets, going towards Craiglockhart where there were green stretches. I arrived back at the flat at about eleven thirty, expecting to find him worrying about me – and he wasn't even back yet! Such an effort for a big gesture and it was totally lost on him! When he did come in I exploded. He had bought a box of Maltesers as a propitiatory offering, which I rejected, and he slammed it on the floor. When we discussed this episode in the future, he would always insist that I had slung the Maltesers on the floor; this guilt-transference was a recurrent theme.

Before our marriage I was sufficiently aware that his attitude to money differed radically from mine, and so from the start in order to minimise tension we had separate bank accounts. This was to prove a mixed blessing, as although I had control over my own income it meant we did not automatically know of each other's. And since he would never talk about money, this led to problems. My salary was higher than his and I paid our rent and the housekeeping but left him the electricity and phone bills. One evening I arrived home to find our electricity cut off as he had failed to pay the bill. I organised the reconnection and took over the payment of these quarterly bills also.

Thinking back, it was odd how I took these inadequacies in my stride. But at home, Mum had always been the manager, the one in charge, which had meant in the latter years that she worked much harder than my father as she had both domestic and work responsibilities; and I just followed in her footsteps.

Robin's father was coming for lunch one Saturday and I was anxious to make a good impression. I didn't know it but he was terribly fussy and conservative about food, convinced that certain things were bad for him. I came across him in the kitchen having a surreptitious look in the pots and pans to see what he was to be fed. Many months later I learned that I had given him several items, including sprouts, bananas and strawberries, that he did not usually eat. When I knew him better we would look back to this occasion and laugh about it.

At work I was discovering that many medical colleagues were natural conservatives and were not at all impressed by my husband's budding political ambitions. There was a strong antipathy to trades unions and any strike action raised unbounded fury, with highly charged phrases such as 'Holding the country to ransom' being cast in my direction. One colleague propounded the view that 'Labour equals selfishness' which I thought exceedingly bizarre since the virtue of self-reliance is generally a tenet of Tory faith. I began to perceive that a person's perspective of politics was often firmly rooted in self-interest, and altruism was rare indeed.

During this year a severe outbreak of hepatitis developed in Edinburgh, affecting staff working in labs and renal units. It led to heightened awareness of blood-borne viruses and the dangers of blood generally, and safety measures were intensified accordingly. A sixteen-year-old clerkess in our lab caught hepatitis and within days she died, to the grief and shock of us all. It so happened that all the senior doctors in the department were absent and it fell to me and the Chief Scientific Officer to break the news, console the staff as well as we could, and to begin the round of protective injections for everyone.

As the general election in June 1970 approached I had planned to take a chunk of holidays (ten days) and work in the constituency of North Edinburgh. Even before then I was out canvassing and leafleting and so on, every evening. There was an unspoken assumption that I would give myself heart and soul to this effort, and I did. Robin and his agent, Sandy Ross, attracted a team of predominantly young enthusiasts, all of whom were convinced that if dedication and energy were all that was required to win then we could not fail. The sitting MP was the then Earl of Dalkeith and I was reminded more times than I care to count of what an asset he had in his wife, who, being an ex-model, was very lovely and very gracious.

In the previous general election campaign, Robin and Martin O'Neill had visited one of the earl's meetings with a view to disrupting it by asking awkward questions. The earl had organisation down to a fine art, but not too many facts at his fingertips. When a question was asked he would begin with a little flannel while his agent riffled through a file of cards till the correct subject was found, handed it to the earl who would then deliver the facts verbatim. To a couple of mentally adroit intellectuals it was child's play to make mincemeat of this arrangement, and they did. But they reckoned without the countess. At the end she forestalled them at the door and overwhelmed them with her charm. She was delighted to see young people so active and interested, prepared to give up their time and speak out, and so on. In the end they slunk away quite ashamed of themselves and left his meetings alone after that. Robin would often tell this tale against himself.

Sandy now issued a leaflet with a picture of the earl out hunting with hounds, and the query, 'Can this man represent you?' On the back was a list of 'Sayings of the Earl'. Certainly he had made some bloomers, like the one about living in subsidised council accommodation being a sap to one's moral fibre. But this leaflet offended a number of people who were impressed with their MP and one was sent back to us with 'Do not knock a man what is a better man than you are' scribbled on it. Everyone was getting a good lesson in political psychology.

One day when I was on a walkabout with Robin we met a group of housewives who were Labour supporters and interested in him and his beliefs. One of them nudged me accusingly. 'Look at his shoes, hen. You'd better make a better job of cleaning them than that. He's to look smart!' And they all peered at his shoes and tut-tutted at me. Emancipation was light-years away in this street and I made no attempt to argue the point.

We bought a car, an ancient Rover. On polling day a dustcart tried to turn left from a right-hand lane and gouged a huge hole in its side. The press had a field day.

Robin didn't win North Edinburgh from the Earl of Dalkeith, not in the least surprisingly, but we were still unreasonably disappointed. We consoled ourselves with a 'moral victory' party. A Conservative government was elected, under the helmsmanship of Edward Heath.

14

Nest-building

I passed my driving test, which straight away gave cause for stress, because naturally I now expected to use the car on occasions. After a little resistance, Robin gave in over this one. He got a new job as a tutor-organiser with the Workers' Education Association, working with Jack Kane, and with an office in Heriot Row, so this made car-sharing easier. Then I moved to the university pathology department for a few months, within walking distance from the flat, a pleasant stroll across the Meadows. My days began with post-mortem examinations and I would rush out of the house exclaiming that I must dash or I wouldn't get a good body.

I'd made up my mind that haematology was my subject and planned over the next years to take the two required membership exams: of the Royal Colleges of Physicians and Pathologists. I would be able to take the first part of the latter in a year's time, so began to study seriously. Besides haematology and histopathology, the multiple-choice paper covered microbology and clinical chemistry, and as I did not plan to do jobs in these departments needed to read widely.

Our financial situation improved to the extent that we could look around for a flat to buy. It amazes me how non-traumatic our first house purchase was. One advantage in this was that Robin would have to shoulder the mortgage payments, this being accepted practice at the time, his first significant input into our combined domestic expenses. We bought a spacious five-room second-floor flat in East Mayfield and set about making our first real home. Peter and Ina were generous and helpful as always, paying for some carpets and giving us some surplus furniture from the Edinburgh flat. Best of all, they gave me their piano. After all the years of longing for an instrument, this was the first time I'd had my own, under my own roof. We sanded some floors, probably doing dreadful things to our lungs, but the result was very beautiful.

Robin was elected to the Edinburgh City Council in 1971 and embarked on the over-driven lifestyle he has pursued ever since.

Essentially he was doing two jobs: his WEA work and his council work. I became used to his routine of disappearing after supper and returning late at night. He began to put on rather a lot of weight, as on council meeting days the lunches were generous, and he did not want to disrupt my habit of making the evening meal – no doubt for a mix of motives. One of his council colleagues was a train driver, and he would relate in tones of horror how this man lived his life in a perpetual alcoholic haze. At lunch one day he had planted his elbow in the bowl of soup and was so fuddled he could not work out why he couldn't get his spoon into the bowl. Robin developed the habit, when travelling by train, of checking that this city father was not driving the engine, before boarding. It was clear however that hospitality on the council was over-generous and may have started a number of people on the slippery slopes of an alcohol habit.

One thing I could do to occupy those empty evenings was to attend the well-run classes organised by Robin's WEA group; and so I joined the music class which was entertaining but not informative, and Russian literature which was both.

We were invited to a Holyrood Garden Party to meet the Queen, but before I could embark on the delicious process of planning and buying an outfit, a nasty little note was sent to all the guests. It suggested that anyone invited who happened also to be a divorcee should consider the wisdom of declining the invitation. This created a furore, and resulted in the Labour group boycotting the party.

I spent a great deal of the summer with my nose in books, trying to encompass a sufficient breadth of knowledge for the forthcoming exam. I recall a weekend of glorious sunshine spent in Kirkcudbright when I had a streaming cold and stayed in bed all day mainly to get peace to study. The rest of the family were in the garden picking apples and I longed to join them; so I did at the day's end, still warm with the sun's oblique rays.

The exam consisted of a written part, including the multiple-subject multiple choice; then a couple of days in London doing practicals, clinicals and oral. We took as much equipment as we could carry, microscope, automatic pipettes and so on. It's much easier doing practicals with familiar gear. I passed and rejoiced: another milestone. I had now worked in blood transfusion, then returned to haematology, first at the Royal Infirmary, then back to the Western. The next hurdle was even more tricky, as I had to get the MRCP but without having done a general medical job. This meant gleaning experience on the side, as it were. I adjusted my timetable, extending the hours rather, in order to spend time in cardiology and neurology clinics. Also I joined a Sunday morning teaching session at the Eastern General, specially organised with considerable dedication for specialists like me by John Munro.

A vacancy arose in my department for a senior registrar, just at a time when there was a shortage of candidates. My hopes and ambitions rose, but I had not been qualified for long enough to be eligible. But to use the vacancy it was changed to locum registrar and I was given the post, being assured that as soon as I had passed the magic four-year mark I would stand a very good chance of promotion to SR. No one ever actually promised you a job, life was too uncertain. It did not occur to me at the time that I could be at a disadvantage from the relative insecurity of a locum job, and I welcomed the promotion and half-promise with delight.

I vividly recall the horror at this time of the events of 30 January which later became known as Bloody Sunday, when thirteen demonstrators were shot dead by British soldiers in Derry. This had echoes of previous massacres on innocents including Amritsar, and the Black and Tans. And yet people with whom I discussed this at work were so complacent in their assumption that the soldiers must have been under control, obeyed the rules; people talked of 'discipline, training, lines of communication', as if these things could never go wrong. And here we are twenty-six years later still discussing and still doubting.

I was now twenty-seven years old and if anyone asked me I said I wasn't interested in having children, that I'd prefer a dog. But as so often happens there was a divergence between my intellectual and instinctive opinions, and the instinctive one proved the stronger. Robin and I had a day out in the country together, driving down to the Borders and beyond, to the Holy Isle and to Bamburgh Castle. A memorable, idyllic day made up of contented togetherness, freedom, leisure, new places to explore, delight in each other's company, youthful madness. And we ended the happy day as couples often do; except that accidentally or on purpose, I made a rather crucial miscalculation.

Two or three weeks later I had a vivid dream. I had a child, and though I was filled to the brim with joy and euphoria, I was also very anxious because I hadn't prepared anything, neither clothes nor babyfeed. The mixture of overwhelming joy and piercing anxiety was extremely potent. The sensation was not dispelled with awakening and the advent of daylight, and the expectant happiness persisted. A week later I was pretty sure I was pregnant; and when it was confirmed I could hardly contain my joy. It was so strangely at odds with what I'd believed of myself.

The delight buoyed me up through some difficult times, because I really had to struggle to keep my career on track. I kept it secret as long as I could, hoping I might achieve greater job security before I had to reveal all.

I met a good friend from my medical school class on the stairs one day. He said immediately, 'You look different, Maggie. Are you pregnant?' I was so startled, I said yes. I was only fourteen weeks, so the changes were subtle enough. My work companions were staggeringly unobservant. In the lab we were voracious coffee-drinkers and one of the things I could not face in the early weeks was coffee; but no one noticed.

The issue of my future job began to look complicated. I had already been engaged in discussions with the head of the Blood Transfusion Service in Edinburgh about a research post, which very much interested me. But besides feeling I would have to own up to being pregnant I did want to be sure of a reasonable amount of time off after the birth to establish bonding and satisfactory care arrangements, before returning to work. I felt an absolute minimum of two months' maternity leave was essential.

So then, trying to do the right thing, I rang Dr Cash at the BTS, explaining my dilemma, and asked about leave arrangements. He was tolerant about the pregnancy, but discussing maternity leave was a complete turn-off. 'Oh, I know nothing about that, it's no use talking to me about those things. Speak to my secretary about it. She'll advise you.' This was all the assurance I could get. Secretaries carried no authority on such matters. I tried repeatedly to discuss this issue, got nowhere and felt I could not pursue this option.

As luck would have it, the SR job at the Western was to be readvertised and it was expected I would apply; but so might several other people. And I was aware that my pregnancy would have to be declared, even if it wasn't obvious by then – which was unlikely. And now I realised how insecure my position was: for as soon as the SR was appointed, my post would vanish. This would be fine if I succeeded, but the alternative was instant unemployment.

With all these problems running through my mind, I faced a much more serious and threatening one. Robin had by now thoroughly established himself on the city council as a dynamic and forceful person of some consequence, and with his particular interest in housing had become the convener of the housing committee – at the tender age of twenty-six. A number of Labour-dominated councils dotted around the country, Edinburgh included, found themselves crossing swords with the Heath government on the policy of raising council-house rents. Some councils had blatantly defied the government by not putting up rents in accordance with national policy and individual councillors had been surcharged, notably in Clay Cross. Robin explained all this and admitted that Edinburgh might go the same way. If he was surcharged, we would go bankrupt, we would lose the house and our modest possessions – and all at a time when I was seeking security for my unborn child. I remember the occasion when he was laying out this scenario before me: I was cooking our supper and was so upset that I burned everything. I tried to find ways out of the maze: could we transfer the house and everything to my name? It seemed there was no way to avoid disaster. I could not believe it. And I blamed him, blamed him ferociously. Should not his first consideration be to protect and support his wife and child? But no it wasn't, it was apparently to do the visibly noble and upright thing, and that he was determined to do. The only emollient he applied was that it would come to a vote in council and that not everyone would vote for defying the government, but he would do so. Also the particular council meeting would fall in the middle of August, when many people would be on holiday, ourselves included. That would not however deter his determination to stand up and be counted. We were to be in the Highlands on the relevant date and he intended to return to Edinburgh for the vote.

With this uncertainty suspended over me like a sword of Damocles, we motored north towards Ullapool. I was five months pregnant and beginning to feel delicate flutterings under my belt. As always, I had not let the sun go down on my wrath, but resigned myself to what would come. There was an infinitesimal process of withdrawing, though, where previously there had been total sharing and confidence. The perception of the importance of personal strength and self-sufficiency started here.

He decided we would climb Cul Mor, not quite 3,000 feet, to the north of Ullapool. Knowing by now how he would tax himself to the limit and beyond, never mind me, I equipped myself with a book and waterproofs and dropped out just below the lesser of the two peaks. It was a glorious sunny day and I had a view of Stac Polly, Cul Beag and various lochs, and amused myself till he returned, exulting in his achievement.

We had discovered an exotic fish restaurant in the harbour in Ulla-pool, where we dined that night, after which he drove to Inverness, and caught the train to Edinburgh to be in time for the next day's council meeting. Meanwhile I took myself on a boat trip round the Summer Isles and to Achiltibuie. There were friendly people aboard but I felt introspective and non-communicative. He returned late that night with the news that the defence motion had been defeated by one vote. I was glad, but felt rather too traumatised to feel elated.

After the holiday my next task was the MRCP exam. First came a set of written papers, then, for those deemed to have passed, a clinical exam. A physician at the Western then who was involved with setting and marking the exam was Ted French, and he would periodically ask us to compose questions relating to data interpretation with a haematological bias. These would then be posed to highly placed specialists for model answers. One question I had outlined related to a young woman with severe vitamin deficiencies and related blood problems due to coeliac disease. None of the professors got the right answer, because it was theoretically improbable. Imagine my surprise when this question appeared in my exam paper. Nor was it easy to answer. Should I give the correct but improbable solution? I compromised somehow.

Shortly after this I felt I had to admit to being pregnant, and took everyone by surprise. By the time the clinical exam arrived I was unmistakably rotund.

To my mind, a clinical exam must be one of the most demanding ways to test your self-command. While maintaining a courteous and considerate doctor–patient relationship, you must also communicate with the examiner, trying to establish rapport, and also keep your wits and powers of observation about you. My admiration for overseas candidates is unlimited, for they have to do all this in a foreign language. Anyway, I kept my cool, had a bit of a struggle with the oral, but passed. Ted French told me I'd got the highest mark in the written paper of all the candidates sitting in Edinburgh. All of which, I thought, would help with the SR job.

About this time the department staff had a night out to bid farewell to someone who was leaving. We had a sociable group then. The night started in the local pub, then moved on to Tiffany's, a dance club. I was asked to dance by a stranger, a young fellow who began to get a little too friendly, so I gently waved my wedding ring in front of his nose. Becoming more polite he asked, 'Do you have any children?' I answered, 'I've got one on the way actually.' My friend released me and fled, to the hilarity of my colleagues.

I told Norman Allan, my chief, about the research post in BTS then still under discussion, again simply meaning to be open and above-board. But this was interpreted as manoeuvring on my part; he later told me he thought I was trying to hold a gun to his head. This was incomprehensible to me; I didn't think I had any bargaining power at all. The SR interview came. One other person, David, was interviewed – and he was offered the job.

It is difficult to describe my devastation. It wasn't at all unfair or unreasonable, and David was arguably the better candidate. But in the circumstances one simply has a terrible feeling of rejection, morale collapse and unworthiness; to say nothing of the fact that I faced instant unemployment. That night Robin took me to the cinema to try to cheer me up, but there was too much misery even for me to overcome so soon.

Luck had not completely deserted me. Our lecturer, Keith, who had secured a consultant post, vacated his job and I was appointed unopposed.

Looking back I realise I handled all this very badly, largely owing to lack of self-esteem and lack of confidence in my worth. I should have been more assertive, should have formally sat down with these men and made them listen rationally to my problems. The climate was different then, admittedly, and you did feel vulnerable during the child-bearing years. This underestimating by women of their strength and value is one feature in which they differ significantly from men. Most men who rise to positions of power, in my view, do so not because they have exceptional ability but because they think they have – which is far more influential than the genuine article.

Robin was certainly not hindered by a lack of self-belief, and that autumn he was chosen as parliamentary candidate by Central Edinburgh Labour Party, in place of Tom Oswald who was the retiring MP. This was by no means an automatic selection. Although Central

Edinburgh was not a safe seat in terms of a majority at previous elections, indeed could be regarded as a marginal, in practice it had remained in Labour hands. There was intense competition for the nomination and it was widely expected that George Foulkes would be chosen; even I had not expected Robin to win. The path of his career progression in politics now lay clear.

Towards the end of my pregnancy I was having problems with swollen ankles and legs and spent as much time as possible with my feet up. In practice there wasn't very much time to do this as I continued to work, feeling I'd prefer more time off after the birth than before. A week before the expected date my blood pressure was too high – perhaps not surprisingly given the eventful few months we'd had – and I was admitted to the Simpson Maternity Hospital. This was like heaven. Lying with my feet up, reading, knitting, chatting, being looked after: it was a brief oasis of calm in my hectic life. I looked sorrowfully at my now bloated and shapeless legs, fearful that they'd never be the same again.

In spite of all the external problems I found pregnancy an enthralling experience. Like listening to music while following the score, when you have insight into what is happening the whole process grips the attention with fascination. Similarly the process of labour. I won't dwell on the details for fear of losing my male readers. When I walked into my individual labour room, my stomach gave a little lurch at the sight of the tiny cot all warm and ready down to the minuscule hot-water bottle, realising that I would not leave the room until I had provided an occupant for that cot.

It was a long-drawn-out day and Robin sat beside me reading political papers for much of the time, periodically disappearing to get some refreshment. We discussed names. Being a traditionalist, he liked the Scottish custom of sequential family names, starting with the paternal grandfather. But I would not hear of naming my child according to a formula. We settled on Christopher, then came to the second name. He was quite forceful in wanting Alexander, after Sandy his agent. I was mystified. Why had Sandy become so important, so close to us as a family? I thought it quite inappropriate. I suppose there was with Robin a debt of gratitude, presumably for support in the Central Edinburgh nomination. In the middle of the discussion I developed a labour pain, and had to concentrate on other things for a moment. We each thought we'd won the argument, and since it fell to him to register the birth, his choice prevailed. Looking back, though I did not perceive it at the time, this typifies Robin's short-term and somewhat spurious loyalties.

Shifts came and went. A young man, looking less busy than the rest of the staff, sauntered in and riffled through the charts. He was obviously a student. He politely asked if he could palpate my abdomen. 'Feel free,' I said. Then, thinking he looked familiar, 'Do I know you?'

'Yes,' he said. 'You gave me a tutorial just about a week ago.'

It was a curious reversal of roles.

After a few hours I gave in and accepted some analgesia. The Simpson routinely used diamorphine (heroin) for this purpose and I actually fell asleep for two or three hours, then awoke babbling nonsense, of which oddly I was totally conscious. I didn't get any more diamorphine after that. Robin had agreed with some trepidation that he would be present at the birth but was chased away as forceps were required.

Chris made his appearance at 1.15 a.m. on 7 February 1973. I held him in my arms and marvelled at his delicate features, how startled and cross he looked, how bloodshot his eyes were. And all too soon he was taken away for a quick wash and bundled into his crib.

Robin staggered home, looking haggard and found his mum (who had come to stay) waiting up for him. They rang Peter in Kirkcudbright. Chris's birth was announced in the school assembly next morning; or rather Peter's elevation to the honourable company of grandfathers. And the school flag was flown in his honour!

Robin was sufficiently well known to merit a short piece in the *Evening News*, headed, 'Daddy Now!'

For a week or so I was queenly and contented with my son, showing off to visitors who came with flowers and gifts. Jack Kane (Robin's boss) who was now Lord Provost, and his wife Anne came in state in the Rolls-Royce to visit, creating quite a stir. Then one snowy morning the Cook family carefully drove home to begin life as a threesome.

15

Problems for the Working Mum

Of all the things I have done in my life, motherhood is top of the list in terms of the pride and happiness it produced. I believe I have been a good mother too, and certainly Robin would frequently say so. I had done all the right things like attending relaxation and child-care classes before the birth. People tended to assume that because of my profession I would know all about looking after babies, which certainly was not true. For this reason I sometimes didn't admit to being a doctor, for instance when the district midwife came to visit. My mother had come to stay for a while. The midwife was a muscular, no-nonsense Australian girl who steam-rollered in with instructions, seemingly working on the principle that I was a complete idiot. Tiring of this tirade, I said, 'Oh, by the way, I'm a doctor and my mother here is a nursing sister.'

There was a pause.

'You stinker!' she said.

Then we all burst out laughing, and got on much better together.

I had cleared out, decorated and furnished one of the bedrooms as a nursery. I had always been determined to breast-feed and in spite of the stories of failure one hears, found no difficulty at all. I can't understand why some women don't, as it proved the most satisfying experience. I'd assumed that when I went back to work I would have to stop but in practice didn't need to. I'd considered carefully all the various options for child care, and had advertised for and appointed a nanny. The first (of several) was Jeannette, a trained nurse. Robin shied away from this process and left it entirely in my hands. Jeannette came in the morning and went away after I arrived home. She also came every third Saturday morning as I worked a one-in-three on-call rota, though non-resident. There were occasions when I had to go to the hospital out of hours and take Chris with me, which was not a problem when he was tiny as one of the nurses was always delighted to look after him.

Relationships changed within the family. Hitherto Robin and I had been the younger generation, the children. I had never been quite at ease with calling his parents Mum and Dad, but now the problem was solved, for they became Granny and Grandpa, even to Robin.

I had to live with a strong feeling of guilt about going back to work so soon. One neighbour said dubiously, 'I suppose if you need the money . . .' I said, unwisely, that I wasn't doing it for the money, that I wanted to work. She said in shocked tones, 'What, more than looking after your own child?' There was a prevailing opinion then that if you really wanted to go on working you were not a good or natural mother. None of which I believed, but one didn't like to be told these things. One of my colleagues said, 'Of course you have to accept that someone else is bringing up your children.' I didn't believe that either, was determined that my influence would still be strong. The people who made this sort of comment would often be those who were happy to send their children to boarding school.

On my return to work I knew that there would be no flexibility on the part of my colleagues, who took the view that as I was being paid the same as them, so my contribution should be exactly equivalent. They had had to do a one-in-two rota in my absence, and I discovered that the first two consecutive weekends had been assigned to me. Looking back I think this was disgraceful, but at the time didn't dream of complaining; not because I was awed by them, simply determined to do my bit and not expect privileges.

I had fantasies of having a close woman-to-woman or mother–daughter relationship with the nanny but it never quite worked out like that. We didn't get off to a flying start with the first two Saturdays being working days. Also her working day encompassed all the time I was away at work, including travelling, so it was of necessity rather long and we had minimal time to communicate. Jeannette gave in her notice after six months which was worrying as I didn't want the disruption of frequent changes.

Certainly there was no shortage of applicants. I chose Bernadette who had done a course in residential child care, and who was to stay with us for four years. She was quiet, sweet-natured and biddable but rather slow. She could not put on a nappy to my exacting standards, so I made her practise with a teddy bear. Everything new needed to be taught with patience and frequent reiteration, and I worried at first about leaving her alone.

In the summer we planned to leave Chris with the grandparents in

Kirkcudbright for a few days, then motor to the Cotswolds and have a brief holiday by ourselves. It was a wrench leaving Chris and I gave poor Granny pages and pages of instructions. I weaned him from the breast just in time. It was on this holiday in Broadway that I persuaded Robin to mount a horse for the first time. I had been on a few pony treks before, so was hardly more experienced, but much more confident. He was quite resistant to the idea, but reluctantly and rather tetchily let himself be persuaded after a stiff double whisky. He was worried about appearing foolish in front of competent young girls, not at all concerned about the physical dangers of riding. In fact, he is brave to the point of recklessness over ordinary dangers, but has always been socially nervous and thin-skinned.

On the journey back north, our car broke down; not an uncommon event. It was beginning to dawn on me that the car, that symbol of masculinity, was not an object on which he lavished his care and attention, as many men did. It was simply a means of getting from A to B. And like many other things, he did not see the job of maintenance as his concern. I tried to prod him into being more disciplined about it, but he would jokingly portray himself as a mechanical ignoramus, with the result that this was yet one more responsibility that was left to me. Indeed the inconvenience and frustration of having an unreliable car in a crowded lifestyle was such that I was certainly motivated to keep it in working order.

Opportunities for an active social life were obviously fewer now, though there were plenty of friends willing to baby-sit. I remember a Labour Party social gathering somewhere in Edinburgh, and meeting Gordon Brown for the first time with his girlfriend Margarita, Crown Princess of Romania. This was during his three years as student rector. Robin was doubtless already involved in his contribution to Brown's 'Red Paper on Scotland', an unredeemedly Old Labour production. I have little remaining impression of Gordon, whom I have met only once or twice since then, and he seems, like many famous people who start their careers almost as child prodigies, to have suffered burn-out of his private personality. This may be an erroneous impression, fostered by years of Robin's unconcealed antipathy. I remember Margarita much better, as a lively and amusing companion. Faced with the buffet, provided inexpensively so as to be accessible to all, we dubiously accepted the Scotch pies and courageously bit into them. The grease poured out unappetisingly. We both did our best to suppress expressions of disgust, but our eyes met and we dissolved into girlish giggles. The five-hundred-pound dinners had not been invented then.

Gavin Strang I also met around this time, or a little later. It is a strange feature of memory that it retains the most bizarre happenings rather than the most worthy. I recall Gavin proffering a piece of advice as we all three sat in a pub somewhere clutching our pint glasses, to the effect that after a night's heavy drinking and before getting into the car to drive home one should always remember to empty one's bladder. In the event of being involved in a car crash with abdominal injury, the risk of bladder rupture would thereby be minimised. I was speechless at the logic of this opinion, and was reminded of it recently in a tribute to the late Enoch Powell. He equated nervousness before making a speech with having a full bladder, and believed in maximising his creative artistry by never voiding before speaking; another piece of distorted logic.

When under stress Robin would occasionally talk in his sleep. I would listen avidly on these occasions, wondering what piece of political wisdom might be caught and handed down through the generations. But sometimes the utterings were heretical, maybe reflecting inner turmoil, notably when he said with piercing clarity, 'We're going to string them up from every lamp-post!'

I was reading quietly beside him at the time, and asked gently, 'Who do you mean, dear?'

'Those ghastly anti-apartheid women!'

Heaven knows what was going on in his subconscious mind. He had no recollection or explanation for this when I told him of it later.

Thinking back to how disorganised I had been over my first child and how I had come so close to ruining my career, I gave some serious thought to the timing of the next one. It seemed wise to have another relatively soon. Robin had strong views about limiting one's family to two children, though I knew I would be the final arbiter of our family size. Having decided that our next family member was to be welcomed, lo and behold, he was on his way. I made no secret of this one. Again there were some long faces at work; while I can fully comprehend the stresses my absence imposed, it was after all only two months each time. My colleagues had wives to do these things for them, and nobody glowered at them and suggested they had been less than public-spirited when they decided to beget their children!

At Christmas we stayed at Kirkcudbright and had a wonderful three-generation family Christmas. Chris was quite alive to the fact that something unusual was going on, and being from the start a happy-natured, sociable child, we had some difficulty in settling him to sleep at night. He was alert and observant, and noticing my swelling tummy would put his hands out to pat it gently. Peter had been offered a senior job at Moray House College of Further Education training potential rectors (headmasters in Scotland), and we were aware that this might be the last Christmas in their lovely house.

So dawned the start of 1974, which was probably the most stressful and eventful year of our marriage (until 1997, that is). Industrial unrest had been brewing for a month or two in the shape of the miners' overtime ban, the resultant state of emergency and restriction in the use of electricity; then, of course, the three-day working week in January 1974. We girded ourselves for a change in lifestyle.

On Chris's first birthday, 7 February, Edward Heath called a general election. Robin and I had planned to take the afternoon off and have a little tea-party, with just the three of us. But it was not to be, understandably. The three-week campaign would culminate in polling day on 28 February, Robin's twenty-eighth birthday. This time, as he was expected to take the seat, though it was marginal and had recently lost a long-term member, it was likely to be a fierce battle, a time of non-stop pressure. I was glad to have that peaceful afternoon before action stations began in earnest.

We organised baby-sitters and I spent my spare time in the committee rooms on George IV Bridge, again arranging to take the final week of the campaign off work. I refrained from too much climbing of three-storey tenements to chap on doors, given my six-month pregnancy. This was a boon to Robin of course: a small child and a visibly pregnant wife go down well with voters, and his election leaflet portrayed us to maximum advantage. Another supporter, Jill, was at the same stage of pregnancy as myself. I eyed her girth critically and suggested she might be a month out in her calculations, as she was much bigger than me. A few days later a scan showed she was carrying twins! My reputation as a diagnostician went up a notch or two.

Nigel Griffiths, now MP for Edinburgh South, came to work for the Central Edinburgh campaign. He seemed very young and naïve then, and his attitude to Robin was one of abject hero-worship, which was extended to me as to a member of the holy family. I found this rather irksome and felt it was bad for Robin. Thus began my role of attempting to keep his feet firmly on the ground and his head of normal size. One day a phone call came for Dr Cook. The young man who took the message looked for Robin, assuming he was the person named. The feminists on the premises gave him a hard time.

I saw rather little of Robin except when I was required for photo-calls or other wifely functions. Occasionally he would call at lunchtime and we would go for a quick snack. He felt obliged to extend the invitation to other people who seemed at a loose end, especially a quiet, attractive girl called Alison, who accepted with alacrity, though she never returned the compliment. I could see the stress taking its toll with Robin, but could do little to help. The weight fell off him visibly, his brow was perpetually furrowed, he was in his inaccessible mode. I dreaded being in the car with him, for his mind was anywhere but on his driving. During the three-week campaign he lost a stone and a half in weight; he needed to do so though perhaps not quite so drastically. On polling day I drove out with him and Sandy with the loudhailer, exhorting people to come out and vote. I appealed to the women, asking them to be sure and get their menfolk to the polls.

The count, which was always a tense time, especially on that par-ticular occasion, Robin's first attempt in a winnable seat, was held in one of the schools. You are supposed to watch like a hawk to ensure that votes go into the correct pile. You seldom pick up mistakes, but one pile of ten votes nearly went astray. If there is a big majority it becomes obvious quickly, but on this occasion it was impossible to predict the result. One other useful job is to take sample counts of votes from various parts of the constituency, to see where the weak spots are for future reference.

In the event, his majority was tiny, less than 1,000 votes, reflecting the national ambivalence. And so he won his first parliamentary seat with a tenuous foothold, and with the clear likelihood that there would be another election in a very short time indeed. I reflected on this: it was possible that, having given up his WEA job, he might be unem-ployed later in the year. But like every other uncertainty we'd faced so far, we could only grin and hope for the best.

After the euphoria these sobering thoughts were joined by others. He would be away in London for most of the week, and I would be left on my own with one, soon to be two, young babies; a demanding job with an on-call commitment and only a daytime nanny. Very opportunely, Peter had accepted the Moray House job so he and Ina were in the process of moving. They bought a house in Dalkeith and were able to offer me support, which they did unstintingly in those demanding years. I felt a close bond with them, and liked the feeling of an extended family. On my week-night on call, Ina would come and stay overnight in case I needed to go into work.

Robin unwound, and went on a shopping spree, most unusual for him, augmenting and improving his wardrobe. Then off he flew on his southerly migration. We soon got used to the new pattern of life. He would travel to Edinburgh on the sleeper over Thursday night, or occasionally fly up on Friday, then in his eagerness to be at work he would return to London by sleeper on Sunday night. He rented a flatlet just off the King's Road and was given an office adjacent to Westminster Hall. Shortly before my baby was due I flew down with him for a few days to view and admire these arrangements, and to dine with him in the House of Commons. I could see how much he loved being part of this imposing and historic institution. He revelled in even meaningless traditions, such as being given a pink ribbon and a peg on which to hang his sword. He described the unnerving experience of sitting, having his face memorised by half a dozen policemen whose job it was to recognise members so that they were never challenged. They were surprisingly good at it. This was a time of heightened security because of the bombing campaign on mainland Britain.

His maiden speech on 14 March 1974 was as non-controversial as maiden speeches are meant to be. He paid tribute to his predecessor, spoke about his constituency on a subject he knew well: housing.

My baby was due on 17 May. The day before I had conducted the consultant's ward round, then on the day itself I was to present myself for induction of labour because of previous blood-pressure problems. Robin was due back on the overnight train in time to take me in to the maternity unit, but the train was delayed. Grandpa drove me in, then vanished hastily. Robin appeared later, equipped with books and papers, anticipating a long day like the last one. Much to the disapproval of the ward staff, as soon as labour was established he took himself off to have a meal. This time I didn't hang about, and the baby arrived within the hour; so quickly that I had no time for any pain relief, not even a whiff of gas! Robin arrived back to a fait accompli.

The baby when I first saw him held up for my inspection, even before the umbilical cord was cut, looked so like Grandpa Cook that I decided he had to be called Peter too. He was a real throwback because he also closely resembled my father as a young man. Like Chris he was a good and contented baby – but greedier.

Chris was fifteen months by now, and still not walking, though he was very mobile by dint of rolling and crawling. The small gap between the two of them meant that there was no jealousy. Chris did not immediately recognise this new being as the same species as himself, and when he did so the time for rivalry was past.

A month after Peter's birth, Robin broke his habit of returning to Westminster on the Sunday night, flying down instead early on Monday morning. That morning, at 8 a.m., an IRA bomb exploded in Westminster Hall, yards away from his office. If he had travelled by sleeper he would have been at his desk at the time. The bomb blast did not damage the office, but the resulting fire did. The room and all his files were destroyed. When he surveyed the blackened hole later that day the only recognisable document was a singed visiting card lying in the corner.

A month later I was back at work, managing again to breast-feed, though Peter was much more difficult to satisfy, and needed supplementary feeds.

With our improved income we began to look around for a larger house, having uppermost in mind the schools that the boys would attend. Robin was adamant that they should go to state schools but we could compromise to the extent of choosing in which catchment area we lived. He longed for a New Town flat or house. One in Danube Street was underpriced because of its proximity to a well-known house of ill-repute. I was determined to have a garden. Living in flats in the centre of town for so long, I had yearned to be able to step out of the door and smell earth and see green things. I felt the boys should be able to do that, and also be able to run out to play without being threatened by traffic and other urban hazards. We finally compromised by choosing the Mill in Clermiston, a seventeenth-century converted stone farm building with a huge circular main room, and a large garden surrounded by trees. Robin made it clear that he intended to have nothing to do with the garden.

This was the time of escalating house prices, so the market was sluggish. Having offered for the Mill, our own flat seemed to take an eternity to get itself sold. In fact it was only five weeks, but I was convinced we faced disaster and ruin. This was not wholly fanciful as many people at the time could not sell and ruined themselves with bridging loans. We also had problems with delay with our mortgage, and wondered if the building society was watching to see which way the political wind was blowing, and since the mortgage was allowed a few days before polling day of the second general election in 1974 when prospects looked promising, we may have been right.

We moved in, and as Robin used to describe dramatically, 'dropped everything and ran out to fight an election'. I remember little of this campaign but still have an election leaflet showing the family in picturesque happiness with a toddler and a tiny babe in arms, strolling in the sunshine in the Queen's Park. His majority quadrupled (Labour also getting in on a small majority) and we heaved a sigh of relief, though he continued to feel insecure about his seat. After so much excitement I longed for a period of monotonous harmony. We had stretched ourselves beyond the limit financially and so had the senior Cooks in their house move. Everything about our new home involved greater expense: the rates, the electricity bills, to say nothing of decorating, furnishing and gardening. As the house had lain empty all summer the garden was like a jungle by autumn. Grandpa helped me to reduce it to a semi-civilised state but until such time as I could afford a gardener this was yet another job to add to my list. Money was so tight that I realised with horror that I should have to budget very strictly indeed if I was not to get into a Micawber-type situation and progressively overspend. I was aware of a contrast between Robin's lifestyle and mine: he would enjoy his dinner with a carafe of wine in the House of Commons dining room; my main meal was in the hospital canteen at lunchtime, very cheap fare. Once the boys' requirements were met, there was little to spend on myself, though of course I provided better meals at weekends.

During the week, Robin phoned me every night unless he was particularly tied up. This habit he kept up throughout all our years together.

At Hallowe'en I was enchanted to be visited by local children in fancy dress coming house-to-house guising. In those days they still called out, 'Penny for the Guisers!' rather than the American 'Trick or treat'. They were uninhibited with their songs and jokes, and I brought them in to amuse Chris and Peter. Then I gave them apples, sweets and pennies, and the word rapidly flashed round Clermiston that Mrs Cook's was the place to go. I was besieged the whole evening. After that, high jinks at Hallowe'en became customary, part of the long run-up to Christmas. I had already got into the habit of reading to the boys, a little story every night before tucking them in, long before either could understand. Around this time Chris started actually string-ing words together. Trundling along the hall, he stumbled and fell. I heard him mutter, 'Oh dear, fa' down! Up!' Another time when Robin was clowning around to amuse him, he said with a chuckle, 'Daddy fa' down,' then with a sudden change of expression to one of concern, 'Daddy broken?'

Perhaps mothers of young children all have a heightened sense of anxiety, as I did, but maybe mine was because there had been so much civic violence and especially IRA activity. I armed myself mentally against wholesale disturbance and was fiercely protective. Once when the neighbour's dog, a friendly Irish setter called Rebel, came gam-bolling into the garden he knocked over Chris who gave a little yell of protest. I launched myself like a fury, screeching, punching, kicking at the poor harmless animal who fled in terror. I stood for a moment, trembling in instinctive rage, marvelling at the totally disproportionate reaction. Chris later tried to relate the story; again all we could make out was, 'Mummy push; Rebel go 'way.'

I had dreams of bombs demolishing buildings, widespread destruc-tion, snatching the boys from their burning cots. Maybe it reflected personal anxieties, maybe all mothers do this. In these days of global warming it is strange to remember that then, some erudite scientists were agitatedly predicting another ice age. At the end of Clermiston Road, hidden by the trees, was a bunker, designed as a seat of govern-ment in the event of a nuclear war. No wonder I behaved like a she-bear with cubs.

16

Careers Intertwine

In our temporary state of poverty – or restricted cash flow – the difference between our attitudes to money became more obvious. If Robin felt he needed or wanted something, he would have it regardless of whether or not he could afford it. I would just go without, retrench in some way, be parsimonious until I could afford the desired object. He in his younger days was generous to the point of prodigality; something that may have been motivated by insecurity and appearances. He was also crazily careless about money and possessions. I was once (correctly) quoted as saying that if he ever became Chancellor of the Exchequer I'd advise my friends to emigrate. He never carried a wallet, stuffing notes and coins in his back pocket and frequently losing significant sums. Gifts from me such as cuff-links, pens, gloves, bought with care and affection, never stayed with him for more than a few months. They would be mislaid, or left lying around so they got stolen. This used to infuriate me, but it was useless to remonstrate. It was never his fault, somehow. We were both inclined to shy away from quarrels and hard words; and I never nagged, but did believe in clearing the air rather than letting an issue rankle. But he was evasive and clever at ducking out of any unpleasant discussion. This was unwise as it left issues unresolved. He might disappear for a few days, but the problem remained. In particular he would never be pinned down to a discussion about money.

My chief, Norman Allan, was asked to supervise the department of haematology at Bangour General Hospital in West Lothian. David, my colleague, and I frequently deputised for him there, covering both laboratory and clinical work. We soon developed a strong affection for the place and enjoyed our trips to the country. Bangour had been built on an exposed remote hillside to cope with wartime civilian casualties, and, being supposedly a temporary expedient, was composed of long barrack-like buildings. In the winter you needed stout boots just to go from one department to another. It had a well-deserved reputation for friendliness and courtesy and for providing a concentration of fascinating and mind-bending clinical problems. Norman mentioned to me that there was every possibility of a new consultant post being created there in about a year, and would I be interested? Of course I was extremely interested. Then it behoved me to get my last and most difficult qualification, the Final MRC Path. exam, reputedly the most difficult and demanding post-graduate exam of all. Nor was it easy finding time to study with my life structured as it was. I would return home, make a meal for myself and the boys, read to them, bath them and put them to bed; then collapse in a chair for an hour or two's oblivion. After this I would wake up and start studying. I was resigned to having no social life, and very little leisure, but was intensely motivated by the thought of a consultant post so soon.

Granny Cook required two hip replacements which were to be done in June, with a break of two weeks between them. She was taken into the Princess Margaret Rose Hospital in south Edinburgh. Grandpa would sometimes come and baby-sit so I could go and visit in the evening. A few days after her second operation she mentioned in passing that her ankle was a little swollen. Alarm bells started to ring, not surprisingly. I rang the surgeon who was horrified that it hadn't been noticed. She was transferred to the Western, where she was found to have an extensive leg thrombosis. Poor Granny thought her days were numbered, knowing the condition was potentially fatal. As she was now in my hospital with a haematological condition, it fell to my lot to control her anti-coagulant dosage. By the time she'd endured all this, she had seen quite enough of hospitals, and marvelled at how I could bear to spend my days working in such places. But she was deeply grateful too and convinced that I'd saved her life. Which may have been true.

For the rest of the year my plans to forward my career progressed without a hitch. I spent some time in Blood Transfusion again, and in the Sick Children's haematology department to complete training requirements; then was directed to Manchester for the practicals, clinicals and orals for the final, three days in all. This tests your toughness and resilience as much as anything, for it is incredibly stressful. Both David and I passed. To my disgust he toyed with applying for the Bangour job, but thought better of it. I could barely believe how lucky I was that a job had become available locally at just the right time, and one where I already had a toe-hold. Most people had to travel the length of the country and not be too choosy about location. I suppose London was another option for me but would be highly competitive, and we felt the quality of life would be less desirable there, especially for the boys.

I was appointed against one other applicant, becoming a consultant at thirty-one years of age. I felt like a bird that has just discovered the power of flight.

I was now empowered to restore the family's fortunes a little, so set about some home improvements and gave Bernadette an overdue rise in pay, but most importantly pensioned off our dilapidated car. Robin took a rather perverse delight in this car, perhaps because it fitted in with his image as a man of the people. I'd given up all hope that his masculine pride might persuade him that we needed to buy a better one. Feeling I needed a man in tow, I took Grandpa Cook to help me choose and negotiate for a respectable used car, for which I paid and arranged servicing and repairs, though Robin shared in its use.

Before taking up the new post I took the boys to Bristol on the overnight sleeper to see my parents. We had a second-class berth with myself in the top bunk and the two of them at either end of the bottom bunk. This was immensely exciting to them, in fact they could hardly wait for the return journey. We made this trip several times, until sadly they became too big to share a bunk. Even their first experience of flying did not create as much pleasure. The car attendants were particularly attentive and kindly; perhaps because they were fathers.

From this point my salary moved progressively ahead of Robin's. At least I think so. There were times when he earned a lot extra in journalism and on TV, or radio, but he never discussed his earnings. Anyway I was the chief breadwinner and also I was simply always there. If the boys needed anything, if there were house repairs, car expenses, nanny-related costs, I met them all. He paid the mortgage, insurance policies and holidays. He was generous, all the same, especially with presents at Christmas and birthdays and even at other times when the mood took him. He would be overcome with affection after some bibulous occasion and arrive home with an expensive item of jewellery, or flowers and chocolates.

The work at Bangour kept me happily occupied without being overly stressful. The clinical side I was to build up from scratch. There had been protracted negotiations to provide in-patient beds directly under the care of the haematologist, in line with modern practice. I also had out-patient clinics. Then there was the laboratory work, samples from all West Lothian hospitals and from general practice to interpret. In my ubiquitous role I soon came to know many colleagues in all departments and to forge useful links. The system was still rather hierarchical then, doctors having a separate dining room with linen tablecloths and napkins, and waitress service. One of the surgeons liked to put new consultants through their paces, and over lunch one day started firing questions at me about lab practice. He was hopelessly out of date and I fielded his attacks easily. Henry, one of the anaesthetists, kept the score under his breath. When the defeated surgeon left he gave me a wink. 'You handled that all right.'

One of the problems that vexed me over the next few years was that of nannies. After four years Bernadette left to get married and I explained this carefully to the boys who had known her as long as they could remember. They took all this in and seemed to accept it without a fuss. Then Chris asked me, 'Mummy, when you get married, will you leave us?'

I have had similar holes punched in my communication systems with a single blow by patients, with the same profoundly humbling effect.

I explained to them that I would never leave them, that children and mummies belonged to each other, and of course I was already married to their daddy.

'The family will always stay together,' I said.

With the next round of adverts there was not a superabundance of applicants and I took on a lovely girl, Elizabeth, knowing that she would not be with us for long as she was to train as a nurse. Chris started nursery at four, then primary school the following year, with Peter following just one year behind. After a few months Elizabeth left and I took on an older married woman who brought her son with her. This created tensions and she favoured her son if quarrels arose. Also she threw her weight around until I made it clear that I was the boss even in absentia. She lasted less than a year, and was followed by a woman who was strongly into alternative Christianity, who also brought her small daughter. This was an unqualified disaster. She went off on her social rounds with my children in tow, and saw no reason why she should not do exactly as she pleased. I gave her notice and she flounced out. Granny responded to the emergency and filled in the gap. I was in despair, wondering if I should give up the unequal struggle and become a house mother.

In the end I decided to try a different formula, that of taking a younger person (who hopefully would be more amenable to following my ways), and one who was prepared to live in, at least during the week. This would also relieve stress, as often at the end of the day when work overran I was faced with conflicting responsibilities.

And so we found Lynn, who was a treasure and a delight and a good friend to us all. She was tall, blonde, and extremely pretty. When I interviewed her she was not especially promising, without a consistent work record, little experience and no training. She did, however, have an excellent reference – and when she smiled I got a glimpse of the warmth and depth of character that were there. For once my instincts proved correct.

Chris announced to his teacher, 'We've got a living nanny!'

Lynn was with us for two special years, after which we had one or two further problems, but more of this later.

Robin joined the European Council and Western European Union, which excited him a lot as it meant frequent visits to Strasbourg and Paris, and whenever I could I accompanied him. The autumn trips to Strasbourg were particularly special. I loved the warmth of the Indian summer that prevailed while the seasonal russet colours were in full glow. The first trip there coincided with an air-traffic controllers' strike, so we waited for two hours in the chartered plane for take-off, sitting with Kevin Macnamara, MP for Kingston-upon-Hull Central, and his son. In order to keep us cheerful, drinks were served – and more drinks. The usual cabin discipline was non-existent. Soon after take-off dinner was served, with wine and more drinks. After that, the party hardly seemed to stop. In my hotel room were beautiful red roses with compliments from the mayor of Strasbourg. While Robin was hard at work I enjoyed myself with sightseeing: the cathedral, the streets, the shops, the orangerie. The British delegation hosted a party with traditional national food and drink, at which all the best malt whiskies were available. The effect was dramatic, as virtually everyone except ourselves was legless by the end of the evening. We had to carry a clerk of the House to his room and insert him through the door, shutting the door on him hastily as there was every sign that he was about to throw up. On Sunday a trip to the Vosges Mountains was

Bedtime routine. Peter, Chris, me

Chris and Peter cool off after riding, Dalkeith 1985

The proper doctor, Bangour General Hospital 1987

Robin carves the Christmas goose, Edinburgh, early-1990s

Gala Day in the constituency, Livingston, mid-1980s

Chris, Robin, Peter on a ramble in the New Forest, 1989

A wet Easter in
the New Forest

Fox Sanctuary, New Forest

Free-roaming sow and
piglets, New Forest 1987

Peter and Chris indulge in
horse-play, New Forest 1991

Peter, me, Robin, Kate, Chris at Eyeworth Lodge, New Forest 1989

Chris on Wendy,
Kirkliston 1986

Liz on Bean,
me on Phyllis,
Dunbar, 1995

Heels down, toes in,
sit up! Robin and
hunter, Kirkliston

Me on Carrie holding
Lucky. The Grange,
West Calder 1988

Phyllis and me going well across country, Douglas 1990

undertaken with coaches for the delegates and police outriders all the way. It seemed so strange to me to have such a security presence for this bunch of hearty, singing, drinking merrymakers! Lunch lasted several hours and there was time to take a gentle stroll in the glorious mountain scenery between courses. We then progressed through the villages at the height of the wine harvest, sampling the local produce. Trips to Paris were just as memorable.

Both boys were prone to the usual maladies. As soon as Chris started nursery and brought back all the viruses that were circulating, we all three had colds without a break through the winter. I found it most embarrassing to face the patients with coughs and sneezes, but I could hardly stay off work for weeks on end. Chris was prone to food allergies and often had tummy upsets. When he was five, one weekend he became particularly sick and slightly feverish but by Monday morning had improved enough for me to go off without worrying unduly about him, though he stayed off school. When I returned in the evening, Elizabeth (for she was still with us) said that he really wasn't well, that he couldn't walk properly: his right leg wouldn't straighten at the hip.

In an instant I knew exactly what was wrong.

Elizabeth, with her nurse's instinct, didn't want to go away. I rather bundled her out of the door as I had much to organise. I laid Chris down and felt his tummy which was rigid over the appendix area: muscle spasm was preventing him from straightening his leg. I groaned inwardly, thinking of the two days' delay. We all three went to our local doctor who thought the story strange but agreed we should go to hospital. He gave me a note. I drove home, made Peter and me a quick snack of boiled eggs, rang the ever-ready grandparents, packed a case for Chris. He had had his tonsils out only a month previously and reminded me to sew a label on his teddy bear.

We drove to the Sick Children's, meeting the grandparents at the door. They took charge of Peter and went home with him. Chris was seen by an impatient casualty doctor who also explained that we'd come to the wrong place – the Western was receiving that day. I cursed our doctor inwardly: what excuse could there be for not knowing this vital information? So we trailed off to the Western casualty department and went through the rigmarole again, this time waiting ages because there seemed to be an epidemic of appendicitis; well, three anyway. The registrar went to one, the house officer to another, and we got the medical student. She was taken aback to discover who I was and went off to find someone senior. More delays. A scientific officer came from the lab to do a finger prick. Both he and I knew well that white cell counts were useless in the diagnosis of appendicitis (there being frequent dialogue with the casualty staff about it, but the myth persisted). Chris had been so good and patient, but was getting tired and progressively more uncomfortable. 'Can't we go home?' he pleaded. Eventually he was seen, decisions were taken. They would operate that night. The senior registrar appeared, a Mr Moussa, who told me that if I wanted they'd call in the consultant surgeon as I was a consultant myself. But I wanted no more delays and anyway preferred a young SR who was accustomed to operating at dead of night to an elderly consultant who was more used to being asleep at such times.

Chris had severe appendicitis with a small abscess forming. No one could explain why he had had no tummy pain. He was pretty sick for a couple of days, needing drips and diamorphine, then suddenly bounced back to health again. I was supposed to be going to Paris with Robin the next week but stayed home with Chris instead.

I didn't blame myself for the delay in diagnosis because the presentation had been so bizarre. But Robin somehow did not perceive that this was a sensitive area and liked to make a crass joke in company about my failing to diagnose my son's condition. I winced on these occasions, as did others in our company. Finally I warned him off the subject with sufficient vehemence for him to desist. Such jokes seemed at variance with his usual intelligent wit, but he did allow himself to belittle me in public at times. His humour under other circumstances, notably when he felt ill at ease, could be hearty and quite perplexing to the recipients.

His job and his travelling patterns gave a wonderful excuse for ducking out of obligations. When the children were small, especially before school age, it must be said that the support I had from Robin was patchy, sometimes minimal. He was very good with the boys themselves, always taking time to play with them and take them on a variety of expeditions. But in the day-to-day duties of living and particularly in matters of discipline, he was nowhere to be found. Once I had just embarked on a talking-to with Chris for a misdemeanour that I regarded as potentially serious. Robin cut across this as he wanted to play with them, only had so much time, didn't want a nasty atmosphere. This particular fault reared its head a week or two later at school with a much more troublesome situation for correction. And so I perceived that he was, on occasions, making my process of upbringing more difficult. Also this theme, that he had priority in all things, was an overriding and progressive one, which I resisted as much as possible. If he had been the consultant and I had been the MP he would have behaved exactly the same. The assumption was promoted that he worked harder and endured more stress than anyone else. He bitterly resented any attempt on my part to match his arduous life with accounts of my own. I was told brusquely not to be competitive about it. I almost never got a partner's support for my demanding life – because he was always several notches further up.

Yet he wanted my wifely ministrations, but only when it was convenient for him. He would arrive home in the usual flat spin, brushing me aside with comments like, 'I'll make a fuss of you later. Just now I've got a couple of phone calls to make,' and vanish into his study without even a kiss. Later he would expect me to drop everything and dance attendance. There were also times of pressure when we hardly seemed to communicate in any but the most functional terms for weeks on end. I would wait patiently until he emerged and became approachable again.

He was certainly energetic in his sphere, and was known as a left-wing rebellious backbencher. He was active and eloquent in the Campaign for Nuclear Disarmament, notably stating that it was a crime against humanity to drop a nuclear bomb in any context, and inspiring prominent people to join CND. He notoriously vacillated about devolution. In the election leaflet for October 1974 he made a special point of the promise of a Scottish parliament with full powers for law-making; then in the mid to late seventies risked further unpopularity by opposing devolution. Later in the eighties he was to turn again. Ah well, anyone can change his mind, of course. He linked his voice with those seeking to liberalise homosexuality laws, notably with David Steel whom he joined as an honorary figure attached to the Scottish Minorities Group (a euphemism for Gay Rights Group), and this was certainly courageous at that time. He had been invited to a formal dinner of this group on a Saturday, to which I objected for once; weekends got progressively invaded by responsibilities. I fumed, 'Why can't I come too?' So he asked, and I was invited. I had a very enjoyable evening in lovely company, though recall being frankly rude about psychiatrists and causing an emotional crisis in my neighbour, who was one. This group was not widely known at the time, and I was able to rescue at least one person from depression and despair by putting her in touch with them.

Holidays were good times for us, and, no matter what the stresses and strains had been, Robin and I always seemed to find what we loved and enjoyed in each other then. We favoured self-catering holidays and he showed remarkable skill in discovering idyllic places for us to stay. When the children were tiny, for two or three years, Granny and Grandpa came too, a great boon to me, though Robin was a little uneasy in his relationship with them. We stayed in the Cotswolds, the Forest of Dean, Suffolk, Dartmoor, Somerset.

The referendum on devolution came in 1979. I was aware that this was a stressful topic as he was opposed to the Wilson government's plans and in a minority group of like-minded people. And as usual he was vociferous and prominent. The consequences of the failure in Scotland to achieve a sufficient vote to implement devolution led to an opposition vote of no-confidence, and thence to the general election. He was undoubtedly worried about how much he had injured his personal prospects with this stand. I think that this phase coincided with his sincere beliefs. He adopted a pattern of behaviour I came to recognise when things were not going well: he drank too regularly – there was always a glass of whisky on his desk – and he became childishly sorry for himself and wanted to be mothered. By contrast, Gordon Brown, as yet only a prospective parliamentary candidate, had been a staunch pro-devolutionist and had run Labour's campaign for a 'Yes' vote. He did a sterling job and was smiled upon by the senior hierarchy. I feel pretty sure that this polarisation of views and its consequences sowed the seeds of enmity in Robin's heart for Gordon.

With the general election coming round again, the family went through the routine of being photographed, this time in the Meadows. The boys were taken out campaigning in Gorgie-Dalry, clutching their banners and entering into the spirit of enthusiastic vote-catching. Ever-optimistic, we expected Labour to win, and were disappointed; but Robin kept his seat and was now able to experience life as an opposition backbencher.

Under Mrs Thatcher's government we rapidly noticed our lifestyle improve owing to Geoffrey Howe's cut in income tax in June. Friends teased us, saying that we supported the wrong party. Self-seeking again was expected to triumph over principle! It's human nature, I suppose, and you can't legislate against that.

Rather to my surprise, we were invited to a post-wedding celebratory party by Norman Fowler, who was the new Transport Secretary, and his wife to-be, Fiona.

Contrary to popular belief, there is not much socialising across party lines. Fiona was responsible for our invitation, as she and Robin had become first acquaintances, then friends, through contact in the House of Commons library where she was a librarian. Robin was ever bookish and used the library as freely as anyone, getting locked in one night when he was tucked away in a corner, wrapped up in his book. Apparently, Fiona and Norman had been encouraged by Mrs Thatcher to regularise their relationship now that he was a senior minister. I took the opportunity, which I did whenever occasion offered, to spend a day or two in London; we had a delightful dinner at Walton's of Walton Street, celebrating our new-found affluence. Then we joined the party in Harley Street Mews, at which most people arrived in chauffeur-driven cars.

As soon as we arrived, to the strain of a string quartet playing on the mezzanine floor, Fiona separated us and conducted me across the room, announcing that I absolutely must meet the only other doctor present. Rapid introductions were made and she disappeared, leaving me facing a man in a tweed jacket whose name I had failed to digest.

'Er ... what sort of doctor are you?' I asked. 'Are you in general practice?' Because that is how he seemed to me.

He looked mildly disdainful, replying, 'No. I'm the Minister of State for Health actually. And I'm not responsible for Scotland.'

With that, Gerard Vaughan – for it was he – turned abruptly and moved away. I chuckled to myself, and stored the story for future use.

Fiona came back to the rescue and introduced me to her mother this time. Her mother knew I employed a nanny and wanted to know all about it. She and her friend, formidably groomed society ladies, pumped me mercilessly and I got the impression that they pulled me to pieces as soon as my back was turned. I moved away as soon as I decently could.

17

Pastoral Interlude and a Winning Move

Robin was a staunch supporter of Michael Foot and was comfortable when he was appointed Labour leader in 1980. He continued to identify himself with the cause of unilateral nuclear disarmament and this was in line with party policy. He joined Peter Shore's shadow Treasury team along with Jack Straw and Bob Sheldon, and I met socially with the team and its wives on a number of occasions. Bob in particular was a kindly, soft-spoken man whom I liked a lot. Jack Straw, who had divorced his first wife in 1978, asked my husband, 'Are you still on your first marriage, Robin?' He was a little taken aback at the implications, and replied, 'Jack, I am on my only marriage.'

At home the habit of reading to the boys at night had persisted and whenever Robin was available he would choose his own book to read to them. They were of course well able to read themselves, but there is something special about listening to a story. Indeed I would usually join the group (on rare occasions I could still persuade Robin to read poetry to me). By a happy chance he read to them *Children of the New Forest*, and we were all so enchanted with the tale that we decided to go there in the summer holidays. This was a decision that changed our lives magically in more than one way.

We – or rather I – had packed cases, prepared picnics for the day, provided essential groceries for the self-catering holiday, and miraculously positioned everything in the car while still leaving space for four bodies. Robin emerged from his study looking perplexed. 'I seem to have got the date wrong,' he said. 'We go tomorrow.'

'We go today,' I said firmly, which meant he had to find us a place to stay for one night, in a village called Fairford near the Vale of the White Horse in the south. Next day we moved on to the most idyllic and beautiful place on earth, Forest Brook Farm at the edge of the

New Forest, near Fordingbridge. We loved it so much we returned year after year, in either spring or summer, and came to know it in different moods and seasons. It wasn't a real farm at all, but a rambling old family home with terrace, lawns, overhanging trees, shrubs, all stretching away to a ha-ha wall, then to meadows, a tree-lined brook and beyond to the wide-open heath. We loved to ramble, discovering the enclosures of forest scattered between stretches of bracken-covered moorland, with magical names like Amberwood, Broad Bottom, Smuggler's Way, Nomansland, Bramble Hill. In a changing world, how wonderful it was to return and find it unaltered, still rural and free of concrete and tarmac, and populated by the wildlife we loved to watch as if they were characters from *The Wind in the Willows*. Here we relearned the capacity to stand and stare; for the more quiet and still you were, the more you were likely to see. Herds of fallow deer, seen in the open at any time, came up to the house at dusk. Semi-wild ponies roamed everywhere, tending to look rather thin and shabby; and at Easter time the yearly foals appeared, wobbling beside their mothers. In some parts, donkeys wandered freely, as did many domestic animals, for citizens have the right to graze their animals on the common land. I remember the delight of coming across a prostrate pink sow suckling seven or eight scrabbling youngsters. Foxes, adders, badgers, voles were our neighbours; there were varieties of butterflies and moths which at last I had patience and time to pursue and identify, including purple emperors once I had been shown where to look. Hundreds of tunnel spiders lurked in the depths of their cylindrical webs, camping out on the heath; and in the damp places you could find the ground carpeted with the carnivorous sundew and the elegant bog asphodel. I kept looking for the very rare Dartford warbler but regret I have not seen one; not yet.

Chris and Peter would bring toys and books aplenty to occupy rainy days. With car space limited I rationed them to three cuddly toys each, and it was a source of endless delight for them to see how many more they could smuggle in undetected. When planning the holiday we considered a number of trips to places of interest; but by happy chance discovered that just two fields away lay a riding stable. This time no one needed a whisky to encourage him to ride. The stable girls sized us up as complete beginners, got us mounted up on suitably quiet ponies and packed us off to the paddock to await our escorts. Peter was small enough to need a lead rein. Robin's horse decided to have a roll, so he became aware of the saddle sliding from underneath him, and having hastily to scramble out of the way of the grunting mass of horseflesh. A nimble young lady of about eight leaped over the gate, gave the horse a hearty kick in the ribs and a barked order. The animal respectfully got to his feet and allowed Robin to remount. The little girl gave him a stick with instructions to wallop the beast if he misbehaved, but the horse was wise enough to know he'd been sussed.

I'm afraid the Cook family did not cover themselves with glory that day. Chris was at the back of the ride of about ten people and as we climbed a little hill managed to fall off his pony. The leader, who had Peter in tow, dropped the lead-rein and rode back to rescue Chris. The senior Cooks were quite incapable of rendering any assistance as they had incomplete control of their mounts: that is to say, they could not make them do anything at all. Meanwhile, Peter's pony got bored and decided to lurch on to the top of the hill, much to his alarm. Again, his useless parents were unable to help. At last, Chris was remounted, Peter rescued, peace restored and we continued our stroll. And very surprisingly, in spite of the trauma, everyone at the end thought it was wonderful and yes, we'd love to do it again please. All other plans were forgotten and we spent the whole holiday learning to ride. I remember the overgrown, lush, damp, leafy walk of about a mile, over stiles and streams, in a state of excited anticipation on the way to the stable, and the feeling of contented satisfaction and wellbeing on the way back.

On future holidays when we had become more competent riders we could go on faster and longer rides, and discovered yet more of the wild and empty places. We loved the sandy gallops around Hasley Hill, and even dared the little rustic jumps we found there. Peter, ever the dreamer, would forget he was supposed to be in charge of the small pony allotted to him, who was as often as not a wily creature with a touch of impishness. Once as we rode along a wide avenue in the woods, I was keeping an eye on Peter as usual as he trailed behind, deep in thought. In the wide-open space I saw his pony change course so that his path took him under an overhanging prickly profusion of holly bush. Meanwhile, Peter disappeared from view as the pony walked unscathed underneath the spiky tree, losing his rider in the process. Then a pair of boots appeared, followed rapidly by Peter's form which landed, flump, on the soft ground. We rounded up the pony, brushed Peter down and gave him a cuddle to restore him a little, for I have to confess we could not help laughing – once we discovered he was not hurt, of course.

Peter said in tones of offended surprise, 'He did it on purpose!'

'Of course. Ponies have as much of a sense of mischief as small boys.'

None of us was immune from being made to look a little foolish by the horses. That was one of their delights. They can refuse to go forward at your bidding, or, worse, fail to slow down and stop when you ask. Sometimes they buck – out of wickedness, or *joie die vivre*, or reaction to a whack with a stick – and the rider may or may not hit the ground, rolling. You like a horse to show spirit, but not too much! Their patience and obedience are more remarkable than their wilfulness, given their size and strength. We quickly learned that trying to show off on a horse was asking for trouble.

Exploring the forest on horseback was rewarding because wild animals, especially deer, were less likely to take fright of mounted humans. Robin's interest in matters of the countryside was kindled and fanned here and he began to inform himself about hunting. He had a certain moth-to-the-flame, ambivalent attraction to activities traditionally associated with the upper classes, and that included racing which also began to catch his notice at this time and which over the next years became an all-absorbing enthusiasm, though he never gambled seriously. A Labour MP who showed sympathy for country sports could not be ignored and we were invited to meets of foxhounds in the New Forest and of staghounds in Somerset. We met a delightfully charming couple, the Fitzpatricks, in this connection, and lunching with them I had my first experience of rising with the ladies to leave the men to their brandy and cigars. Mrs Fitzpatrick chatted to one of her guests about MPs: 'My dear, they all have affairs with their secretaries, don't they?' Whereupon a look of anguish crossed her face, for she was the soul of kindness, as she glanced at me and realised she'd made a *faux pas*. I affected not to have heard. Robin also made contact with Captain Ronnie Wallace, Master of the Exmoor foxhounds, whom we visited. I don't think the lobbying did the country sport enthusiasts much good, as Robin was far too wily a politician to risk his career on such an issue. But socialising with and being courted by these people was a boost to his frail social confidence.

Looking back, you realise how happy times are composed of small, relatively ordinary pleasures: the country walks, the huge log fires we made on cold March days, toasted buttery hot-cross buns and steaming mugs of tea after wet rides, visits to the Fordingbridge bookshop, cream teas at the innumerable delightful cafés found in the most remote places. And fish and chips on the last night of the holiday. No matter how cold it was the boys always insisted on consuming this meal from newspaper while strolling along the street.

To my dismay, Lynn found herself another job nearer home, and I faced the troublesome task of replacing her. With a not very promising field I selected a girl by exclusion whose intelligence I seriously overestimated. She was the product of a small Edinburgh private school and had a polished accent which Robin was convinced had misled me. Chris at eight found he could dominate her easily and was soon handing out the orders. One day she said to me timidly, 'Mrs Cook, is Chris really supposed to have all his class round to tea each day?' But I had realised even before this that she had no control, so I gave her the sack without delay.

The next nanny had only been with us for a few hours before it dawned on me that she had anorexia nervosa. I was to learn about that condition by first-hand experience over the next year. Fortunately she related well to the boys, which was the most important consideration. She gave me a good deal of stress and vexation however. Knowing that she liked to bake, I asked her one morning to make something for tea, gave her some money and a free hand, and went off to work. On my return I found every surface in the kitchen covered with cakes, scones, buns, tarts of every possible variety. When were we going to consume all these? I had forgotten the obsession that some anorexics have with food, as long as they are not obliged to eat it. This extended to her knowing the calorific value of any food or meal you could name. She was also rather anti-man and infuriated Robin and even Grandpa Cook, who was the mildest and most kindly of men. He referred to her as a 'surly tink'.

One day as we sat chatting at the table after supper, Chris came running in and flung himself on my lap, affecting histrionics. He tore at his hair and gasped, 'Oh, whatever shall I do? I've just weighed myself and I've put on a pound!' I realised he was taking the mickey, and chided him but grinned to myself. Chris later told me that the nanny spoke of Princess Diana having anorexia, and being proud of having the same condition.

She left rather abruptly after I'd told her in exasperation that I employed her to help me, not to give me extra worries. There was little doubt that some of her behaviour was manipulative. After leaving she wrote an aggressive letter accusing me of not giving her paid holiday leave at the time of her departure; I reminded her of the four or five weeks she had been allowed over the course of the year, and heard no more.

The next girl was young, sweet-natured and reserved, so that I never felt I quite made contact with her. She worried me by forging a friendship with a young man known to have a drug problem, but I think the attraction sprang more from curiosity and a reforming zeal than a wish to share his habit. She left also after a year, but kept in contact (as also did Lynn) to my gratification, and returned some years later to show me her first baby. Our last nanny was Elaine, who was with us for four years, bless her, and brought an era of much-needed stability; for me, if not for the boys.

I had been steering the haematology department at Bangour for around six years, had presided over a number of changes and fought over others. The clinical service in particular had increased its activity exponentially, so that I now ran two full out-patient clinics per week. I generally had a handful of in-patients under my direct care, but in addition was much in demand by all the other departments. Bleeding and clotting problems after surgery or giving birth, and mysteriously abnormal blood counts at any time were triggers for my intervention. While enjoying the challenge of disentangling diagnostic problems I was conscious of the terrible weight of responsibility until that challenge was met, especially in a critically sick patient. The job satisfaction was enormous. A perplexed colleague sought your help, and you were able to give something positive. I became aware as I had never been as a junior of the considerable influence on patient care of having a tidily and logically filed set of case notes. This sounds boring, but isn't. By quietly leafing through a patient's past history you could unearth highly relevant nuggets of information about him; this could even provide the key to understanding the current problem. I'm a firm believer that medical records should never be destroyed; but alas, the logistics of that belief prevent it from ever being put into practice.

I rediscovered the importance of thinking: just going away with a problem and mulling it over. This was not really part of the culture of the time; you were expected to be a whizz-kid with instant answers.

So much so that I recall a time when a management fad dictated that doctors didn't need offices; they should be perpetually on the wards! Someone seems to have had enough sense to scotch that one.

I did so much complaining about medical records that I was pushed into chairing a newly constituted records committee and the first thing we did was to standardise the format of the case note. I managed to get a consensus view of all my senior colleagues on this, no mean feat, the reader may be assured. I learned from this process that by far the best way of getting people to agree with you was the courteous, pleasant approach.

With no funding available to put this standard principle into practice, I had an inspiration to organise a voluntary day, a Sunday, of record reorganisation, in which motivated people, of which there was a surprising number, could devote an hour or two to this clerical job. But I was told that the unions would object strongly to the work being diverted from regular staff. The idea of the MP's wife precipitating a strike made me back off in alarm, and I dropped the idea. Still, our new case-note design was strongly influential when the Lothian Area attempted to do the same thing on a wider basis a year or two later.

With my busy life I never worried about what Robin was doing in mid-week, though he phoned almost every night. Occasionally journalists would ring, wanting to contact him urgently, and would get exasperated with me for not knowing precisely where he was. I recall one particularly irate and impatient man, who asked with laboured patience, 'Is there an assistant? a secretary? anyone? who knows where he is?' The implications were clear as a bell. 'You are obviously a neglectful wife and there must be a devoted mistress somewhere who could tell me where he is.'

Around this time he had a weekend conference at the Ditchley Foundation in Oxfordshire. This was a beautiful country house and garden, with interesting associations as it had provided Churchill with a country retreat during the war years as an alternative to Chequers, when moonlight and clear skies made that house a potential target for bombers. There were photographs of him on display, taken in those days. With a history of American connections going back for several hundred years, Ditchley Park now hosted Anglo-American conferences on international affairs and in particular nuclear deterrence. So I went with Robin and enjoyed the facilities but did not join in the conference, feeling the need of mental recreation. He observed an American

delegate doodling throughout one session and, out of curiosity, sur-
reptitiously lifted the page of scribbles. He found it covered with
drawings of tanks, machine-guns and other weapons of mass destruc-
tion. Ted Heath was present and Robin offered to introduce me to
him. As we walked across the hall with this intention I saw a look of
almost terror cross Heath's face. He gave me the most perfunctory of
handshakes before turning away quite rudely and escaping. I divined
that he was terrified of women, or at least of me. The Social Democratic
Party had recently been launched and I sat next to Bill Rodgers of the
'Gang of Four' at lunch; conscious of his celebrity status, he was affable
but tedious.

Constituency boundary changes had meant that Central Edinburgh
would now be highly marginal, and it was clear to me that Robin
would find himself a safer seat if it was humanly possible. In fact he
had been nurturing the new West Lothian constituency Labour Party
for some time. This constituency had been created by chopping in half
Tam Dalyell's erstwhile huge domain, and Tam would continue to
stand in the Linlithgow portion. I was vaguely aware of the *sotto voce*
plottings rumbling on. But there were other predators, dispossessed
and looking for safe seats, notably Tony Benn, who also showed an
interest in West Lothian. Robin went through a number of degrees of
agony. Benn's profile had been high and Robin's left leanings had
made him a sympathiser. He said at one point that perhaps his duty lay
in yielding to Benn. I knew him well enough by now to appreciate
that this was only soliloquising, and I was right, for he gave no
quarter. Robin was also pressed hard about moving the family into the
constituency, his friends offering to find him another converted mill
there. But I refused point-blank to consider this, for we had chosen
the site of our house with the express purpose of sending the boys to
a good council school, and I was not now prepared to change all that.

Robin was uneasy and worried, and talked about his extreme sorrow
in leaving his city-centre constituency which he felt to be his natural
habitat, and how he doubted whether he would feel so comfortable in
a new town and a rural community. I have since discovered that there
was a strong body of opinion which considered he should have stayed
in Central Edinburgh, which was in theory winnable, and would have
to be taken if a Labour government was ever to be returned. So it
seems clear to me that the thoughts he expressed were the reflections
of others rather than his own, and that his concern was how much his

principled and dedicated image would be diminished. I felt that personal ambition took precedence over devotion to party.

One of the deciding factors that won him the nomination, possibly the most important one, was the role I had played and reputation I had gained working in West Lothian over the past six years. I had smoothed the way for him to the safe seat that would be his stepping-stone to high office in future years.

Once he had secured the nomination and began to get to know the electorate, Robin was amazed and gratified to discover the degree of respect I was accorded, and of which he had evidence both from members of the public and from Tam Dalyell. This was perhaps quite revelatory for him because, though he had been supportive with the development of my career, he did not show much interest in my daily activities. I had learned that sharing my work-related problems with him was a turn-off. This worked both ways, for I don't suppose I was riveted by accounts of his political life. In the early days he would sometimes joke, 'You're not a proper doctor.' Interestingly enough, the children had little perception of me as a professional person. Chris one day, chatting about himself and a girl friend Jill, described how they were going to marry and he would become a doctor and she a nurse. Robin said carefully, 'Chris, why can Jill not be the doctor?'

Chris said (I fear it's true), 'Oh, she can't. She's a girl!'

'But your mummy's a doctor.'

'Well, she's different!'

I did notice when I visited their primary school that the old conditioning was still in force. There were pictures of Grandpa doing the garden, Granny knitting, Father tinkering with the car and Mummy in the kitchen cooking. In my household, I reflected, Mummy did all four jobs. I was an all-powerful, problem-solving, Mother Earth figure. There was a significant shift in my relationship with Robin around this time, or a little earlier. He had earned a degree of smouldering resentment from me in the children's pre-school years because he was so elusive and unavailable. Now he observed the strong mother–son bonding, my intensely affectionate but also vigilant and disciplined care of the boys and he liked it; indeed he was a little envious. Ever so gradually he began to move in again, to insert himself under my maternal umbrella, almost to identify himself as a third son. There was more than one reason for this perhaps, as Robin had been an only child and missed the sharing of many childish games, especially with an academic father who tended to encourage his more bookish tendencies. Robin's games with the boys were as boisterous and physical as you could imagine: rough-and-tumbles, pillow fights, water-pistol fights, sword fights with rolled-up newspapers, Red Indian games with ambushes and blood-curdling shrieks. Often I had to be a spoil-sport when over-excitement threatened damage to person or property. Later they would wait till I was out of the house, though I always knew what had been going on. He also shared their quieter games, in particular board-games, which for a while became quite a family obsession.

Unfortunately, all the male members of my family, even Grandpa, were ferociously competitive. I recall one Christmas Eve session of Monopoly before going off to sing carols at St Mary's. The game was played with unredeemed ruthlessness, and at the end we were all cross and disgruntled, a poor preparation for the most magical moment of Christmas. I swore to myself I would never play Monopoly again, and I haven't.

Though I joined in games and reading, sometimes I left the three of them to their own masculine devices, but sat nearby engrossed in some embroidery, tapestry or fine crochet. We would have musical moments too, as the boys learned to play recorders and were quite uninhibited about playing and singing around the piano.

Robin brought me a present home from Strasbourg which he handed me rather tentatively, saying, 'I'm not sure if you'll love and adore me for this or if you'll want to wrap it round my neck!'

It was a very beautiful and enormous tablecloth with a complex floral pattern requiring to be embroidered. I was delighted. At Easter 1982 I took it with me to Forest Brook Farm and listened to the radio bulletins of the start of the Falklands War as I worked on the first corner. The tablecloth was finished some two years later, and every time I look at the colourful pattern I am instantly reminded of those wartime broadcasts.

The next most important event in our lives was the 1983 general election. More than most, an MP's family sees the battle at two levels, local and national. For once I did not feel obliged to spend every free waking hour involved in electioneering; indeed I was rather weary of the process and felt that if everyone would just go to bed for the duration of the campaign the result would probably be just the same. Also there was an element of dishonesty and hypocrisy about the whole business which I found increasingly distasteful. I knew my greatest value to Robin was my working role, but I still put in a few hours on the door-to-door routine.

He returned one evening having spent time in the Addiewell Miners' Club, making himself known. One solitary wizened man, seated at a table bearing witness to the consumption of several halves and pints, accosted him.

'Is that your wife then? That Dr Cook up at Bangour?'

Robin, accustomed to receiving plaudits on my behalf, readily assented.

'Tell her she's a crabbit auld besom!'

Rapidly recovering from this assault, Robin divined that I had seen this man with some alcohol-related disorder and had been only too blunt about explaining to him the remedy.

18

Living with Ambition

After the débâcle for Labour that was the 1983 general election result, Michael Foot resigned as party leader and the new machinery ground into action to replace him. Robin, who had been comfortably elected, enthusiastically became Neil Kinnock's campaign manager. It looked like a natural alliance, for they were both Celts, supporters of CND, public ownership and other left-wing policies, including withdrawal from Europe. Our families met in Edinburgh and in the Kinnock home in Ealing, west London, with a fair degree of amity, for both Neil and Glenys possessed natural warmth, charm and humour. Neil was elected and Robin achieved a seat on the shadow cabinet after party conference that autumn.

I should mention that I never went to party conference with Robin, a source of some surprise to our friends. This was a mutually acceptable arrangement. On these occasions, and usually for a week beforehand, the stress levels hit the top of the Richter scale and he was pretty unbearable. He generally shut himself away in the study to prepare speeches but the phone would go incessantly until he fumed with frustration. I heaved a sigh of relief when he departed. We both knew I did not function well as an appendage, and if disenchanted or bored would not trouble to hide the feeling. And he was constantly engaged with speaking, contriving, scheming, so I would have been *de trop*.

After such a disastrous election result, it was natural that policy restructuring would take place, and by means of some nimble footwork a turn-around on Europe was effected. Neil and Robin forged links with the socialist group of MEPs, seeking a common manifesto for the next year's European elections. And when those elections had taken place it was clear that Labour had recovered to a significant extent with Kinnock as leader. In recognition of his support, Robin was invited to a meeting of the recently elected European parliament in Florence in 1984, and I accompanied him. Also on the trip were Janey and Norman Buchan. Norman, who was MP for a Glasgow constituency, was there like myself purely in the capacity of accompanying spouse, for Janey was a newly elected MEP. Robin and Janey went into a huddle over some policy issue while Norman and I made plans to do some sightseeing together. Robin was always very fond of Norman, seeing in him some of the characteristics of probity and commitment to duty he so admired in his own father.

In the heat of the Florentine summer, we arrived to find the water supply throughout the city disconnected: a not uncommon event. For twenty-four hours we were unable to shower or flush the loos! As Norman and I climbed the narrow winding stairs in the cathedral dome, he lightly mentioned that he had had heart surgery a few months previously, and was very glad to be doing this climb with a doctor on hand, in case of problems. There were none, luckily. This trip was nothing like party conference: Robin was an honoured guest with few commitments, which left us ample time to enjoy the cultural and epicurean aspects of Florence.

The Labour Party still sanctioned unilateral disarmament and Robin continued to be strongly identified with the peace movement, signing petitions against cruise missiles along with other public figures, speaking and appearing at venues around the country and writing articles for the press. He served on the co-ordinating committee of the European Nuclear Disarmament movement, a group of academics and intellectuals which included Mary Kaldor of the European Institute, Sussex University, and Meg Beresford, who became general secretary of CND after Monsignor Bruce Kent. With Mary, a prolific writer on all matters opposed to peace, he had very frequent contact in the early and mid-eighties. She is still speaking and writing on these issues, and must wonder what has caused the metamorphosis of her old comrade-in-arms, if that is not too inappropriate a term.

Sometimes it seemed that Robin had to identify a rival, on whom to concentrate his antipathy, or against whom to match himself. In the early days of his parliamentary career it was Bob Cryer, MP for Keighley from 1974, like himself a new and ambitious member, who was tragically killed in a car accident and whose wife is now member for the same constituency. Possibly I am the only person who knew of this particular tension. In the noise and commotion of rutting-time, no one notices what the juveniles are doing. But now he came up against a heavyweight, namely Roy Hattersley who was both deputy leader and shadow Chancellor. Rivalry is probably not the correct

word to apply to the friction between them as Robin was an inexperienced and junior member of the shadow cabinet. Try as I may, I
cannot remember what the agony was all about, and agony is not too
strong a word, for it plunged him into morose brooding for the greater
part of a New Forest holiday. No doubt some personal slight, magnified
by vanity, was the only explanation and the ripples have long since
disappeared amongst the waves of other ferments.

After the first holiday when we began to ride we had continued taking
riding lessons and going out hacking in the countryside, and it was
good to pursue an outdoor activity that could be enjoyed by all four
of us together. We were soon deemed capable of taking ourselves out
without an escort, which was probably ill-advised, and sometimes
frankly dangerous. One Remembrance Sunday when flooding had
blocked our usual off-the-road route, we redirected our way through
Loanhead, just at the very moment when the massed pipe-bands
emerged with loud skirling and flapping banners, to the alarm of our
horses who took off at speed down the main street. I vividly remember
the humiliation – and the bruises – of the first time I fell off; also the
exhilaration of the first canter, when the centrifugal force as you career
round a comer is only resisted because you hear the teacher's voice
shouting, 'Yes, wonderful – super – heels DOWN, hang on – great,
just great! – sit UP! – terrific!' Enthusiastic encouragement is everything. All the things you do automatically in precarious moments on
horseback are wrong and have to be consciously counteracted.

Robin and I had agreed that we wouldn't learn to jump: we were
too old; it would be irresponsible; we had too well-developed a sense
of self-preservation. In a few weeks, however, we were persuaded to
join a jumping class, and the excitement went up a few notches. Our
enthusiasm increased with the passage of time and the accumulation
of stories of narrowly missed disasters. There is no doubt that the
danger added to the fun. Robin's lifestyle prevented him from riding
as regularly as the rest of us which annoyed him as he loved the idea of
looking good on a horse and being able to ride a difficult animal. For
the Easter break of 1984 we took our holiday in the Cotswolds and
discovered Badminton Horse Trials took place almost on our doorstep.
We took in every exciting moment of it, and it became a regular fixture
in our family calendar.

That summer my fortieth birthday fell in the middle of the holiday at Forest Brook and Robin had planned a special day with a ride and a party jointly arranged with our landlady Ilne, and freedom from any chores. The day began with Chris coming into our bedroom at about seven o'clock to announce he had just been sick in the washbasin. Aware that Robin was extremely squeamish about such matters, I sat up. He groaned. I said, 'Look, don't worry, I'll sort it. The birthday doesn't begin till eight o'clock,' and started to get out of bed.

But to my utter amazement, he pulled me back and said, 'No. I can't have that. I'll do it.' And off he went, perfectly graciously, to attend to Chris's little problem. I was deeply touched.

Chris began secondary school at Craigmount the next year, such a different environment from the sheltered primary school, but he seemed to take it in his stride. He was a sociable and gregarious boy with a sunny nature and always seemed to land on his feet. I had been to view the school and was very impressed with the facilities. In his first year he was given a part in *Bugsy Malone* which played to packed houses for several nights in their fully equipped theatre. The free-for-all custard-pie-slinging scene at the end was played with gusto and each night I had to clean up his suit in time for the next day's performance. Peter followed him to Craigmount the following year, and I was much more worried about his capacity to cope, though having an older brother a year ahead was a help. I needn't have worried. Peter was quieter and more reserved than Chris, but beneath a sensitive and sometimes vulnerable exterior there was an independent toughness about him. He also adapted without any trauma. Parents were involved at every stage, and I went to regular yearly meetings to discuss their progress; always rather melancholy occasions for me because everyone else seemed to be there as a couple. These events focused my attention on how much of a single parent I was.

One source of friction between Robin and me had been removed at a stroke after the 1983 general election, and that was the necessity for him to have a car to himself. Car-sharing in the preceding years had led to endless problems. I needed it for work of course, and that was clearly understood. But he tended to assume that he could have it at all other times, while I struggled with the chores like the weekly shopping, conveying sons to cubs/scouts, swimming and so on. I fought my corner with vigour and had some strength since the car was financed by me. When he was in Central Edinburgh he grumbled, but took taxis. This, however, was impractical in the wider geographical spread of Livingston. With separate cars, relationships took a significant turn for the better.

My sense of fair play prompts me to elaborate on some of the things he did well. I've mentioned that he was very imaginative and generous with choosing presents. Granny used to get quite envious because this was not one of Grandpa's strong points. He would leave it till the last possible minute, then rush out and buy some expensive and hideous brooch, trying to make up in value what the gift lacked in everything else. Robin by contrast would buy frilly feminine things, especially nightdresses and underwear and would seek out small specialist and very expensive shops for the purpose. It was a custom to bring back some such item from party conference each year. One of the best presents was a box containing six or seven books by Anthony Trollope. In the days when the only recent editions were the Barchester series and the Political series, he had to comb the second-hand bookshops for the lesser-known novels. It was a very real pleasure to receive a present that promised so many hours of enjoyment, but also to know that so much effort and thought had gone into it. At such times, and in spite of other marital stresses, I felt anew a sense of being loved and cherished.

When time allowed, and usually on holiday, he liked to try his hand at cooking a meal. Having no idea of the basics of cookery, it was truly amazing how well he managed, and again his secret was to buy very costly ingredients which, thrown together for a certain time, could hardly fail to taste good. But still, often a considerable effort went into these creative meals, including the preparation of ornate menus in mangled French, some of which I still have.

With both these acts of generosity, present-giving and preparing a banquet, he expected to be thoroughly appreciated. The gifts and the creative cookery had to be admired, and discussed in depth, and gratitude had to be bottomless. At Christmas time, my gifts to him might sometimes receive scant attention; I became rather used to this. It was competitiveness in another guise. I think a really sensitive, generous person is equally alive to the importance of giving and receiving graciously. His fondness for the pleasures of the table led him, as with so many people with stressed lifestyles, to use this as a form of comfort. He was nearly always overweight, and on occasions would determine to be strict and slim down. I found if I tried to help he would become antagonistic and break the rules, presumably just to defy me. Not surprisingly, he never lost any weight by intention.

Because he felt a little pressurised to keep pace with the family's improving equestrian ability, Robin began to take private lessons with Celia, who came to the riding school for that purpose. Celia lived in a basement flat of Hope's House in East Lothian, a beautiful manor in a sheltered hollow in lovely countryside. She had horses of her own and also took care of those belonging to Dorrie who owned the house. We became friends with Celia and her husband, also called Robin, and her two children, meeting for dinners, weekend parties and outings to local equestrian events such as the horse trials at Thirlestane and Dalmahoy. We began to ponder whether it would be a good idea or utter mad folly to become horse-owners ourselves.

About this time, Robin developed another problem, superficially stress-related, that of occasionally failing potency. This troubled him greatly and inevitably a vicious cycle was engendered of mounting stress and worsening problem. I didn't make an issue of it, but he began to accuse me of not helping to solve the problem, not being sufficiently concerned or active – and so on. Thus it became my fault. I was distressed that this aspect of our lives was transformed to yet another stressful duty to be added to the daily round.

I attributed the problem to personal pressure which had become – perhaps always had been – a way of life with him. He had no idea of how to pace himself and always tried to pack more things in than he had any hope of accomplishing. He would dash in, ignore the usual greetings, growl like a bear if impeded in his precipitate course, chuck things to left and right for anyone else to clear up, then barge out of the house, leap into the car and with a skidding start and clashing of gears, accelerate violently up the lane. Another reason why I was relieved when he got his own car was that with his perpetual haste he was forever denting the car; he just would not take the trouble to check for obstacles or do a graduated turn. This unremitting scramble, which did awful things to his temper, was one of the most difficult things to live with. Sometimes if he was late (as so often happened; I must have wasted months of my life waiting around for him) for an engagement, he would arrive hurried and impatient, and I would be enveloped in his tension. The only way I could deal with him in these moods was to withdraw into myself. The children, when tiny, had taught me to match my pace to theirs, and I never forgot that. Patients also remind you: you can't rush a sick person.

If we ever managed to have a discussion about ourselves, he would sometimes say that he felt I didn't need him. I reminded him that I had had to learn to do without him, most of the time, whether I liked it or not. With regard to the haste and the corrosive effect on his temper I think he had almost no insight. He thought that when gruff and bearish he was lovable.

His post in the shadow cabinet, which was created especially for him, was campaign co-ordinator. He was not very enamoured of this role, which effectively prevented him from performing and starring on the floor of the Commons. His misgivings proved correct, as the following year he lost his seat on the shadow cabinet by virtue of not getting enough MPs to vote for him. This rejection was deeply felt, and attributed to his low profile; but Robin has no natural courtesy and tended to favour those who would be useful to him.

On the last day of the summer holiday at Forest Brook in 1986, Peter became unwell with fever and sickness. The weather was stifling and we had a 400-mile drive ahead of us, so I worried about his comfort. Usually on these mammoth treks we stopped at a Happy Eater for breakfast, some scenic spot for a picnic lunch, then at Lanark for a Chinese meal before the last stretch home. But Peter had no interest in food at all. I expected his malaise to last twenty-four hours as these episodes usually did, but this one dragged on. Poor Peter could keep nothing down, and he actually began to lose weight. It is quite impossible to make a rational judgement on your child's illness, as I well knew, but I could not prevent my mind prowling about amongst serious and threatening diagnoses, and completely ignoring the most likely one. Peter was normally very fond of his food, and became very depressed with the loss of this daily pleasure. One evening he was sitting miserably in the kitchen while I hovered, observing him. And then as I caught his gaze I realised that the whites of his eyes were not white at all but a faint yellow colour. Before I could stop myself I said, 'Peter! You're jaundiced!'

Now although I knew instantly that he almost certainly had hepatitis A, a nasty enough infectious condition, very common in institutions such as schools, and almost invariably running a short, benign course; and though jaundice was a topic on which I could have lectured a class of medical students, or post-graduates, with details of clinical, diagnostic, pathological, social and therapeutic aspects; yet when I was faced with the condition in my son, I was almost completely demolished by it. Not fear, not worry, just dreadfully and illogically upset and emotional about it. I phoned our GP and a very nice lady doctor came. I took her into the kitchen, away from Peter, till I had told the story, for I knew I wouldn't cope with dignity. I burst into floods, positively tidal waves, of tears. No, I wasn't thinking he might have the much more dangerous hepatitis B, my reaction was purely visceral. Once it was over, I pulled myself together and behaved rationally.

Peter became intensely yellow over the next few days, but his appetite returned and so he cheered up. The diagnosis was confirmed, and the health visitors were obliged to come. It was thought the source of infection may have been raspberries in the Highlands. He recovered.

Then I bought my first horse. She was a Welsh cob called Wendy, not very elegant but with a down-to-earth nature and a very nice jump. Robin did not feel he had the time to have his own horse but bought a small gymkhana pony with the regrettable name of Winkie for Chris and Peter to share. We realised we were taking on quite a responsibility here and it certainly changed our lives. It was not unlike having children.

At first they lived in a small livery stable at Kirkliston, a short distance away, under the supervision of Garnet, who recently had been trying to improve our riding. It had become apparent, to me at least, that no further progress would be made unless I had a horse of my own.

Now almost everyone I know who takes on a horse for the first time in middle life has a complete disaster at the beginning. Almost you might think that some mean-minded hobgoblin is determined that you shall know the downside of horse-owning before you experience the heady delights. After a few weeks Wendy, who seemed accident-prone, came in from the field very lame indeed. And after much veterinary attention, rest and all sorts of other measures, and a diagnosis of suspensory-ligament strain, it became apparent that she was not going to recover sufficiently to be ridden again. It seemed dreadful that my first horse should face the knackery after only a year, but Celia came to the rescue with the suggestion that she be sent to a farm in Alloa as a blood donor (for quality-control purposes); this is a lifeline for horses who cannot be ridden but who are not otherwise in discomfort. So that is what happened.

Nothing daunted, I set out on the road looking for another horse; meanwhile the boys were having a lot of fun with Winkie, whom we had moved to a bigger stable, the Grange, at West Calder. Soon, with much help and advice, I bought Brunhilde, a beautiful, sweet-natured roan mare who was just perfect in every way. She was a real school-mistress, and my skills began to improve; I entered some local jumping competitions – very low-key. I adored her, and could think of nothing else. I went around at work with a perpetual glow inside and could hardly wait to be at the stable again. I was obsessed; not unlike being in love.

I would have been perfectly happy staying at home for Easter 1987, but Robin needed to get away from the phone and the demands made on him, so we took a cottage in Wiltshire. Though as a family, as always, we had a happy time, I was conscious of something amiss between me and Robin; something undefinable. Some resentment he felt against me, but I had no idea why. It was as if I had failed him in some way, and he was trying his best to forgive me. It was subtle and I'm sure the boys were not aware of it. People are astonished when I say we (almost) never had rows or harsh words. We were courteous. I realised when I could not influence things, and put up with the deficit. Or I made a strong stand and he knew from experience the immutability of my stubbornness.

On our return, things began to go wrong with Bruni. She developed a cough. We took the usual measures, but it was bad enough to call the vet. Not many months previously she had been vetted as sound for purchase, but now to our collective horror he identified a very abnormal second heart sound. Horse heart sounds are just like humans', only much slower and more resonant: lub-dup, lub-dup, lub-dup. Hers sounded more like lub-dusshh, lub-dusshhh, lub-dusshh, with a harsh metallic ring to the second component. You could hear it without a stethoscope, just with your ear applied to the chest wall. She was sent to the University Bush Field Station, where a defective heart valve was diagnosed; prognosis very uncertain. I would just have to see how she progressed, and clearly she could never be sold. For her dust-related cough she lived in a field with the school ponies, and had a rest from being ridden. The fates seemed to be treating me particularly cruelly, though I have since found out that many people have a similar sequence of distressing events.

Meanwhile the general election of 1987 was fast approaching. I made myself available to do a little constituency wooing, but my offers were turned down – rather casually. I was surprised and questioned this response. Off-handedly he shrugged and said that the party machine was so efficient and he had so many party workers that my assistance was not required. The boys now being in their teens were not considered vote-attracters and they were sidelined also, for the first time not appearing on the election leaflet. There was a huge difference in Robin on this occasion from all previous elections, which worried me deeply. There was no drive, no verve, no ebullience. And he was clearly drinking heavily. His mood was one of weary depression and going through the motions, but his heart was not in it. I asked if he was worried about the outcome. No, he was as confident as he'd ever been about his own seat, though Labour was clearly not heading for victory.

The puzzle remained unsolved. I did nothing at all to help the campaign and felt guilty, but really it was not for lack of offering. On the evening of polling day I met Robin and Jim, his agent, at a country hotel for dinner, before proceeding to the count. I had bought an apple-green dress, not wanting my clothes to indicate my party allegiance. His troubled and withdrawn mood continued through the count at Bathgate Academy. He kept his seat and in his acceptance speech did not acknowledge me. I put it down to oversight.

19

Two Disasters and the Aftermath

One Sunday in June a week or two after the election, the boys and I planned to visit the Highland Show at Ingliston. We had prepared a picnic and were intending to go to the stable to exercise Winkie and see how Brunhilde was faring before driving to the showground. We got up early and were in high spirits. Robin was tied up with some other business matter that day and had set off even earlier.

Just as we were piling into the car, the phone rang. It was Grant from the stable; whenever anyone called from there my heart sank, for it usually spelled some problem with the horses.

Time stood still when I heard his voice say, 'Margaret, Bruni has had an accident. I think ... she may have broken a leg.'

Everything froze. I didn't react emotionally but was icy calm and businesslike. 'Where is she?'

'In the field.'

'Have you called the vet?'

'Yes, he's on his way.'

'Shall I come to the field directly?'

'Yes, we'll meet you there.'

I was in such a daze that I continued from where I left off when interrupted by the phone, organising things as if there had been no catastrophic change to the day. I told the boys about the mare's accident and that it was serious, but did not immediately reveal that she was almost certainly doomed. The twenty-five-minute journey passed in almost unbroken silence. As we drew up to the field I told them to sit tight; that this could be distressing.

Grant and the vet, Ian, waylaid me as I entered the field. They did not want me to see Bruni in her pitiable condition. I didn't say anything, just looked and waited, though their faces and attitudes told me everything.

'It's no good,' said Ian. 'It's a bad break, a spiral fracture. There's nothing can be done.'

So then the reaction took over and I wept bitter tears, hanging on to a fence post for support and covering my face with my other hand, ashamed of such a stormy display of emotion. When the first violence had subsided, I became aware of the two of them standing by uneasily, unsure of how to handle this sensitive situation. Grant said in obvious distress, 'Margaret, whatever can I say?'

Ian said, 'I don't know what it is with you and horses, lass.'

No one had any idea of how the accident happened; certainly not a kick from another horse. Then I gave permission for Ian to destroy her and he went off hastily, for she was in a lot of pain. I really wanted to see her to say farewell, but realised that I was not going to be allowed. Grant summoned one of the girls to go back to the yard with me and hastened off to give Ian a hand.

The stable yard was milling with the usual crowd of folk on a Sunday. The boys and I were ushered into the house and given mugs of tea and coffee. Everyone tried to be nice and tactful but I had got to the numb, unresponsive phase. The boys were wonderful; they sat one on either side of me and gave comfort with their presence and touch. I felt a pang when Ian and Grant returned, knowing that it was all over, and thought it better to take myself and my sorrow away.

We drove home and unpacked the car. Then, without a murmur about missing the Highland Show, Chris and Peter went off and amused themselves very quietly. Later I left them with the picnic spread out in the kitchen and went off for a walk up Clermiston Hill. It was a comfort to sit on a stone under the trees, gazing into the misty distance and just musing and mourning. Deep down inside I could not help being aware that this tragedy could be a blessing in disguise, as the heart problem had given her a very uncertain future. But why had she had to have this sequence of disasters at all? Along with many others in a situation of personal suffering, I asked, 'Why me?' and could find no answer.

Later that afternoon I was sitting alone in a state of torpor in the kitchen when Robin returned. He did not require much clairvoyance to see that all was not well.

'What's the matter?' he asked.

'Bruni broke a leg in the field this morning and had to be put down.'

Silence.

Then he came and sat beside me.

'Margaret. Look, I'm sorry. I'm really sorry. I think, though, since you are obviously so upset, I may as well tell you some other bad news. As you suspected, I've been having an affair.'

We looked at each other and I found I had nothing left with which to react to this startling announcement.

'Who with?'

'Oh, you know very well who with.'

I should explain that while trying to find out the cause of his depression I had questioned him about a certain lady, a friend to both of us, who shall be named Thelma for the purpose of this account. I don't know anyone of that name, so hope it causes no embarrassment. Anyway, I was aware that he was fonder of her than he perhaps should be; indeed he made no effort to disguise the fact. Almost he flaunted it. Once when we had all called round at her house he set about putting cups and spoons on a tray for coffee, putting on the kettle, searching in the fridge for milk, for all the world as if he were in his own kitchen at home. I was aghast at his easy familiarity. Knowing how sensitive the children could be to certain nuances, I glanced at them but they seemed not to notice. And when we left the house, by chance I turned at the wrong moment and intercepted a brilliant smile and affectionate but furtive wave, obviously destined for someone other than me. We had dined out with this couple recently and Robin kept muttering under his breath how delightful it could have been if Thelma's husband could have excused himself. Hardly the behaviour of someone anxious to keep a guilty secret.

Previously when I had challenged him about her, he had said, 'No, I'm not having an affair with her. Mind you, I could if I wanted to.'

So now, when I was breaking my heart over the horse, why did he decide to own up to the affair, and admit he had lied to me? It seemed that Thelma had decided to give him up, some weeks ago, although they had had agonised encounters and discussions since then. This was indeed the cause of his dreary mood and his excess alcohol consumption. I think he had probably been with her that day and she'd made it clear that this was the end. He talked on about his own personal catastrophe completely forgetting mine. Thelma had a young child and at one point there was some doubt as to who was the father, though I think by now his looks favoured the husband. The affair had drifted on for some years, and she had never pressurised him to leave me. The reason for the break was, apparently, that after some tiff Robin had compared her mothering skills unfavourably with mine, causing much offence. No doubt the story was fed to me selectively.

There was a great deal here for me to digest, and, bewildered as I was with my own grief, I was in no rush to do so. His attitude to me changed instantly, and he became affectionate and communicative again. In a week's time he planned to host a social gathering for his party workers to show his gratitude. He suggested that once this was over we should take a long weekend in the Lake District while the grandparents looked after the boys.

I went to his thank-you party, where he made a speech containing warm words of praise for me and expressed the gratitude that had been missing from his speech at the post-election count. Then we drove off to the Lakes and stayed for a few nights at a small hotel off the beaten track.

Our relationship felt as if it had been tossed about by an earth tremor and I didn't know how things were going to settle down. One notion kept attracting my attention like a red flag: that I was now released from my vows of fidelity and could have an affair if I so wished. I found this idea unexpectedly exciting. Robin was eager to explain to me that his sexual difficulties had sprung from guilt over his affair; they had only occurred with me, not with Thelma, and unsurprisingly they now disappeared.

While we were pursuing some activity such as hill-walking the relationship was easy enough; but I found the sudden return of his full-time attention, dependence and anxiety to please a little cloying and intrusive, so begged some time to myself. I looked for craft sales where you could sometimes pick up old lace and other interesting antique fabric-work. On my own, my thoughts returned to Bruni, but I knew this was something I just had to work through.

On Saturday night we dined at the Miller Howe on Lake Winder-mere, a world-class experience in dining which we had discovered some years previously. We drank considerably more than was good for us. And then the revelations began.

With no hint of regret or apology, but rather like an indulged naughty schoolboy confessing to a favourite and tolerant aunt, he related the catalogue of previous affairs. Most of them were women I didn't know, or only knew by name or a voice on the telephone, and they dated back to a time when I was pregnant with Peter. One girl from Glasgow I had labelled 'Heather Honey' because of her sugary telephone voice. Including her and Thelma, he named five women that I can recall, but apart from being drunk I was soon sated with information and may not remember all the confessions.

The following day he continued his little-boy act, until I rounded on him impatiently, told him that I did not want to mother him, that I wanted a husband, not a third juvenile. He replied petulantly, 'All right, I'll never do that again.' Apart from moments of brief forgetfulness, he never did. I think my refusal to act out the mother role may have been one very significant factor in the ultimate breakdown of our marriage.

When we returned home I felt I needed a spell apart from him, but I was terribly anxious to shield the boys from any whisper of a suspicion that all was not well between us, so this was scarcely possible. Even though they were both in their teens, I was still fiercely protective. Parliament was still sitting, so he was away for part of the week. I noticed with considerable anxiety that he was drinking regularly and was often the worse for drink. Others might not notice because he had enough self-command to conceal it. Then I found that he had been taking sleeping pills since Thelma's defection. His restlessness at night was disturbing and I found difficulty in sleeping also; I suppose the old empathy between us was still there – certainly his taut nerves communicated themselves to me.

The combination of sleeping pills and alcohol was highly detrimental, and to my unbounded horror his memory began to show gaping hiatuses, mostly about recent events. I took him to task over both the pills and the drink and he meekly agreed to try to do without; with very limited success as far as I could see. He was not eating properly and the weight fell off him like snow in a sharp thaw. His mood continued to be low, his wit and conversational ability vanished beneath a ponderous self-pity, and I began to have doubts about his judgement in some matters. He seemed to teeter perilously on the brink of total mental and physical collapse.

I should like to say I stood by him staunchly and nursed him through this, but in truth I wavered a little, and it was at least two years before he was rehabilitated. With his personality change I wondered if I could tolerate the continuance of our marriage. For the boys' sakes I would do almost anything to keep us together, but my professional work had shown me the tragic disintegration of an alcoholic's personality, and if progressive deterioration occurred I knew I would leave him. I flirted with the idea of an affair. Although my first reaction to his revelation was icy cold, I was deeply injured and felt the need for support from somewhere. But there was none to be had. I found my role of respectable MP's wife, mother, professional person of repute in the community something of a strait-jacket, from which it was impossible to release myself. I joined a correspondence club, hoping to make new friends, but none of the contacts inspired any other emotion than pity. I did not want to be part of this scene. I wanted to be successful in my marriage as I had been in most other things. I desperately wanted someone in whom to confide. But who? I couldn't talk to my family, who all thought I had a marvellous marriage. I couldn't disillusion his own parents; that was unthinkable. I had no friend close enough to share my troubles and give valued advice. In any case, natural reserve and pride were hard barriers to overcome. I even thought of referring myself to a psychiatrist.

In the end I sublimated my sorrows in a number of ways: first by making stronger links with my colleagues at work. We were always a friendly and supportive group of consultants and had a regular meeting place for coffee and talk, which I began to attend more regularly. Secondly, I adopted a more businesslike attitude to tidying up various neglected aspects of my life. This sounds perfectly crazy; but it helps. I had an overhaul at the dentist's and the optician's, got the car serviced and smartened up, bought some new clothes, took advice on a troublesome bunion. And there was the question of another horse. Immediately after losing Bruni I did not know if I could face all those traumas again. But my friends at the stable were all very sympathetic and supportive about this problem which I could discuss, and soon I felt, yes, let's have another go. The boys were growing out of Winkie and needed a fourteen hands two inch pony to move on to; but to start with, I could ride him. One advantage of being lightly built is that you can enjoy the fun of riding ponies, quite a different experience from horses.

On holiday at Forest Brook, Robin and I felt the need to widen our social circle, given the continuing fragility of our relationship. The New Forest provided country homes for a number of his acquaintances, within hailing distance of London. We began to meet Clive Hollick, the Labour-supporting multi-millionaire media tycoon, now Lord Hollick, his wife Sue and their delightful trio of daughters, who shared our love of riding and had their own horses. They had a small cottage at Hale, but needed somewhere larger. When they visited us at Forest Brook, like us they were enchanted by the place and were envious. I knew that Ilne, the owner, was toying with the idea of selling and getting a smaller cottage just for herself, and mentioned to Sue and Clive that if they made her a suitable offer, I felt sure she could be persuaded to sell. In no time they got down to business and became the new owners. They were guilty about spiriting away our holiday home, and were superbly generous in their offers to us to come and stay. Other holiday friends included Arthur Davidson, legal adviser to the *Mirror*, and his wife Joan; Chris Powell, advertising executive and brother of Charles Powell, Mrs Thatcher's adviser, but unlike him a Labour supporter, Rosie his wife, and their families. With so many children, parties usually ended up with cricket or rounders on the village green. Robin threw a birthday party for me, bringing in caterers and trying to pass off the wonderful spread as his own creation. No one took him seriously. Amidst the fun, I could not help noticing his conversation, usually so sparkling and informative, was ponderous and dull.

One day, after we had had an exciting jumping lesson, Robin and I nipped into the pub to quench our considerable thirst. I had a whisky and chaser; then another, and another, in quick succession. The barman who had been affable, became rather disapproving. Robin said he probably thought I was a dumb stable girl in the process of being debauched. Back at the house, he took over making the lunch of sausages and beans for all of us, and gave me a large orange juice to sober me up. I was delighted. Perhaps this was the beginning of his recovery. Alas, later in the afternoon I found him flat out on the dining room floor with a brandy bottle. We had a very long way to go, and I was ashamed of my own lapse that day. It didn't happen again.

Back at home in Edinburgh, Peter gave us further cause for anxiety. A cold progressed to wheezy bronchitis, to which he was prone. Having apparently recovered, he would complain of feeling cold and shivery in the evening. I was actually laid up after my bunion operation, but got Robin to take him down to our doctor's and organise a chest X-ray which showed broncho-pneumonia. On antibiotics he improved dramatically. My partial incapacity meant Robin had to muck in with domestic chores, a useful part of his therapy.

Then we bought our new pony, Third Time Lucky, or just Lucky for short. He had a fair component of Arab in him, and an interesting 'thumb-print of Allah' on his neck. He was quite spirited and a more demanding ride than Winkie. The first time I took him out hacking and moved up a gear to canter, he took off at breakneck speed for about half a mile until I found the brakes. However once we'd given him plenty of work he became more manageable. As soon as I took him into jumping competitions it was clear that he was a star, and I actually began to win things. Dressage wasn't a strong point: he got too strung up in a discipline where calmness is everything.

And so life settled down to an even keel again. In the summer Robin weighed less than ten stone. Once parliament returned in October he began slowly to get back to normal though there were to be lapses for well over a year. He regained his seat in the shadow cabinet and to my delight Neil Kinnock appointed him shadow health spokesman, a post he held throughout the duration of that parliament (1987–92). Neil told me himself of this appointment, and clearly there was potential here for some interesting co-operative teamwork. Our working lives had hardly touched before; I felt this could only be for our mutual benefit. From this time on, his profile began to be more prominent in the public domain and increasingly he began to be recognised out in the streets. Naturally he liked this and found it flattering.

I didn't talk to Robin much about political matters and if anyone asked me what my husband thought of such-and-such, I carefully avoided voicing his opinions as I would invariably get the nuances wrong or fail to appreciate some subtle emphasis. Occasionally I would take courage in both hands and tell him what I thought. I did this once, around the time of the 1987 election, or a bit before, on the subject of nuclear disarmament. It's easy to forget, in the post-Cold War climate, of how fearful people were then of a nuclear war or nuclear blackmail. From an impression of the prevailing view, I voiced the opinion that Labour would never be elected on a policy of unilateral disarmament, which they still supported, even with promises of strengthening the conventional armed forces as in the 1987 manifesto. With so much fear and perceived threat to survival, people reacted instinctively rather than logically. I recalled a prayer from my religious days which said, 'Deliver us from the FEAR of our enemies' – not the enemies themselves, and this is very profound. Anyway, Robin did not want to hear my views at all and positively bristled with rage though he had no logical rejoinder. It was clear I had touched a very sensitive nerve. In 1989 Chris had to make a ten-minute speech in connection with his Standard Grade English continuous assessment, and after conferring with his father took up the theme of nuclear disarmament. He made an excellent attempt and got a good mark. However, shortly after this the Labour policy document, 'Meet the Challenge, Meet the Change' was published, in which, amongst other changes, unilateralism was abandoned and a multilateral approach adopted. One may only imagine Robin's inner torment about this, but Chris came in for some light-hearted teasing at school for being behind the times.

At the time of his revelation, Robin had asked me what I thought would become of us. I answered gloomily that I expected to get more involved with horse matters and he would probably have another affair. He thought this was an unduly pessimistic prognostication. I told myself that another affair would certainly put an end to the marriage; I didn't see how it could survive. But over the next year or two our mutual convalescence progressed satisfactorily. He became a loving husband again, showering me with gifts and affectionate tokens, and rapport was re-established. In an obvious attempt to rehabilitate himself within the family he took on an extra mortgage, installed a more efficient central-heating system and a brand-new kitchen. I took this to be a sign of emotional maturing and sincere intention to reform, and was glad.

In 1988 there was a flurry of posturing and antler-clashing within the parliamentary Labour Party, as challengers for the leadership and deputy presented themselves and were seen off. Robin offended John Prescott for failing to support him. No doubt he ground his teeth when Gordon Brown topped the poll in the shadow cabinet elections that autumn. John Smith had his first heart attack, and I must have known him reasonably well, for I went to visit him a few days later when he was still in coronary care in the Edinburgh Royal Infirmary. He looked well and ebullient, and was filled to the brim with gratitude for the devoted care he had received from the staff, as most people are who receive NHS care in a crisis. He was already making enthusiastic plans to alter his lifestyle: to lose weight, take exercise, take time off work.

Not many weeks after, the Smith and the Cook families and journalist friend Ruth Wishart had a night out at the uniquely exotic Armenian restaurant in Edinburgh. We had been occasional clients for some years of Petros, who is owner, chef, waiter and master of ceremonies all combined. The evening's entertainment there evolved, was never planned. Sometimes the theme was politics; but more often it was Armenian dancing, which got wilder and wilder, with occasional breaks for further courses or more cups of sweet Turkish coffee. John and Robin danced with as much vigour and abandon as anyone, and Ruth and I wished we could call in the television cameras.

20

Health and Horses

In tandem with the switchback relationship with my husband, with children, horses and holidays, I still spent the greater part of my working life trying to restore health and happiness to my patients in West Lothian. When I was first appointed a consultant, some senior colleagues thought I would acquire a few years' experience, then try for a more prestigious post in Edinburgh. I suppose I did entertain the idea, but with so much on hand to fulfil and satisfy, I never felt the need to move away. And in a so-called caring profession, surely the greatest accolades should go to those who do the most basic work, and those who have the most direct and hands-on contact with patients? Of course it doesn't work like that, as I well knew. But I did see a degree of disillusion amongst colleagues elsewhere, and felt content to be where I was.

Over the years I had become a Fellow of the two Royal Colleges (of Physicians and of Pathologists); also an honorary Senior Lecturer in the Faculty of Medicine, Edinburgh University, because of significant input to the teaching of medical students.

The people who work in the health service are not a random cross-section of the population. People are attracted to the service at all levels often by motives of altruism and beneficence, though there may be a falling-off of those motives in inverse proportion to the salary size. But you do find that most people you work with are congenial and pleasant. And almost everywhere, certainly in places I've worked, there is a sense of responsibility and commitment that ensures most staff would go the further mile, give of themselves to a level way beyond the call of duty, as occasion demanded. So that when Mrs Thatcher determined to introduce market principles to the NHS with the 1989 White Paper, it was clear that she and her advisers were ignorant of this most basic fact, which hitherto had enabled the service to run on highly efficient, well-oiled wheels.

Over the next few years the imposed business ethos had disastrous effects. By competitive tendering, lowly paid workers were paid even less and some ancillary services such as cleaning were less satisfactorily delivered. The numbers of managers, and the cost of managing, rose exponentially. I was outraged at the slogan that appeared on letter paper and elsewhere: 'Putting Patients First'. From the taking of the Hippocratic oath this is a doctor's most basic principle; and when there is a perceived need to advertise this adage, it probably means that it is being pushed down the list of priorities. And it was perfectly clear what the new priority was amongst the hierarchy of general managers: money and savings.

Within Lothian medical circles, and no doubt elsewhere, there was an intricate network of co-operative contacts, ensuring cohesion of specialties and sharing of information, long-established and still evolving. With advancing knowledge and expertise, no one could stand alone, but absolutely had to tap into the locally available sources of expertise for any individual patient's benefit. But the new competitive ideology was to bulldoze through this elaborate mesh-work. Hospitals (soon to be Trusts) would compete against other hospitals in order to cut costs, attract 'clients', do each other out of business! Which meant an ivory tower philosophy, self-sufficiency in services, duplication of expensive equipment and loss of dialogue with colleagues since we could not share with business rivals. Doctors were told to see more patients; but patients wanted doctors to spend more time with them, and no one had a solution to this conflict. The impossibility of conducting a humane service where quality was the most fundamental requirement as a business, where making parsimonious ends meet was the first objective, was a paradox which ensured unceasing skirmishing between managers and health workers for the next eight years. The goodwill of the NHS staff – those who remain – has survived intact; though most have borne the burden of trying to maintain standards in the face of constant erosion in support and finance.

Advertisements for private health care seemed to proliferate. Watching TV ads, I fumed at the implicit assumption that private care was better than NHS care. There were plenty of anecdotes from the US and the UK presenting evidence that the absolute necessity in a business-run hospital to cut costs leads to some dangerous and uncaring practices. The public seems to be brainwashed on this issue. It is erroneous to assume that private practice attracts the best doctors – it doesn't: it attracts those who most want to make a lot of money.

I shall tell my own favourite anecdote. A GP rang me one day, many years ago, to talk about a man in his fifties with a large, hard lump in his neck; almost certainly malignant. The patient was clearly worried and distressed. Could I expedite his diagnosis?

My next clinic slot was a week away; but I could fit him in as an extra the following morning. I contacted a surgical colleague, as the patient would require a biopsy for diagnosis. Yes, the operation could also be done the next day on an afternoon theatre list. In order to have no unforeseen snags, I asked my secretary and records staff to dig out all available information on the patient. I saw him as planned, talked to him, examined him, arranged blood tests and X-rays. I explained the likely diagnosis and the need for biopsy.

He looked uneasy. He apologised, but could he ask me a question?

'I've been paying into private insurance. If I went private, could I get this done more quickly?'

I paused, till I could recover my breath, then answered him, very kindly. The poor man was just totally unaware that he was getting a Rolls-Royce service on the NHS.

In my opinion private medicine is incompatible with a doctor's duty to give of his or her best according to need. It seems to me that a contract with a private patient implies that you will give a better service if he pays for it, which is immoral. But if you are not giving him a better service for his money then you are guilty of deception.

At the first five-hundred-pound dinner thrown by Labour to attract the well-known and wealthy to its ranks and swell its coffers, I sat between agony aunt Claire Rayner and the best-selling author Ken Follett. Ken was enthusiastic about the notion of providing private, celebrity hotel services for those health-service patients, like himself who could afford them. He protested that he would want to take his coffee and meals to suit himself, not according to a rigid timetable. Claire Rayner chimed in with the same theme. Frankly, I found the idea so preposterous I hardly wanted to discuss it. You cannot readily separate hotel services from nursing, medical and other clinical provision without escalating costs and producing a two-tier or multiple-tier arrangement. We don't have too many people in West Lothian with Ken Follett's income. I enjoyed the dinner nevertheless. We actually arrived with Ken and Barbara Follett, who were friends at the time. I met Dickie Attenborough and his wife, both of whom were completely charming. Stephen Fry was there, also John Sessions who had a long and boring conversation with Robin about some union matter. Meanwhile I had been talking to Robbie Coltrane, and asked him to dance – thinking I could boast about it later – but he refused! Robin reminded me afterwards that Coltrane had described his acting as cerebral, whereupon I had laughed, so maybe I had offended him.

The poll tax was introduced in Scotland in 1989, a year ahead of England. Robin decided to make a stand and not pay. I had always paid our rates bill, which was massive, and my poll tax was small by comparison. Without noticing, I signed two debit slips and only discovered some months after that my bank had quietly assumed I was paying Robin's as well. I related this tale to Neil Kinnock at a dinner party in Edinburgh, and got a telling-off from Robin, for I believe Neil did not support the 'refuseniks' over the poll tax.

Robin was sensitive about exposing the family to media attention, and I certainly valued my privacy and did not want to become a public figure. Most people who recognised him in public would say briefly that they thought he was doing a good job and pass on. But some people were unbelievably insensitive and would commandeer his attention and bombard him with their views. He was more tolerant than me. Once when we had dined out together, just the two of us, as he went to the bar he was collared by two party workers. They engaged him in keen conversation and the minutes ticked by. I waited, patiently at first; the time passed when he could reasonably excuse himself. I became irritated. Emancipated I may be, but a woman sitting alone in a bar always feels a little awkward. When I saw the gestures indicating they were settling down to another round of drinks I saw red. I stalked over to the trio, said stiffly, 'Do you think I could have my husband back? We were supposed to be having a private night out together.'

They were most apologetic and Robin came away, but he was mortified. He excused his conduct by the fact that they were party workers and had to be humoured at all costs. We left soon afterwards.

The emphasis on privacy did not, however, deter the family from agreeing to be the subject of an illustrated interview which appeared in *You* magazine, part of the *Mail on Sunday*. It was a very sympathetic portrayal of a happy, interactive family with some lovely photographs of us at home and with the horses. Interestingly the interviewer remarked upon my vehement negative when she asked if I mothered my husband.

★

We sold Winkie and I reluctantly let the boys take over Lucky. Then for once I did something incomprehensibly foolish: perhaps feeling over confident from our success with Lucky I went out and bought a mare without taking anyone with me for an experienced and unbiased opinion. The new mare, an elegant grey called Carissima, proved a disaster. She was extremely highly strung and overreactive, and though her flat-work showed potential, she was impetuous and precipitate in her jumping. I struggled along with her for a few months and gamely took her into a jumping competition, when after completing the course she took off and did two circuits of the school at top speed before I could pull her up. Then I planned to do a dressage test; just a prelim riding club competition. I had grave misgivings about this, wondering if I was going to get killed before I was much older. It was customary to dress smartly, which I did, and as we walked into the school to warm up prior to our test presented quite a fine appearance. Alas for spin over substance. Someone just raised her voice to convey a message, Carrie boiled over and set off like a streak of lightning, and with equally erratic sense of direction. She skidded and tripped; I came flying out of the saddle, observing as I rolled over in the dirt a grey shape leap-frogging over me.

To fall off your horse in a dressage test is humiliating; to do so in the warm-up is lamentable. Besides, my confidence was already shot to pieces and I decided there and then that she would have to go. The misery of owning a horse of which you have become frightened, but still have to exercise each day, is not to be endured for long.

I was reading in bed later that evening, feeling down in the mouth, when Robin arrived home. I heard his key in the front door and his footsteps on the stairs, then he came into the room. I knew from his facial expression and his body language that he'd heard the story of my disastrous dressage test. He said something anodyne, but I hate delicacy under these circumstances and growled, 'Don't be so bloody tactful!'

So I sold Carrie, losing a fair bit in the transaction, and restored my confidence by riding Lucky for a while. And then I heard about Phyllis.

Did you ever hear of such an odd, unhorsy name? Yet it's not really; it's related to Philip which means a lover of horses. A friend recommended her. She was eleven years old, a little small, a pure thoroughbred with a classy pedigree, a beautiful dark chocolate colour, and her complete history of owners available. Her present owner declared she was so good she was almost boring! When I brought her back to the Grange, Grant said, 'Fourth time lucky, we hope!'

And so she was. She was nearly perfect.

At Easter in 1989 we rented a cottage in the wilds of Exmoor, arriving as the snowflakes started to fall, presaging one of the coldest Easter holidays we could remember. Not that it mattered to us. There were newborn lambs in their hundreds in the fields, wrapped in blue and orange waterproof coats. The boys and I went out riding with an eccentric man whose clothes were held together with string and who took one look at us and attached three lead reins to his horse. He clearly didn't believe we could ride. The weather was cold and wild. As we reached the crest of a hill the wind hit us with maximum force; not a place to hang about. But would you believe it? Our escort mumbled that his saddle was slipping, dismounted and untied his girth! With the wind behind him the girth blew away out of his reach on the far side of his horse. The boys and I stared in disbelief and mounting (though silent) merriment as he fished ineffectually under the horse, trying to catch the wayward and flapping girth. After a while it occurred to him to turn the horse through 180 degrees to effect repairs. There was absolutely no shelter, so we were glad enough to move on.

We were invited to see Captain Ronnie Wallace who lived nearby in Dulverton and I was pressed (with very little resistance) into riding to hounds with the Exmoor Fox Hunt. This was the one and only time I have hunted on horseback and it was a thrilling experience. The terrain there is hard on the horses, so there is no jumping. The steep downhill runs worried me a little, as I wondered whether my balance would be good enough. I need not have worried, as my horse knew exactly what to do. The uphill gallops were more likely to cause an upset: it was almost like climbing vertically and I leaned well forward, grasping a handful of mane, and was relieved to see everyone else doing the same. We were out for five hours, and the family kept pace with us as well as they could in the car.

On the way back to the cottage we stopped at a shop in a tiny hamlet in the middle of nowhere, and who should we see but Jean, my flatmate from university days! We hadn't seen each other for over twenty years, and flew into each other's arms with exclamations about the other being instantly recognisable in voice and looks. Jean had her husband and twin children with her. It was really good to make contact again and to plan a reunion.

Then we dined with Ronnie and his wife. I had extracted the car key from Robin early in the evening before the first drink made him careless about risk-taking. This holiday was the last time he gave me cause for concern about his drinking, and it is to his credit that he dragged himself out of that particular slough of despond.

Just after New Year in 1989 I had had a further toe operation. On admission, Robin sat nearby while the nurse came to take basic details. She asked about drinking habits of course, and I answered (truthfully) that I usually took eight or nine glasses of wine a week and seldom anything else. But Robin chimed in with a contradiction, making a great thing of adding up and claiming I'd taken double that over the festive season. This may well have been true, but in making such an issue of it he made me look like a liar and a furtive drinker. When the nurse went away I was furious and let him know it. This was another instance of his guilt transference and tendency to denigrating me in front of other people.

This same year brought a huge change in my working life. For years, a spanking new hospital in Livingston had been planned to replace decrepit old Bangour, and finally Phase One was completed. Laboratories were in Phase Two. But the difficulties of providing blood transfusion for acute surgical specialties from a distance of seven miles filled everyone concerned with horror. With some difficulty I persuaded managers of our case to move into the first phase. We redesigned a basement ward area as a temporary haematology department. The move to Livingston had to be effected while still carrying on routine work, and was managed one Sunday with everyone (and in some cases their families also) working overtime to get everything in working order. I often wondered what the move would have cost if there had not been this goodwill by staff in all departments.

The Queen and Prince Philip came to open Phase One of St John's in the summer of 1989, and of my two local roles, the wifely one took precedence. I stood at the entrance in the line-up of officialdom next to my husband, wearing a new outfit and broad-brimmed hat, to shake hands, smile, curtsey and utter banalities.

That summer we found another wonderfully magical place to stay in the New Forest, Eyeworth Lodge near Fritham. It was entirely surrounded by beautiful woodlands and at night the multitude of interesting sounds that emanated from the darkness and vibrated on the still night air sent shivers down my spine. I imagined it was like being in the jungle. There was a particularly scenic walk through deciduous woodland, over streams, stiles and heathland to the Hollicks at Forest Brook with whom we joined on numerous social occasions. I met John Eatwell, academic and economic adviser to Neil Kinnock. He described to me how he divided his time between various activities, and I rather ungraciously retorted that you wouldn't get away with that in the health service, much to Robin's entertainment. I was beginning to feel the pressures, I guess. This year we celebrated our twentieth wedding anniversary for which the Hollicks generously lent us their Paris flat for a long weekend.

Phyllis and I had been forging an effective working relationship throughout the year with enormous enjoyment. We entered a number of riding-club competitions, dressage and show-jumping with a degree of success. She had been a cross-country star with previous owners and I longed to have a go myself. I heard of a novice course in Lanarkshire, on the Douglas and Angus estate, and I bravely entered the trial held there in October, my first cross-country at the tender age of forty-five. The course was very well made, with Badminton-like fences but a fraction of the size and complexity. I learned a huge amount that day: that cross-country jumping is totally different from show-jumping; that it's vital to ride the horse at the middle of the fence; that the outward journey may require some encouragement of horse by rider, but the return journey requires none; and finally that it was one of the most exciting things I've ever done in all my life. We collected quite a few penalty points owing to my lack of experience, but we finished the course. Some days later I was sent a photograph showing a horse and rider leaping in grand style over a gallows-type fence. I mused over it, misty-eyed, thinking, isn't that beautiful? I wish I could do that. And then I realised that it was actually Phyllis and me sailing over the last fence at Douglas. I learned that in the summer a one-day event was held here (with the three disciplines of dressage, show-jumping and cross-country); it had been beyond my wildest dreams that I would ever take part in an event, and here was one that was within my capabilities. Phyllis and I attempted one or two small cross-country courses and I continued to learn the art of conveying one's deter-mination to the horse while containing energy and eagerness. She was doing well with her dressage and I joined our riding-club team for inter-club competitions.

At Douglas the following summer we had a wonderful day. Phyllis did a brilliant dressage test, coming second or third. She skimmed effortlessly round the show-jumping course; and then remembering all my newly learned lessons, we set off on the cross-country. Usually I wasn't very good at judging the time, so put up my internal pacemaker by a notch or two. Phyllis enjoyed herself as much as I did. Just after the point on the course at which you turn for home, you face a water jump, which causes hydrophobic horses a few problems. But Phyllis moved up a gear, bounced through the water, taking out a stride. Then we were power-striding across a field and I was exerting my utmost to stay in command so that I had steering control. As long as you keep that, you feel as if you can jump anything in your path. We sailed over a corner, a coffin, downhill and sloping jumps, spreads, a ski-jump, and on to the final, solid-looking gallows jump; just inside the time. And, wonder of wonders, we were first in our class of twenty-four!

We attempted a number of other cross-country courses. At Lanark racecourse there was a notorious quarry jump with a drop, two steps and a downhill slope followed by an uphill track. On our approach I noted with trepidation the presence of St John's ambulancemen looking expectant. I slowed Phyllis to a trot so that she dropped down the steps with immaculate control and though our pace became a little precipitate on the slope, the upward track acted as an effective brake.

Over the next few years we had enormous fun and quite a few triumphs. We joined the club show-jumping team as well as the dressage team. By the skin of our teeth we managed to qualify for the national riding club championships and the entire family came down to Malvern for the weekend. The ground was iron hard in the September Indian summer, and Phyllis didn't perform well, but to me it was just wonderful to have been there and taken part. She won a third in dressage at Holyrood and a second in the Caledonian championships at Scone. She was overall champion of our club one year and won other annual points championships. All the family were very tolerant during this phase of my riding career and would turn out to help with grooming and handling, a role which Robin termed 'being the grubby'. Peter even got up at three in the morning to accompany me to Scone in Perthshire. And on Sunday afternoons in winter, always taken up with show-jumping at the Grange, Robin had the task at home of putting the joint in the oven and bringing me a glass of wine as I bathed the horsy smells away before dinner. It was a very happy time.

The boys also had a number of successes with Lucky, but were not enthusiastic about travelling around the countryside to compete. As Chris approached his Standard Grade exams, they were growing too big for the pony, perhaps opportunely. After a family conference they decided not to have another horse as they were both entering an exam-intensive time and did not want extra obligations. So Lucky was sold and not replaced.

At Christmas, the riding club would arrange frivolous high jinks such as parties with gymkhana games and fancy-dress competitions in which the horse had to be an integral part of the character. I had a brainwave and went as Tam O'Shanter on his old grey mare Meg, covering Phyllis with talcum powder to achieve a suitably dappled effect, and attaching a rag-doll to her rump to portray the witch, Cutty Sark. It was a matter of no great difficulty to make myself up as a drunken old reprobate. We won the class and Robin took photos.

A week or two later, he came to talk to all the consultants at St John's about the health service changes; a serious occasion at which everyone was professional and dignified. Robin was competent at holding the floor on these occasions, and even as he spoke with grave mien, he passed along an envelope to me, sitting at the other side of the room. As I opened it, the photographs of Phyllis and me in fancy dress fell into my lap, with a note saying, 'How much will you give me, not to show these around?' With difficulty I gulped back my mirth, while he continued speaking, poker-faced.

We were invited to Ken Follett's fiftieth birthday party which took place on a boat on the Thames, a lavish affair with many beautiful and famous people present. I sat between Hanif Kureishi, who was a lively and interesting conversationalist, and Bill Owen who portrays Compo in *The Last of the Summer Wine*. This was a favourite programme of the boys, so I had watched it on television. I had fully expected Bill Owen to be a laugh a minute but it was not so. He was an extremely serious-minded, soft-spoken, unsmiling companion. I had to bend close to catch his words and he spoke mainly of some social work in which he was engaged. I also met Donald Woods, the journalist friend of the black martyr Steve Biko, who became a banned person in South Africa and later fled the country with his family. He began to explain to me who he was, but I had both seen the film *Cry Freedom* and read his book *Biko*, and was excited to meet him in person. He seemed very weary and older than his years, which was perhaps understandable.

I had some correspondence with Ken on the fascinating excavations at the medieval hospital at Soutra, south Scotland. I had read his book *The Pillars of the Earth* and rather wondered if this archaeological site might provide inspiration for another historical novel. He sent me an article on the topic outlining how blood-letting was widely practised by monks to quell sexual desires. This is one of the explanations for the finding of deposits of blood preserved in clay at the site.

My parents' golden wedding anniversary fell in August 1990, for which we planned a family get-together. There were some difficulties, for my father at seventy-eight had become a bit of a recluse and was difficult to winkle out of the house. They now lived in Trowbridge. Jenny's two sons, both unmarried, tended to wander erratically round the world, so she could not guarantee their availability. In the end we decided on a party at the parents' home, and I would bring in a caterer so that we could enjoy the occasion without worry and frenzied organisation. All of which came to fruition in the most delightful party on a beautiful summer's day. Robin organised some photographs with a time-lapse switch so that everyone is recorded, looking cheerful and happy in bright summer clothes and with sunny smiles.

We were based at Downton near the New Forest for that holiday, memories of which are indelibly marked by the Iraqi invasion of Kuwait. Another incident rather marred the end of the holiday for me. Regrettably, money discussions still raised tension between Robin and me, especially in recent years when my salary had risen faster than his at a time when some of my financial outlays had fallen. In particular I had stopped employing nannies in 1987, though still had someone in for a few hours a week to housekeep. Also the poll tax had relieved me of a huge burden; and because of Robin's heavy dependence on the phone, had seen fit to trust him with that particular account. He had realised that his domestic outlays were now at least the same as mine, if not more. He objected to this, and was more than ready to discuss money, holding that I should pay more in proportion to my salary.

For once I dug my heels in and said no; we were equal partners (were we not?) and costs would be equally divided. One of the most important reasons for making this stand was that very shortly Chris would be going to university and would receive no maintenance grant. Peter was planning to follow a year later, and with the courses they planned I would have to finance them both together for four years. I knew full well I could expect little input from Robin – unless Labour got in at the next election, but one couldn't depend on that. My income as it was could not cope with all this outlay and so I was saving like mad to have a fund to support them. Robin never saved a penny in all his married life, and this concept seemed to be quite alien to him. I certainly got no encouragement from him in this endeavour. He became rather aggressive about our relative inputs, so I suggested that since I ran all our domestic affairs, maybe I should charge him a nominal sum for that. He was aghast at this idea, and talked about marriage being a partnership – sharing – not a thing you put a price on. I remarked drily that that was a convenient argument when the partnership was so unequally slanted in his favour.

So there developed a paranoia about the subject of money in him and he began to propagate the notion that I was miserly. At the end of our holiday in Downton I sat him down to the usual reckoning-up, of which the net result was that he owed me. His reaction was startling. He lost his temper, scribbled out a cheque and slammed it down on the table with a harsh string of expletives. The boys were present and looked in amazement. I spat out, 'How dare you speak to me like that in front of the boys!'

His temper cooled quickly, for he did not like scenes any more than I did; but everyone was upset by his vicious outburst, and I was deeply troubled. This was a complete contrast to his once careless but generous habits, and his paranoia verged on the pathological.

My problems with funding for the boys' student careers was solved as if by magic in 1992 when I was awarded a C merit award, back paid for one year. Quite apart from the money, the recognition gave a substantial boost to morale. Chris started at Aberdeen that autumn, studying law; a four-year course plus a year's diploma. I paid his living expenses but he earned some extra money by researching for Robin's regular Saturday racing column in the *Glasgow Herald*. They shared this activity for several years.

21

The Invisible Barrier

That year, 1992, there was to be yet another election, and with the extensive policy review and redefining of socialist aims and values, Kinnock's Labour Party seemed to be approaching this assessment of its popular appeal with confidence. But there were many unknown factors, notably John Major's leadership. Defence had dropped out of sight as an issue, but taxation and the NHS were crucial and it is difficult to judge in retrospect how influential the persistently anti-pathetic tabloid press was.

People asked me if I had plans to move to London and patients anxiously enquired if the election results would influence my working life. It seemed to be popularly supposed that Labour would get in. Oddly, though I accepted the general optimism, I didn't review my lifestyle or make any provisional plans. Deep inside I accepted I would go on doing things as before; maybe the old premonitory powers were still at work. Even before the campaign began Robin and I were going through one of those phases of never seeing each other long enough to communicate at any depth. I was made poignantly aware of this because about the end of February I discovered a breast lump. Every woman who has ever made this discovery will sympathise with the first reaction of heartsink and fear. I knew the odds were against it being malignant. It was the worst possible time to be going through diagnostic tests, and the most baneful aspect was the waiting. Usually I do not like to pull rank with medical problems, but this time I did. I phoned one of my trusted surgical colleagues who arranged for me to be seen the next day in the Breast Unit at the Royal; and the lump proved to be a cyst which was aspirated on the spot. My problems were over – in less than twenty-four hours! I was sincerely grateful. However, the point that struck me so forcibly was that I had not shared my discovery with Robin, having not found a suitable moment to do so, and it was over a year before I told him. And when I did, it was to illustrate to him how unsatisfactory a husband he was at times. He should have been the first person to know. There was nothing to stop me except the invisible barrier he set up around himself at times of stress. The message on the barrier was loud and clear: don't come inside without removing your shoes, treat me gently, don't add to my burdens and above all, don't expect anything from me to you.

Unlike the previous election campaign, my offers of help were accepted. Chris gave generously of his time and was invaluable, especially in his role as a chauffeur, which relieved me of worrying about Robin's tendency to smash up his car. Chris and I did some canvassing together. He was far too headstrong in argument and nearly came to blows with an SNP supporter. As I dragged him away I tried to suggest that he had to be a little tolerant of other folks' views.

'But, Mum,' he argued, 'he's wrong, and if I explain it all to him, he'll see more clearly.' Ah, the mistaken self-confidence of youth!

For my part, on the doorstep I stuck entirely to health issues, foreseeing the irreversible damage the current trends would inflict if allowed to continue. I could talk about this with deeply held conviction.

On the evening of polling day, Jim, Robin, Chris and I, with some other party workers, met for a meal before the long night of the count. The mood was upbeat, before the slow dawning of failure yet again. More years in the wilderness. My gloom was one hundred per cent for the health service. Robin was returned, and yet again in his acceptance speech made no acknowledgement of me. This wound, I believe intentional, struck home, though I didn't mention it till five years later, at the next general election.

The Easter holiday followed immediately after polling day and a somewhat dispirited Cook family settled into Allum Green Farm near Lyndhurst for a fortnight. I wished in vain that Robin and his colleagues would give themselves a break. They had spent weeks in frenetic, non-productive activity and needed to unwind, to crawl away and lick their wounds; pause, think, cool off. These were terms they did not understand. Robin seemed to spend the entire fortnight on the phone, intriguing and scheming over the leadership campaign, which hardly seemed necessary. With strong union support, John Smith was the new leader-in-waiting. I wish now I'd listened to some of the discussions, as doubtless there were sub-agendas. Robin was a personal friend of John's, and his campaign manager, but it was difficult to comprehend the need for so much discussion.

Though this behaviour was irritating, the boys and I did not let it interfere with our holiday activities. I did not know how much longer the boys would want to accompany us on holiday, and, as I revelled in their joyous and youthful company, made the most of it while I could.

Within three weeks of the election our chief executive at St John's had called a meeting in which he intimated that St John's would declare an interest in becoming a Trust. So much for democracy. Previously the prevailing mood had opposed Trust status; but now with another Conservative government we had to submit to the inevitable.

John Smith was confirmed as leader and Robin became shadow chief trade and industry spokesman, a role in which he was to consolidate an already formidable reputation both as a debater and as a man in total command of his brief. When he had been shadow health spokesman I would sometimes be congratulated on how well informed he was, for which I certainly could not accept any credit. He did of course have five years to get to know his sphere, and there were some issues, notably the professional role of laboratory personnel, where I was useful to him; also I functioned as a general sounding board. We discussed a number of local problems as they arose, when there could be an interesting polarisation of attitudes. If patients took their complaints to him about the hospital he would assume they had all the right on their side. I would tend to see the point of view of my colleagues more clearly, though hope I kept a balanced outlook. I certainly modified his attitudes before he went in to challenge people in his usual uncompromising manner.

Robin's political aspirations, which still drove him relentlessly, now became tinged with ambivalence because, I suppose, his party had given up on so many policies he had made his own, notably on defence. Sometimes he pondered whether he would not, in the future, like to concentrate his endeavours in Scotland: a small country, where you could actually care about things, achieve something tangible for the people. I was with him entirely, and felt I should like him to be Secretary of State for Scotland, if Labour ever got back in, or maybe Prime Minister, if Scotland achieved its own Parliament. Indeed I mentioned this to John Smith, who was not inclined to concur. He said that, for the present, Robin was needed in the thick of things; he was a fighter, a terrier, snapping at the heels of government and giving them no peace. In truth I doubted whether Robin's love affair with Westminster was waning. He probably had enough insight to recognise that ambition was likely to drive him on even when the principles he had worn like a toga were slipping away from him.

Since the early days of speaking from the heart at CND rallies, he had enjoyed holding an audience, the feeling of power that filled him after a good performance, reinforced by widespread approbation and an admiring press. He loved to be recognised and courted, he loved to take the stage. It is worthy of note that when he won the *Spectator* Parliamentarian of the Year award in 1991, for his 'indefatigable, relentless and pungent' debating style, he expressed his pleasure at being known as a parliamentarian rather than as a politician. I saw clearly that this public adulation was highly addictive. He appeared regularly on television programmes such as *Question Time* and on radio in *Any Questions?*. I praised him whole-heartedly, for he generally did well, even outstandingly; but he didn't like even valid criticism. And there were times when he was cocky and overbearing, prickly and ungenerous. Sometimes when impassioned he would swallow his word-endings, but any suggestion of mine that he should consider diction lessons was resented.

When the family first went horse-mad, he used to spend time at the stables, mucking out and helping with mundane tasks. One of the attractions was that no one was particularly impressed by his public role and no one treated him as a special person. He and I felt this was a healthy counterbalance. But as pressures grew he left all this behind.

Over all the years we had kept close ties with Robin's parents and saw them frequently. Grandpa kept up the habit of saying grace before meals, to which we graciously submitted, though four of us were agnostic. All the same, I liked to hear him say, 'Thank you for bringing us together as a family,' because he so obviously relished the communion we had. Christmas, New Year and birthdays were special get-togethers. The noise generated with just the six of us could be astounding. One Christmas morning Robin covertly tape-recorded the hour-long present-unwrapping session, which was hilarious when played back and enabled us to enjoy it all a second time. On these occasions we played noisy games such as charades and masquerade, which were good for lifting us out of post-prandial torpor. Family discussions were lively and Robin, perhaps used to being treated with deference elsewhere, had to struggle sometimes to get his word in edgeways. In moments of frankness he would say that I was the natural leader of the family; also that I was one of the most intelligent women he had ever met (distinctly sexist, that), and never in my life bored him but that I was not easy to live with and few men could handle me as well as he did (note the equine allusion here). I thought this was nonsense, as it seemed to me that I did all the adapting, but I could be intransigent over important issues. Once on a Friday evening at six o'clock, which was his usual time for phoning in his *Glasgow Herald* racing article, I needed the phone for an urgent hospital call to organise blood products for a bleeding obstetric patient, details of whom had been phoned to me. Robin made a terrible fuss, saying that he absolutely had to have the phone right then, and would not immediately be persuaded that my patient's needs obviously took priority. I did not give way.

Grandpa Cook's health began to fail a little. He had prostatic cancer and was on treatment for this, and, possibly connected with this, had a heart attack that summer, though appeared to recover well enough. My own father had his eightieth birthday in 1992 and we gave him a party similar to the anniversary celebration two years before.

The year previously we had broken with tradition and taken a family holiday in France, near Le Mans in Sarthe. This year we took a house in Tuscany, near Siena, called Castello di Montalto. The first night was memorable for the most magnificent thunder and lightning storm I've ever witnessed. Chris, who had been at university for a year, was feeling his independence; he and I had a few head-on collisions which were perhaps inevitable. He was going through the power-without-responsibility stage. However our differences were benign and no lasting damage was done.

The next year Chris went into a flat with three other lads, and I felt there was an immense change in him, in terms of greater tolerance and consideration. With Peter, I never had any battles. I think he just learned, at a very early age, how to wind me round his little finger. He now started at Newcastle University, studying electronic and electrical engineering. For the first time in nearly twenty years I found myself living alone for part of the week. I missed the boys' company, naturally, but didn't go through any major crisis. Chris was two and a half hours' drive to the north, Peter the same to the south. They kept in touch by phone and came home for odd weekends, and all their vacations. My life was very full, but I was glad to have Robin's company at the weekends. For the last few years I had taken to exercising Phyllis in the early morning, which meant rising at six, getting to the stable by seven, riding for an hour or so, then after settling her in her box I would drive to St John's (less than five minutes from the Grange), have a shower and complete change of clothes, and arrive glowing at my desk.

Earlier in the year Phyllis had fractured a pedal bone (a small bone in the foot) while playing in the field. She had required two to three months' rest, but had made a remarkably full recovery and was now competing as well as ever.

It seemed a good idea to celebrate my newly found freedom by joining the British Society for Haematology visit to India in December 1992. I think Robin was rather nonplussed that I'd decided to take off on my own. For part of the time we joined the equivalent Indian society's annual conference in Hyderabad where I read a research paper, but for the most part we toured around that fascinating city and its surroundings, notably the Golconda Fort and royal tombs, the tiny shops where we bought pearls and hand-embroidered silk. Our travels took us also to Delhi, Jaipur, Agra, Khajuràho. Wandering around the teeming, colourful, noisy, smelly streets of Old Delhi took us off our usual privileged beaten track, carefully picking our way between sacred cows and trying to avoid being mown down by bicycles and other traffic; and above all, trying not to lose our guide. We learned how to put on a sari, something of the religions of India, observed extreme poverty and tragically disabled people begging. We were discouraged from giving money to beggars, but were expected to give tips for the least little service, which I gladly did. Once I had no rupees and gave some sterling silver coins instead, which were received with great delight! You quickly learn that western attitudes and values do not apply here. In a carpet factory in Jaipur an eight-year-old boy was weaving a pattern with nimble fingers. I sat down beside him and allowed him to guide my hands for a few stitches, becoming aware of his softly murmured, 'Twenty rupees, madam, twenty rupees, madam.' I was careful not to let the manager see the exchange. And I came away feeling glad that he had work and a craft, and would not end up on the streets begging.

We saw the Taj Mahal as the moon was just rising in the early evening, and returned the next morning to see it again as the sun rose; and yes, it is incomparably beautiful, and mystical too. The whole exotic trip was only enough to give a tantalising taste of the country, and make me long to go back. I later told Robin I wouldn't take him though; I don't think he could cope with the poverty and the distressingly disabled and disfigured people. Our last weekend coincided with the riots caused by the sacking of the Ayodhya mosque, and security at airports was stern. I was frisked by a fierce military woman in a khaki sari. We saw no other disturbance, but everyone at home was getting a little anxious.

Robin met me at Heathrow where we had breakfast and I talked non-stop for about an hour. It was strange to come back to a cold climate and Christmas decorations.

Just before Christmas we drove from Edinburgh to Newcastle to collect Peter for the holiday. On the way we looked for a suitable restaurant or inn to have dinner on the return journey. Robin, with his eye for the lavish, espied an expensive-looking hotel, set in its own grounds, so we drove in and booked a table for later. I murmured in his ear, 'Don't you think this is a little grand? Peter will be wearing scruffy jeans and trainers. I doubt if they'll let him in.'

Robin dismissed my misgivings with the view that nobody stood on that sort of ceremony nowadays.

As predicted, Peter was dressed in the usual barely hygienic student gear. Everything else he had was bundled up in a case, needing to be washed. Well, I thought, let's see what happens. Maybe his parents' respectability will make up for his lack of it. Arrived at the hotel, we settled into the cocktail bar and I told Peter to order whatever he liked – which proved to be a champagne cocktail costing six pounds! The boy had style. The head waiter came in, paused, scratched his chin.

'There is a leetle problem, but we can get round it,' he said, measuring Peter with his eye. Then he brought in a jacket and tie and helped Peter into them, later positioning him in a corner seat in the dining room so that the jeans and trainers were not on display.

'It's as well you ordered the expensive cocktail,' I teased him. 'Otherwise they'd have turned you away.'

In his early years in London Robin had rented a flat. Later he found it more congenial and economic to stay in a hotel. He now felt he was in a position to get a mortgage for a flat. This concerned me greatly, for many reasons, not least the ease with which he would be able to conduct a covert affair. I also worried about the financial side. He was so feckless about personal matters, all of which could be shelved till the mould grew if his political work demanded it. Then I discovered he wanted to use our Edinburgh home as security. Alarm bells rang in several discordant intervals when he suggested this. However he had no other security and I could hardly refuse, so unwillingly signed the papers. He bought a very nice flat in Pimlico, in Sutherland Street, and then realised that he would have to decorate and furnish it. So another loan was required, and another signature for financial security. There was a hiatus before he bestirred himself to organise this, and I pushed him to make progress, aware that he would now be paying both mortgage and the expenses of living elsewhere until he could move in.

Then I asked for a key, and he said, yes, of course, but none ever appeared. Interestingly he had no difficulty about giving Peter a key when he later lived near London. It was a year before I was to visit the flat, and this was probably more to do with my lifestyle than his. In all his years at Westminster I loved to visit London and did so usually several times a year. But now demands at work were such that it was becoming increasingly difficult to get away for a weekend. Still, I bought a number of items for his domestic comfort, things like tea-cosies, towels and trays, that men tend not to think of. When I did visit eventually, I found it very tastefully furnished, airy and comfortable.

Now I must ask the reader to be a little indulgent while I explain why my work was making such unreasonable demands of me. One factor was the new legislation about junior doctors' hours, which put a legal limit on the numbers of hours they could work or be on call. This had potentially huge implications on the need to increase numbers of doctors. But for all sorts of reasons, career opportunities as well as cost, this need could not be met. All kinds of initiatives were put in place, including cross-cover between specialties, but inevitably the burden often fell on senior doctors like myself, for whom there was no equivalent legislation.

My specialty being a hybrid one is complex in requiring two on-call rotas (for out of normal working hours): one to cover in-patients, and a separate rota for covering laboratory advice and interpretation, the latter being more specialised. In both areas serious emergencies can and do arise. Previously I had done a lot of the cover in both aspects myself, but with support from St John's physicians and haematologists at the Western respectively to stand in if I wanted to go away, or visit the theatre, or get a little tipsy, or whatever. Perhaps the public seldom appreciated the extent to which some doctors harness themselves so entirely to their jobs. Anyway, this system worked very well, though was demanding enough.

But with the new legislation, and also with the new Trust status, which meant that co-operation between hospitals was being eroded, the system collapsed. The Western department staff had problems of their own and could no longer give me support. My physicianly colleagues at St John's very helpfully took over my in-patient cover altogether, saying I had enough to do to cover the lab. As indeed I had, for I needed to be available for about eighty per cent of the time – weekends, evenings and nights – outwith normal working hours.

I quailed when I thought of what this entailed. I acquired a mobile phone from our switchboard, which meant that there was at least some freedom. But for the next few years I became almost neurotic with the sensation of being perpetually on tap for advice; at times the burden became almost intolerable, and when I arrived home late and weary and the phone would ring yet again, I would want to scream, 'No! Not again! Leave me alone!'

I became short-tempered and began to get a reputation among the juniors for being difficult. I tried to discuss this with senior managers, wrote letters galore, sat down and had discussions. Before the business era my staffing needs would have been listened to and assessed with an element of trust in my integrity and track record as a hard-working and committed senior consultant; and perhaps after a little delay, additions would have been made. But now people made sympathetic noises but there was no question of increasing staff; haematology did not have a high profile in the new commercial service. In truth, few people understand what is involved in another specialty, and in a complex one like mine this was doubly true. For some unaccountable reason there were unforeseen workload increases, and we were occasionally almost overwhelmed with the demand.

We did fortunately have an arrangement for nominal consultant cover for holidays; if I had not had that outlet, I think I would have been carried out of St John's feet first. Riding Phyllis was also a relief, but from now on I always had a phone somewhere about my person. I have even been known to take part in a show-jumping team competition at Gleneagles with my phone in my pocket.

Robin was asked to appear on the TV programme *Through the Keyhole*, but before he agreed we had a family conference. On the whole we felt we had no skeletons in the cupboard and that it might be fun, so the process was set in motion. None of us would be at home when Loyd Grossman visited, but we arranged that my housekeeper, Mrs Ramsay, would be there to supervise. Anything we did not wish to appear on screen was to be put out of sight. We made no special attempts to tidy up or rearrange things, but I remembered late in the day that I'd left out a cassette of *A Year of the Quorn* (on the subject of hunting) on top of the video recorder. It was too late to do anything about it, so I just prayed; luckily the crew never noticed.

The programme was hugely enjoyed by us and our friends. The camera swam over the shelves and shelves of books, focused on the extensive library of Trollopes, paused over the innumerable political works, picked out the medical tomes, located ornaments relating to red deer and other wildlife, identified a Scottish theme or two and some racing cards. Then it hovered over my embroidery frame bearing the half-completed Tree of Life, admired the spinning wheel, moved on to the piano bestrewn with a wide assortment of musical scores and supporting a few rosettes and equestrian trophies. Willie Rushton and other panel members identified Robin's home with relative ease. Then Robin appeared, had a benign interview with David Frost and received his token key. In the following weeks, Robin was offered advice on the stability of his embroidery frame and was asked to consider performing on the piano at a charity concert. Then the Trollope Society invited him to appear as guest speaker at their annual dinner on some future occasion. The latter he seriously considered accepting, encouraged by me; but I would have to write his speech for him.

One of my colleagues commented, 'It was more about you than him!'

The following year we did attend the Trollope Society's annual dinner as nonspeaking guests on a sort of information-gathering exercise – Ruth Rendell was the main speaker that year – and we took Ken and Barbara Follett with us. In fact, Robin never did take up the invitation to speak as neither he nor I had time to pursue it.

In the spring of 1993 Chris and Robin, as was their unfailing custom, had gone to Liverpool for the Grand National. On occasions in the past I had gone too, but Peter and I were not such racing enthusiasts as the other two, and on that Saturday he and I drove down to Allum Green Farm, our new New Forest holiday haunt. We listened horror-struck to the fiasco of the false start of the race, and wondered how near to being suicidal the other half of the family would be. Chris shared his father's obsession with racing and was very well informed, as a result of his input to Robin's by now well-established Saturday racing column in the *Glasgow Herald*.

Possibly because of our personal sparring in Italy the previous August, Chris did not join the family at Easter, nor in the summer when we planned a holiday in the Canadian Rockies. Our holidays were getting ever more adventurous. About a month before we were due to go I was show-jumping with Phyllis one evening at the Fishcross equestrian centre near Alloa. As I prepared her in the lorry for the journey back home, she was badly startled by some external noise and in the ensuing moment of panic and erratic leaping and pulling, she stamped heavily – twice – on my foot. I knew immediately that some significant damage was done. I was with two friends and did not make a fuss. We arrived back in Mid Calder where I had left my trailer. Elizabeth helped me decant Phyllis into the trailer and I drove back to the Grange. My left foot was sickeningly painful. It was about eleven o'clock by now and quite dark. No one was about. Hobbling and groaning to myself, I settled Phyll for the night, disconnected the trailer and clambered wearily into the car. I knew I should go to Accident and Emergency but did not feel like facing all that. I just wanted my bed as quickly as possible so drove the twenty or so miles home. My riding boot held the foot together and made it possible – just – to drive. Peter was home for his summer vacation but was in bed asleep. I made some tea, removed the boot and admired the bruised and now swelling foot.

The next morning I couldn't put the foot to the ground. There was a choice of Peter or Grandpa to take me to St John's for X-rays, and as Peter was only just qualified to drive and still scared me to death in the driving seat, I gave Grandpa a ring. Granny grumbled, 'I thought urgent calls for help first thing in the morning were a thing of the past.' But he came anyway. I had fractured a metatarsal, and not much could be done except wait for it to get better. I borrowed a pair of elbow crutches, got some painkillers and was back at work the next day. Peter and a colleague, Ray, gave me lifts into work. Hirpling through the main front entrance at eight in the morning I encountered Paul, the chief executive. I hope he's impressed with my devotion to duty, I thought. A number of my patients were quite taken aback to see me disabled, thinking that doctors ought to be indestructible! Robin had been given the news by Peter, and possibly thinking of my previous strictures, was most upset with me for not telling him sooner.

Within a week I was both driving and riding, though mounting the horse was a tricky operation and I limped rather pathetically for a couple of months. I was still very lame as we set off for our Canadian trip. Not that I let such a thing interfere too much with plans, but I wasn't able to do much walking. Most activities such as riding, canoeing and white-water rafting did not require much reliance on feet, fortunately.

We hired a car in Calgary and set off on the wonderfully scenic road from Banff to Jasper, with many stops to admire wildlife such as buffalo, black bear and elk. Crossing the mountain ridge from Jasper and passing Mount Robson, we reached British Columbia and travelled south to Helmcken Falls in Wells Gray Park. The impression of being way out in the wilds was exhilarating, and was reinforced by the ever-present wildlife, some of it potentially dangerous. All the guidebooks gave endless instructions on coping with bears, especially grizzlies. All Canadians, we discovered, had their bear-story. Camping especially required that you knew the rules. Bears like food and foodie smells so never have anything pungent inside your tent, we were told. For the same reason, it was best to avoid sex! We spent our first couple of weeks in comfort in luxurious lodges at Helmcken and then at the aptly named Emerald Lake. Here Robin was determined to go off on a solo hike. Peter was perturbed. 'You know how reckless he is,' he said to me. 'Perhaps I should go along to keep him out of trouble. You know perfectly well he's going looking for his own bear-story!' However Robin went off alone with his belled bear-bracelet, provisions, stick and camera, and with all the latest information about grizzly sightings. He told us to wait till nine in the evening and then ring panic buttons if he was not back. Peter and I were tucking into our dinner at nine, and there was no sign of Robin. We knew that the instructions meant, don't actually do anything till ten, and he appeared about nine thirty.

One day on a white-water rafting trip, we had gone ashore to see some falls and woodland scenery. The terrain was rough and because of my injured foot our guide Scott had the task of supporting me over the most uneven parts. Robin was scrambling along the track with a German student, who exclaimed, 'This Scott! What a cheerful, happy man he is!'

Robin replied, 'Yes, no wonder. That's my wife who is hanging on to him.'

There was a startled pause. Then the German's face cleared with sudden comprehension. 'Ah!' he cried. 'The British sense of humour!'

The white-water rafting experience in Kicking Horse Canyon was one never to be forgotten, with sudden drops of twenty feet and boiling witches' cauldrons − if glacier meltwater can be said to boil − and swirling, lethal vortices. We were told the danger index was four out of six; the definition of five being a fifty per cent chance of loss of life. I didn't enquire about any more definitions.

Then we spent a few days camping way up in the Rockies, miles from civilisation, journeying up on horseback and with mules to carry our luggage. There was a mix of ages and nationalities in our group of about twenty, all of whom enjoyed considerable bonding in those few days. We slept under canvas with extra warm sleeping bags as the temperature fell to zero at night. Going to the toilet at night was scary: you paused till you were sure that black shrub over yonder was not actually a bear. The skies at night were beyond description, so densely populated with stars because of the distance from any artificial light source. The food was excellent and abundant, and we were not required to do anything but enjoy ourselves. We played cards round the stove in the kitchen tent, or told stories and jokes round the campfire. At one camp, a grizzly had established himself close by, having killed an elk. We watched from a vantage point as he gnawed away at his carcase, and was challenged unsuccessfully by another grizzly emerging from the trees, so we witnessed a dramatic trial of strength between them.

22

Encounters with the Pale Horse

In the autumn of 1993 I noticed Grandpa Cook was becoming a little frail, and, observing especially that his ankles were very swollen, I persuaded him to see his doctor. The result of all this was as I had feared, that his cancer was re-emerging after a good two-year remission. Radiotherapy treatment was planned which I hoped would give him temporary relief. Driving wasn't easy for him, so I suggested he should stay with me on weekdays while he was getting the treatment. I was pleased to have him as he was always interesting and relaxed company, and we shared a little friendly rivalry over daily crossword puzzles. I made his favourite dishes, carefully avoiding those foods he thought he couldn't take, and generally fussed over him. He had no illusions, knew he didn't have much time left and talked equably of having had a good life.

Unfortunately the radiotherapy provoked some unpleasant side effects without having any significant beneficial result; the legs continued to swell and he became uncomfortable. He returned home and his deterioration progressed inexorably. Sadly, he was not well enough to come to us at Christmas and for the first time in the boys' lives we were just a foursome at this festival. We visited quietly in the afternoon with presents. I noticed Grandpa's speech was becoming indistinct and he was unsteady on his feet. He seemed to lose his tranquillity of mind and become anxious, looking for improvements that I knew would not happen.

In mid-January he was admitted to the Western General, where he was found to be in severe renal failure. In spite of this his mental processes remained clear almost to the end. Robin later discovered a crossword which he had half completed the day before he died. His doctors told me they could improve his kidney drainage temporarily, but this would only prolong his life for a short time while not alleviating his discomfort. When Robin and I visited, he awoke from an opiate-induced sleep with a smile, looked at us and said, 'I must be in heaven!'

And so he died very peacefully and was sincerely and profoundly mourned by his family. He wanted to be buried in Kirkcudbright, which was arranged and we gave him a very fine send-off. For the first time I met many distant relatives and it made one wonder why it has to be a funeral that brings kith and kin together.

It was to be a year of alternating sadness and celebration. Chris reached his twenty-first birthday in February. I bought him his first suit and Robin gave him a year's subscription to a racing club which involved being in a syndicate owning a racehorse; he claimed a tiny fraction of the animal. Robin once admitted to Princess Anne that his son owned a thousandth part of Mysilv, who was quite successful. Her Royal Highness was convulsed with merriment at such a modest pride of ownership.

On the morning of 12 May someone stopped me in the corridor at St John's. 'Have you heard that John Smith's been taken into hospital with chest pain?' No, I hadn't, but I assumed that they were just taking no chances, especially after his near-demise with the previous attack.

Later I spoke of this with a colleague, Stuart, still taking an optimistic line. He paused, said, 'I'm afraid you haven't heard the whole story. He's dead.'

The impact of this news, as for all his friends and associates, was felt at many levels. There was a feeling that one of the few men of true honour and integrity had been snatched from the political scene, which was several degrees poorer as a result. Thank God the demands of friendship and the effect of shock meant the deferral of the leadership battle for a decent interval. It seemed that all the world would be in Edinburgh that Friday to say farewell at John's funeral and I planned to accompany Robin; indeed I was privileged to be going.

But before then the fates were to deal another blow; isn't it odd how disasters come in runs of three? Coming upstairs from the clinic I was met by my secretary, looking anxious. My mother had been on the phone, sounding distraught and muddled. Would I ring back straight away? I dropped everything and did so. My father had collapsed that morning after a few days of mild malaise. Mum tried unsuccessfully to resuscitate him while simultaneously ringing 999. 'He's gone,' she sobbed. Privately I thought it was as well he hadn't survived with only half of his faculties intact. Mum sounded so agitated I made up my mind to go down to her immediately. In no time I organised staff cover, got the cat into a cattery, phoned Robin and was on my way. From Heathrow I planned to take bus and train connections, but to my delight Robin met me off the plane. He had borrowed a car from Anna, one of his assistants. After delivering me to Mum's house, he had to hasten back to London; we were both grateful to him. Jenny joined us the next day, and it was odd how, out of the blue, we had those few days together in a climate of emotional upheaval. We talked, remembered, re-established relationships, did little things for each other. Quite a happy time, in spite of the sadness. We helped to organise the funeral for the following week. Dad was an atheist but Mum had converted to Catholicism and her priest agreed to conduct the ceremony. I remembered most warmly Dad's unfailing courtesy, an undervalued quality, and the times when he had been especially strong and protective. Mum observed that he would be standing at the pearly gates between John Smith and Jackie Onassis who also died that week, which would be ideal as he'd have one to argue with and one to flirt with.

Letters from both my parents had been so frequent that I usually threw them out after answering them. With the most recent events of my life I have come to value letters so much that I shall never throw any away again. Very fortunately I have Dad's last two letters from March and April, talking about daily affairs and family, also his pleasure in our most recent visit, and an analysis of the Grand National runners and successes. Also there is a letter from Mum expressing much gratitude to both Robin and me for our support in her difficult time. These will go into family archives. Mum gave me a number of mementos, including Dad's RAF service medals and one of his pipes, the smell of which is incredibly evocative of his presence.

Both fathers died full of years and one shouldn't over-regret, but there was a significant contraction of my extended family. I supposed one should now start looking forward to the next generation.

In the aftermath of sorrows and funerals, I began to wonder about Robin's attitude to the leadership election. I well knew that his ambition was unbounded and he would want to be a contender. I had very mixed feelings. By now I had no illusions about the deleterious effect of his aspirations on our relationship, and really believed that our marriage would survive in name only if he were to become leader, or

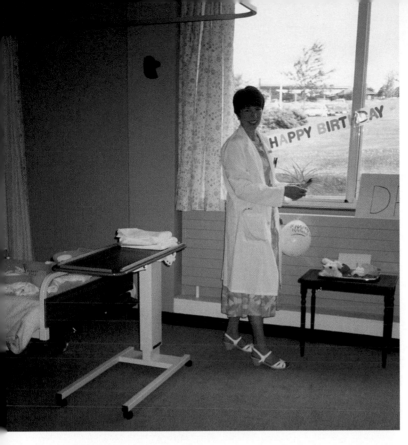

Fiftieth birthday
doesn't go
unnoticed,
St John's
Hospital,
Day Bed Unit,
3 August 1994

Fiftieth birthday party

Golden wedding celebration for Granny and Grandpa Cook

Golden Wedding Celebration for Granny and Grandpa Whitmore.
From left, Peter, me, Jenny, Derek (Jenny's elder son), Mum, Dad,
Chris and Robin in front.

Peter's graduation,
Newcastle 1996

Chris's graduation,
Aberdeen 1995

Water sports. Peter
on the offensive,
Sarthe, France

Breakfast at Helmcken
Falls Lodge, Canada
1993

With
Kate and
Iain on
the Great
Wall of
China,
1995

Peter and Robin
near Grenoble,
France 1995

Climbing in
Connemara,
1995

After a morning's ride in the Picos de Europa, Spain, 1996

In exalted company, on the royal yacht *Britannia*, Hong Kong 1997

Gorky, Gary
and Mike
painted for
hunting in the
Amazon forest

Taking a bath with pirhanas! Me and Sue in the Amazon

Prime Minister. There was a little of the natural wifely ambition to see my man in this elevated role; but it was vestigial by now. I did not believe, frankly, that he was the right person for the job. There was a lot of very foolish talk in the press about his lack of good looks, but this would not have mattered if he had shown greater capacity for relating to people. He had absolutely no natural courtesy or sympathy, and no awareness of the lack of these qualities, though his intelligence and ability were unmatched at Westminster.

He certainly did wish to stand as leader, but after interrogating various sources of information came to the conclusion that he did not have enough support. Those who believed in him did so very staunchly. But Robin was far too wise a politician to stand without a reasonable chance – maybe fifty per cent – of winning. For months afterwards, people in West Lothian would say that he was the obvious choice, and why had he not put himself forward? He sank into the deepest despondency. He was not a particular friend or ally of Tony Blair, still less of Gordon Brown, and would have to start forging links all over again. I had never met Tony, and knew next to nothing about him; indeed, it was my perception that he'd popped up from nowhere with little to recommend him other than a pretty face. I heard Robin speaking to him on the phone and was uncomfortable to hear how deferential and almost subservient he was. If I answered the phone to Tony I would be courteous but not effusive, and Robin would be annoyed that I had not shown greater warmth. Why should I? I asked crossly. I don't know the man. Besides feeling left out in the cold, Robin felt even more out of step with trends in the party.

Chris's dramatic activities led him to direct a production of *Macbeth* in Aberdeen. The setting was the atmospheric university King's Quad. Though it was summer time, we still needed rugs and flasks of coffee to keep us from petrifying for reasons other than fear as we sat on the cold stone steps. He and the Centre Stage group did extraordinarily well, making maximal use of the grey, forbidding environment. Then he was given a part in a Festival Fringe play, written by his friend, Steve Horobin: *That Falls at Eve*. They had a prime venue on Princes Street and very good reviews. The subject was the life of the poet James Elroy Flecker, and Chris played T. E. Lawrence (of Arabia). We were impressed. At one time, Chris had worried us with his ambition to become a jockey; I silently hoped he would not now throw everything over for the stage.

I was now approaching my fiftieth birthday though didn't feel my age in the least, and Robin offered to organise a birthday party. I liked the idea. We had left it rather to the last minute, and I was seized with fright that everyone would be away on holiday, and no one would come. We decided on a lunchtime party, a Sunday, so friends could bring their children. Chris and Peter undertook to entertain the junior element, Mum and Jenny came to stay, and Granny Cook was collected on the day. We were actually very glad to have an opportunity to use the magnum of champagne Robin had won with the Parliamentarian of the Year award, the opening of which afforded a dramatic moment in the garden, with a bucket to catch the overflow. We had caterers to organise the buffet, and Robin even laid on a birthday cake shaped like an ice-bucket with a bottle of champagne in it. On the wall he arranged a frieze of photographs of me through various ages and in a variety of roles and settings. It was very gratifying to be at the centre of such a celebration and I loved receiving my guests and being showered with cards and presents. All the friends there, many of whom I'd known for decades, were from my medical or horse-riding life, or family, or neighbours. No politicians, oddly; I suppose they weren't in my first circle of friends.

There was just one strangely discordant note, which I put down to Robin's lack of awareness of certain raw and tender areas. He made a little speech about me and my achievements, a witty and charming account with a few humorous tales. Then he finished up with the story of my unfortunate dressage disaster with Carrie; I heard the collective horrified intake of breath from my horsy friends, knowing what a blunder this was. I chose to smile and ignore it. To this day I'm not sure if it was crass insensitivity or a subliminal wish to degrade me.

Besides birthdays, this was the year of our silver wedding anniversary, which would fall in the middle of the summer holiday in Hungary. For the first time since 1973, Robin and I would be on holiday without one or both sons, and they were pleasantly concerned about how we would manage without them. Hungarian is easily the most difficult European language, and I made no progress with my phrase book before we touched down in Budapest. By some mischance our hotel was diametrically opposite the airport, on the other side of the city and the Danube, which Robin had to negotiate in the hired car without any assistance from road signs. I was amazed at his patience and courage as we got caught in a loop, crossing and re-crossing the river until I worked out how to extricate ourselves.

Like all our holidays it was packed with incident. On the metro in Budapest there is a complicated system of serial ticket purchase, and hefty fines if you are found without a valid ticket. Purely through failure to understand the instructions we were found wanting by a heavyweight bouncer who demanded our passports. At that very moment a passing student recognised Robin and overwhelmed him with voluble appreciation. I put on a confused and harassed tourist act, which was not far removed from the truth, so the policeman kindly explained the system, reduced the fine to a nominal one, and returned the passports. Turning to Robin, who was just bidding a magisterial farewell to his admirer, I thanked him for his support.

We left Budapest and motored into the countryside. Hungary was remarkably uncommercial, which was refreshing. Each household in the rural areas seemed to be protected by packs of ferocious dogs. We spent some days on a group horseback ride from Epona in the Puszta (or plain). The weather was ferociously hot and the land dry as a desert, but on the morning of our anniversary Robin still managed to arrange delivery of an enormous bouquet of flowers. We spent the evening of that day dining on the balcony of our hotel in Eger, overlooking the market square, vibrant with music and folk-dancing to celebrate the wine harvest. On more than one occasion we were enticed into wine cellars to sample locally made wine, which was excellent. In the heart of the countryside no one spoke English so we relied on my phrase book and smattering of school German.

We returned from Hungary in time for Robin to go to party conference. He was still glum and disillusioned. He talked of the paradox that Labour could well be on line to win the next election, and that he would then be in the cabinet, but he felt anything other than elated. Tony Blair's oblique reference in his conference speech to the abolition of Clause IV, his personal quandary between freedom and equality in regard to the schooling of his children gave Robin digestive problems. I tried to explore with him whether he should not think of making a break, return to the back benches, or even leave parliament altogether. He had long wanted the freedom to write; but he shied away from this option. He became shadow Foreign Secretary and sank further into misery, feeling he was being sidelined, while his long-standing adversary Gordon Brown was shadow Chancellor, the job he most coveted next to leader. He felt this job would take him far from the floor of the House which was the milieu he liked best. Nevertheless, having shouldered the job, he set about exploring its avenues thoroughly. Early in 1995 he embarked on a series of trips to all the trouble spots of the world: Bosnia, then Rwanda, then Moscow. For my part, I was quite excited about his new role, and looked forward to accompanying him in the future. I speculated on whether, when (or if) he became Foreign Secretary proper, I should drop some sessions and travel with him. His reaction was of alarm rather than pleasure, it must be said, but I didn't take too much notice of that.

My working life, which had been getting progressively more demanding, now went through a major crisis. My repeated and urgent requests for help were gallantly listened to and then ignored. Always there seemed to be some new initiative which put greater burdens on to already overloaded backs. There was a trend (very laudable, I'm sure) to formalise training arrangements for middle-grade doctors, and this meant that registrars had protected time for courses in blood transfusion and other areas, especially when exams loomed. I struggled along in the spring of 1995 largely without help while we encountered one of those unexplained mini-epidemics of acute leukaemia and related conditions which play havoc with statistics and almost persuade you that some malign influence is at work. When a holiday was almost due, I despaired of being able to leave the department in anything approaching an organised state to my recently returned registrar, and myself with a clear conscience. When colleagues know you are going away they tend to ask you, as a favour, to fit in this patient or that before you go; we all do this. But you sometimes wonder if it's worth going away at all: you have to jam in so much extra work before and after the release.

The stress I felt at this time made me fully aware I'd reached the end of my tether. I began seriously to look at the adverts in the *British Medical Journal*, wondering whether I could find another job that would not stretch me so painfully on the rack. Only a few years ago I had been so enthusiastic about my job that I'd planned to ignore the retiral age of sixty when it came. Now I began to despair that I'd even last till that watershed. One lifeline I did have, and that was the prospect of partial release if Labour did get into power in a couple of years. In that scenario I felt that my desperate plight would no longer be treated so slightingly. With the fluency of extremity I put my case yet again to our director of clinical services. I sat down with him over coffee, described in graphic detail all the multitudes of onerous and conflicting responsibilities I shouldered, confident that he would have to respond in some way to my cry for help. He listened. And did nothing.

The Easter break at Allum Green was a much-needed balm. I think it took me the entire first week to unwind and feel some release from the strain. The trouble was, you knew you had to go back and face the same problems again. It would not surprise anyone to learn that the strain extended to my personal life, but in fact that particular Easter, Robin and I were on our own and enjoyed a very close and peaceful relationship. He liked to go and look for deer in the dusk, so just to be friendly I went along as well. I was surprised at how well he knew where to find the different species of deer that inhabit the Forest. We had a particularly bewitching encounter one evening, when an albino fallow stag – pure gleaming white – showed himself, glowing like an unearthly apparition in the twilight.

I cannot fix the precise timing of the incident that should have told me without a doubt that he had embarked on another affair, but it was somewhere near the time when he became shadow Foreign Secretary. It was a repetition of the failing capability he had gone through at the start of the Thelma affair, only now he knew I would recognise the pattern and was at pains to conceal it. He became so stressed he was drenched with sweat. It was impossible to ignore, but the soft side of me didn't want to embarrass him. It was possible there was some less culpable explanation. I asked if there was anything wrong but he brushed my concern aside. Yes, I fully admit I was behaving like an ostrich; but who can blame me? Ever since 1987 I had been looking the other way. Whenever he met a woman who was prepared to indulge in a little flirtation, his body language was so explicit, especially if he didn't think I was observing. I think he'd have gone with anyone who was sufficiently compliant and presentable. But I didn't want to know, because one more affair would spell the end of the marriage, without a doubt.

Later in the summer I went with travelling friends Kate and Iain to China; we had met on the India trip in 1992. Robin had been politely asked to come too, but I knew he wouldn't, while parliament was sitting. I was not unduly sorry, for he never mixed well with my friends. He would never bother to put himself out to be sociable, and unless he could appropriate the conversation and hold the floor, rapidly became bored and showed it. This put a constraint on me, for I could seldom persuade him to come with me if I was invited to social gatherings, and if I did I often regretted it. I sometimes thought ruefully that I had all the disadvantages of a marriage and none of the advantages.

So it was better to enjoy my own friends without him. Our stay in China began in Beijing, in a sumptuous hotel; though I found that the veneer of luxury was rather fragile when things like plumbing went wrong. We visited Tiananmen Square (or the Square of Heavenly Peace), of huge interest following the events of 1989, and found it milling with people, including many members of the People's Republican Army, looking quite amateurish in their thin uniforms and sloppy plimsoles. An enormous digital clock ticked away the seconds till the moment when Hong Kong would become Chinese. We queued to have official photographs taken at the foot of the statue of Chairman Mao, with suitably solemn expressions. Some of the older generation still revered him, and wore the traditional Mao suits. We were not allowed to see the embalmed body of the erstwhile leader for some reason; they said because it was Sunday. I sensed a heightened tension at this point, and we were quietly asked not to take photographs of certain signs. Families sauntered in the immense square, always appearing to have their attention focused on the one child in the centre of each unit. The people were friendly, and very interested in us westerners. They were particularly fascinated by one lady in our group who was unusually tall and had a fine head of auburn hair. The Chinese liked to invite one of us to have a photograph taken in the midst of their family, which I thought was very hospitable. We visited some of the main historic sites such as the Forbidden City (or Imperial Palace), the Summer Palace, Temple of Heaven and other temples, wondering that they had survived the worst excesses of the Cultural Revolution. Though our guides told us a lot of history they tended to shy off recent events about which there was much ambivalence; but politics was discussed, especially the 'one-child' policy.

We travelled north to see the Great Wall and the summer hunting retreat at Chengde with its profusion of Buddhist temples and oddly shaped Hammer Mountain, reached by cable-car and an energetic scramble. Then on to Xi'an to see the immensely fascinating Terracotta Army, eerily on guard in their thousands with their horses, chariots and equipment. The thought kept occurring to me that all this effort and artistry had been undertaken for the mythical protection of just one individual; and though he was an emperor, I cannot conceive of how one man can be seen by another as so radically different and so vastly more important than himself. Philosophy apart, the army is an enthralling and awe-inspiring sight, and I felt almost that such heroic repetition of human images in clay could not fail to be accompanied by some spiritual manifestation. My fanciful illusions of course.

After Xi'an we flew to Shanghai where so many cultures and histories merged, and the visual impact was as colourfully exciting as anticipated: the Bund with its imposing British Victorian buildings looking out over the smoky river traffic on the HuangPu River; the teeming streets adorned with lanterns, banners and balloons where it was a wonder no one got lost; the watery, ornate gardens with dragon motifs at every turn. From here we were spirited by train to Suzhou, a centre of silk production and embroidery so exquisitely fine that most British samplers look clumsy and coarse by comparison. We were taken on a freshwater, pearl-fishing trip – decidedly precarious – and we kept any pearls and oyster shells we retrieved. From here we flew to Guilin, where on our first evening we joined the fishermen on the river, observing their highly skilled and ancient method of fishing with cormorants. Then we took an all-day river trip through the beautiful, mountainous and wooded scenery with characteristic steep-sided peaks and pinnacles, sometimes softly rounded, elsewhere sharply jagged.

And finally to Hong Kong for a few days, exposed to a very different culture with extremes of prosperity and dire poverty juxtaposed. We were eager to see and hear as much as we could with the handover being only two years away. After such intensive sightseeing we were very content to lose ourselves in the markets and indulge in shopping for gifts to take home. I found silk jackets and leather rucksacks for the boys, silk shirts and ties for Robin; and a number of gorgeous items for my summer wardrobe.

Then there were thirteen hours of exhausted sleep on the flight home.

23

Family Crises and Celebrations

The boys were really growing up. They would probably say they had already done so, and wouldn't think it relevant that they were still very dependent on their parents. But I was extremely proud of both of them, and in their thoughts and deeds they were everything I could wish for. Besides pursuing his studies and dramatic activities, plus his racing interest, Chris had got himself a holiday job at Burton's in Aberdeen, and also worked on Saturdays to eke out his allowance. I admired his application. Peter had also got holiday jobs, taking on catering work in and around Edinburgh. I knew from my own experience how tough these could be. This year, 1995, there were two important dates in our family calendar: Peter's twenty-first birthday in May and Chris's graduation in July. Peter got a new suit and a planned expedition in a hot-air balloon, apart from the usual jollifications. Robin and I would both attend Chris's graduation and Granny Cook was anxious to be there, but limited space meant she couldn't sit in at the actual ceremony.

The week preceding this big event, Peter left home at the crack of dawn on a bus trip which would take him across the Channel and down to the south of France, to Grenoble. Here he was to spend six months of his student life as part of his electronics course, mainly concerned with computer science. As always with him my anxieties were roused, though he was by now quite a practical and independent boy. But he was still quite reserved, and I wondered how he'd cope with communicating in French.

The following Saturday morning I arrived home from the stable to find Robin looking very concerned. He had had a phone call from Peter, who, within twenty-four hours of his arrival in Grenoble, had been robbed of all his cash, credit cards, passport and the few other valuable items he had with him. He was staying in a student hostel in a rough area of town and security was notoriously poor. Robberies and break-ins took place regularly when there was an intake of foreign students, and Friday night was favoured because the local police office apparently shut down for the weekend. Peter had, very fortunately, bought some provisions but he had absolutely nothing with which to identify himself, so sending a money order was completely pointless.

Robin hastened out to see if he could get hold of some French francs and send them off post-haste by the most expeditious method available.

As any parent will know, under these circumstances, you cannot disengage your mind from worry about your child. We were in daily contact by phone. Only on the Monday was he able to report the affair to the police. He was by now having to borrow money for phone cards, and beginning to run low on food. We hoped the money package would arrive soon – and safely. He'd also been in contact with the consulate in Lyons about a temporary passport, but all these thing seemed to take so much time.

And then with the old familiar pattern of crises never coming singly, something else happened. Late on Monday afternoon I was tidying up at work, anticipating being off on Tuesday for Chris's graduation, when the phone rang; it was Elis from the stable to say that Phyllis was having colic.

She had had this once or twice before, and it was most distressing. There are so many possible causes, and few diagnostic measures to give a clear answer. The present attack was not too severe but came in waves every few minutes, as colic is wont to do. I went straight to the stable after work where Phyll was standing with her head hanging, looking miserable. Every so often she would look round at her belly, then lie down and twitch and grunt. We called the vet who came and undertook various diagnostic and therapeutic procedures. She didn't improve very much and it was thought she might need to go to the Bush Field Station if matters did not take a significant turn for the better. No one mentioned grass-sickness, a frequently fatal scourge of horses, but it was in the back of people's minds.

I spoke to Robin on the phone; our plans till then had been to drive up to Aberdeen early the following day. Granny was to stay with friends, Robin would fly down to London after the celebrations, and I would return to Edinburgh with the car. When I explained to him about Phyllis his reaction was, I suppose, understandable. He said if I couldn't come to Aberdeen he would understand; they'd work out some different strategy for travelling; obviously I couldn't leave Phyllis in her present state, etc., etc. I nearly blew a gasket, that he should so totally fail to understand the awful nature of my conflicting responsibilities, even while I was completely clear where my priority lay. My horse I loved dearly and she was of the utmost importance; but my sons came first, and I would certainly be present at Chris's graduation. I was also determined that on his big day Chris would know nothing of the crises affecting Peter and Phyllis.

In the horse world you make some very good friends, and they can rise to supreme heights of support on occasions, usually having been in some similar predicament themselves. Liz and Moira, fellow horse-owners, realising that crunch-time for decision-making was likely to be early Tuesday morning, offered to take Phyll to the Bush and thus relieve me of an unbelievably stressful time-schedule. I left Phyll late on Monday evening, semi-settled; Elis got up through the night to look at her, and she was still not very happy. So in the morning she was packed off to the Bush, which was a partial relief, to have her in a medicalised environment.

I hadn't had too much sleep, but programmed myself as we set off to Aberdeen to be companionable and cheerful. I phoned for news of Phyll using the mobile, but there was not much information so early in the day.

Chris's graduation year coincided with the university's five hundredth anniversary and he was in good company, as the then Secretary General of the UN, Boutros Boutros Ghali, received an honorary degree. We sat in the historic hall admiring the stained-glass windows and appreciating the baroque organ music. Then the graduands processed in and I embarrassed Chris by catching his eye and aiming the camera at him. We all sang 'Gaudeamus Igitur', which I had never before realised was such a morbid little song in translation. It sounds better in Latin, full of youthful might and optimism. As Chris went up to have his hood arranged and to receive his degree certificate I feasted my eyes on him, wanting to retain the moment.

Then there was a quick sherry with the vice-chancellor and staff as Robin had been recognised, then we joined Chris for hugs and laughing photographs with his friends, followed by a genteel feast of champagne and strawberries. In the evening we took him and his girlfriend, Clare, and Granny for dinner. I am happy to say the photographs of me look remarkably carefree.

I drove back to Edinburgh that evening, arriving home after midnight. On the following day, Wednesday, news of Phyll was encouraging. She was much better and the colic had gradually resolved. News of Peter was most dispiriting. He sounded awfully depressed, poor lad; he was down to his last packet of pasta and no money had arrived. As far as I could gather, no one seemed to be doing much to help. My protective instincts swelled in my maternal bosom and I was furious that the university and the consulate had not been more proactive. I rang the consul at Lyons, only sixty kilometres from Grenoble, who was helpful enough, though inclined to stand on ceremony. We worked out a way I could get money through by Thursday at the latest, and also methods of expediting Peter's temporary passport. I arranged with Peter that if, when I rang on Thursday evening, nothing had happened, I would fly out to him on Friday. I would not have him face another weekend in dire need. I felt guilty every time I sat down to a meal, knowing that he was going hungry.

Aware that I might have to be in France, I arranged to collect Phyllis on Thursday afternoon and bring her home. Liz went with me, and it was good to see the mare back to her normal self. I had checked on plane times, arranged staffing cover and provisionally booked Muscat into her usual cattery. On Thursday evening when I rang Peter, he sounded cheerful; yes, thanks, all the packages and money orders had arrived and he had arranged to collect his temporary passport the next day. And would I excuse him rushing away, as he was cooking his supper? Of course I did, with relief and delight that not only were things resolved, but he did actually seem to have coped with the crisis without going to pieces.

There were sequels to this story. Peter and his friends caught some intruders in the hostel, possibly the same ones who had ransacked his room. There was a scuffle and a chase, in which Peter received a black eye. Amazingly, most of his stuff was eventually recovered. He had a photograph for his temporary passport taken with the black eye and a few days' growth of beard (his shaver having been taken), so must have looked a frightful thug. They complained vociferously about the hostel accommodation, many of the rooms not even having window locks, and were moved as a result to a safer, more respectable area.

I had one further domestic crisis: a tropical-style rainstorm caused a flood in our lane, and as I walked in the front door found my feet squelched on the carpet as if I were sinking into sodden moss. Somehow this seemed the merest nuisance compared with the agony over Peter and Phyllis; to say nothing of the problems elsewhere in the world.

Robin and I felt we should visit Peter for a morale-boost, after his trials and tribulations. We had trouble identifying a mutually convenient weekend. There was one early in August, when we had been invited by Derry Irvine (then shadow Lord Chancellor) to join him at his Highland home. But the invitation had not been confirmed, and since it had been made at a chance encounter in a pub some months previously, when our would-be host was full of the joys and maybe other things too, we assumed it had been forgotten, and went to Grenoble instead.

The night before we flew to France, Chris, Robin and I celebrated my birthday, first in one of a new wave of Irish theme pubs, then moving on to a French restaurant. I was feeling happy and carefree, having cast off the shackles of work for a weekend, and somehow contrived, with the help of our waiter, to have the entire dining clientele sing 'Happy birthday to you'.

The weekend in Grenoble was completely delightful. Peter was in good health and spirits. He had bought a bike to get around town, far and away the cheapest and most efficient mode of travel. It was steamingly hot; no one with any sense stays there in August. We indulged in a gastronomic weekend, enjoying the superb cuisine and wines. I ordered a *Crapaudine de Roger*, only later realising it was toad! Delicious, all the same. As a sop to fitness, we played some table tennis, and I was unbeatable by the other two, singly or together.

Chris was to be in Aberdeen for a further year, doing his diploma. This meant the two of them would finish their student life together in mid-1996. Meanwhile Peter had, unusually, failed an exam and had to return to Newcastle to do a resit in September. Robin hadn't had a summer holiday, so we planned a ten-day trip to Ireland: Dublin and countryside near Galway. We had previously felt deterred from visiting Ireland because of the Troubles and the possible threat to Robin, but now with the peace process begun, we were eager to visit. Chris was persuaded to come too, and as Peter was to return to Newcastle for his resit, he would also be able to join us for part of the time.

I have many happy memories of this time with all the family together, and we undoubtedly enjoyed an energetic and fun-packed holiday, enhanced in particular by the wonderful culture of pub folk music in Ireland. We stayed in a little village on the isthmus that lies between Lough Corrib and Lough Mask. Normally I wouldn't have admitted to anyone that there were also less happy moments. Now, I have to break with the habit of a lifetime and admit not just to those tiresome lapses of a husband which might after all have only amounted to the usual handful of matrimonial disharmonies. But I felt that there were barbs and slights which were the beginnings of a consistently deteriorating pattern of behaviour towards me.

It seemed as if he were driving a wedge between me and the three of them. Talking to the boys, he would refer to me as 'your mother' in the sort of tone that implies 'you can keep her'. He was provoking and contrary and then would treat me with exasperation, as if the fault were mine. Sometimes at mealtimes his conversation and eye contact were so firmly directed to the boys as to exclude me altogether. Once we were rowing on Lough Mask when a storm threatened. He immediately decided he would row to an island, and that come hell or high water he would get there. And he did, oblivious to the fact that the rain was lashing, the wind whipping, the lake treacherous, the distant shore almost invisible, and all of us cold and uncomfortable. It was this latter kind of behaviour, which was not unusual, which rendered the boys insensitive to his particular antagonism to me; at least I suppose so. They had grown so accustomed to me smoothing things over and not provoking him when he was being difficult, that they thought it was my continuing role in life.

Finally, at the usual reckoning-up at the end of our stay, I left it to him to work out the sums, aware that the balance of cash was in his favour. I wrote out the cheque; but something niggled away in the back of my mind. I returned to the sheet on which he'd done his rough reckonings, and discovered that he'd mixed up sums that I owed with sums that should be shared. He showed no remorse when I pointed this out, and did not deny that it was deliberate.

As Christmas approached and the boys were due home again, I did not want a repetition of his disdainful behaviour towards me, and I challenged him on the subject. In a mood of honesty he admitted he knew what I meant. He was much more distressed than me about the boys growing up and loosening ties, and attributed his attitude to this. I had reservations about this explanation.

The final weeks of Peter's stay in France were proving to be almost as much of a crisis as the first, since they coincided with the general strike, and it was not at all clear if he was going to be able to get home. There was even a threat that phone lines would be disconnected. Again I made up my mind that he would be home for Christmas even if I had to go and collect him. I worked out that one of us could fly to Geneva, hire a car, drive to Grenoble and collect him and return the same way; all to the tune of several hundred pounds. As it was, the strike collapsed in time for him to make it home by a more conventional route, to a warm and rapturous welcome.

Robin was invited by the local Labour Party at Kilwinning in Ayrshire to do the Immortal Memory at their Burns' Supper in January 1996. Since this was in Burns' own country, he rather liked the idea and agreed; he suggested I should go with him. Aware that our relationship had been a little rocky and that we had not had much time on our own, he thought it would be a good bonding opportunity, as we could stay the night in a hotel and have a leisurely return journey. I was pleased, and agreed to come.

It so happened that Granny Cook had spent some time in her early married life at Kilwinning and when she heard about the venture was quite effusive. She asked him to look up her old house, earnestly wished she could come – and of course he offered to take her also. Now when I heard this I was furious. Not that I minded Granny coming in principle, but I had only agreed to an evening that held no particular attraction for the sake of some time for us as a couple. I could hardly back out now.

Robin collected me from work on the Friday in question. I had been up since six to exercise the horse, and had worked through the usual demanding day with a bit of a scurry to get finished on time. But there was a two-hour drive in which to unwind and relax. As always I carried the phone.

Alas, Robin's feverish schedule had not included time to write his speech and he needed to do that on the way. I was told brusquely I would have to drive. With Granny smiling away in the back of the car I could only bite my tongue and submit. The weather was bitterly cold and beginning to snow. The route took us over the bleak stretches of Eaglesham Moor, where the light falls turned to blizzards which, combined with the treacherous state of the road, required every ounce of my concentration. Robin demanded complete silence so he could fix his mind on his speech, so there was not even the soothing effect of music available.

The supper, speeches and other entertainment went off as well as such things do. Granny, who is very sociable, enjoyed herself enormously, revelling as she always did in the reflected glory from her famous son. I was dead tired and looking forward to returning to the hotel, getting my feet up, contact lenses out, and the comfort of a large mug of hot chocolate. At the end, we were accompanied back to our hotel, and some of our hosts came in to have coffee. And more coffee. After a while, as graciously as I could, I excused myself and went off to bed.

The next morning, after a good long sleep, I felt vastly better and looked forward to a thoroughly unhealthy breakfast, one of the best reasons for staying in a hotel in my opinion. I thought, maybe we can now have a little of the proposed bonding. But as soon as he was awake he put on the TV racing channel, full blast.

We took Granny on her pilgrimage to places of nostalgia, then headed for home, stopping at the scenic village of Eaglesham to have a light lunch and a look at craft shops.

I was aware as Robin drove homewards that he was getting impatient, no doubt thinking of all the things he wanted to jam into the rest of the weekend. We had to return to St John's so I could pick up my car, and as we turned into the main entrance I told him where it was parked. This supposedly helpful and time-saving remark was greeted by a ferocious explosion.

'Don't bloody tell me where the car park is! I know my own f——— constituency!'

I was stunned by this totally unprovoked and violent outburst. He slammed the car to a stop. As I leaped out I had to restrain him from driving off before I could get my stuff out. He was seething with irritation and I was barely clear before he did one of his skidding starts, accelerating out of the car park in a way that must have had poor Granny's bones rattling.

I was angrier than I'd ever been, almost, thinking of the bonding weekend he'd proffered and the shambles it had turned into; also the way he had treated Granny, apart from anything else. And when we later met at home I gave him the brunt of my wrath for once.

But the unbridled and unreasonable nature of his temper was a new feature, and deeply disturbing.

The boys would finish their formal education in June, and were much occupied in looking for jobs. Chris had been applying to law firms for some months, and was beginning to feel uneasy at the lack of interest they showed in him. It seemed likely that his absence of legal connections and his state-school education worked in his disfavour. He told me that fifty per cent of the law school output each year did not get a traineeship, which was news to me; I thought they would all be virtually assured of the first step on the ladder. Peter also had definite ideas about what he would and would not do in life. It was an anxious time. I tried not to think of everything coming to a grinding halt for them, after so much effort and learning.

But at last, after interviews, nail-biting and tenterhooks, Chris got a traineeship in Edinburgh, starting in July, while Peter landed the option of two jobs, and took a post with Cellnet in Slough. I was so happy and thankful that they would not face the dreary depression of unemployment. With a light heart I took them on shopping expeditions and equipped them with basic wardrobes for the start of their working lives. As they tried things on I hovered, helping to match, assess and admire, creating a great deal of embarrassed consternation amongst the other (male) customers, of which I was totally oblivious.

With my working life still in overdrive, I visited one of the more sympathetic of our managers. Appreciating that his hands were probably tied by the feudal layers above him, I still made it clear that my on-call commitments were criminally excessive and must be addressed; and that I expected to be relieved of the demands by this time next year.

Robin, in his previous role as shadow trade and industry spokesman, had been actively involved in the arms-to-Iraq allegations. He had kept this particular brief, having made it his own, and it sat well with his current role as shadow Foreign Secretary. We were all riveted by the handling of the Scott Report and the unequal access, and were as determined as he was that he would create as much embarrassment as possible for the government in the ensuing debate in February 1996. He did not disappoint us. It was a bravura performance, Robin at his intellectual, analytical, caustic, articulate best. His greatest strength as always was his command of fact, but his position of unassailable moral rectitude from whence to shower his scathing arrows was the one he loved best; he dispensed accusations of arrogance, of failure of accountability, of misleading, of culpable secrecy. Here was the Presbyterian minister manqué in every line. We were enormously proud of him and lauded him to the skies when he came home that week.

At Easter that year he and I did not find the companionable harmony we had enjoyed the previous year. He tended to snore rather badly which disturbed me, so he just moved out to another bedroom for the rest of the holiday. After that there was no finding each other's wavelength. He would pick up things I'd said, simple uncomplicated things, and invest them with all sorts of meanings I did not intend. He would answer questions obliquely as if I had tangential sub-agendas. I found this habit utterly infuriating. I think, in these moods, the person he saw in my place was someone quite different: a projection of his own guilt feelings at whom he could direct his hostility. There was yet another ferocious and illogical outburst at a completely harmless remark I made. I was bewildered and unhappy but, as before, put most of his behaviour down to stress.

He spent a good deal of his time that holiday writing the speech he was to deliver at the Scottish Trades Union Conference in mid-April: a very radical speech, talking of how Labour must support the weak and the vulnerable, pledging also union recognition, an end to NHS Trusts and to the Private Finance Initiatives. He tried some of this out on me and I was enthusiastic. Possibly on that basis I excused some of his contrary behaviour. The preparation and delivery of this speech, which won a standing ovation, may have exorcised some of his ghosts, and was interpreted by some as keeping his claims open for high office in a future Scottish parliament.

Robin's London life for the past few years increasingly took him into contact with wealthy, famous and influential people, and he would tell me of various engagements and encounters he had enjoyed. Sometimes I would be perplexed at the lack of advance information I received, and asked, 'Did no one think of asking me?' He would reply, 'Oh, yes, but I never thought you would be able to come.' The fact was that I was never given the chance and it seemed he wanted it that way. He was a past master at keeping his own freedoms and flexibility and yet blaming me for adverse consequences. For instance he would grumble that the reason we never saw each other was because I was always at the stable with Phyllis, of whom he was keenly jealous.

But we received an invitation in April 1996 that he could not avoid sharing with me, and this was from Her Majesty the Queen, to dine at Windsor Castle. I was entertained by the wording of the missive. It would be a bit too dictatorial for the Queen to command you to be present; so she commands the Master of the Household to invite you.

I was naturally very excited about this and as usual had great enjoyment from buying my dress and planning the ensemble. We were given to understand that normally we would have been invited to spend the night at the castle, but accommodation was difficult in the aftermath of the catastrophic fire a year or two before. So we booked into a hotel in Windsor. With an hour or so before we needed to leave, Robin, as was his usual habit, snuggled down in the bed and was soon dead to the world. I bathed, washed my hair, put on make-up, got dressed, put on jewellery. Still he slept. I knew of old that if I got him up too soon I'd get the full blast of his awakening temper, but time was running short. To be late for the Queen's dinner didn't bear thinking about. At last I persuaded him to make a move, which he did with much grumbling. He had hired a car in central London from which three hub-caps were missing, so we looked a little out of place amongst the other chauffeur-driven cars!

We were ushered into a small drawing room by members of the household who were very good at creating an easy and pleasant atmosphere. After a little small talk and accepting a glass of juice (I was determined to be judicious about drinking), I noticed the seating plan for dinner. Now I had estimated that I would probably be the person of least consequence of the twenty or so present, who mainly consisted of Lords, Sirs and Ladies, with the odd Right or Very Reverend, and would be able to remain in relative obscurity while watching the fun. But when I consulted the plan I discovered I was sitting between the Duke of Edinburgh and Prince Edward, and directly opposite the Queen. Robin was as dumbstruck as me, but inclined to take it as a compliment to himself. He was sitting further down the table, next to Princess Margaret.

Momentarily I was seized with panic: why hadn't I marshalled a few fashionable conversation topics? Still, there was no time to do anything, so it was as well to relax and take what came. As we milled around the room a little bustle was heard. We were politely but expertly manoeuvred into some sort of line and the royal family wandered in, with little ceremony, to allow us to be introduced.

I had time enough to take in the richly royal and resplendent decor, furnishings and appurtenances; imagine what an acceptance of all this as ordinary must do to your perceptions. No wonder the royals seem out of touch. The guests were ushered into the dining room, closely followed by the royal family. There is a precisely observed protocol of conversation: you talk to the person on one side for two courses, then you talk to your other neighbour. Heaven knows who decides the initial pairings. I found myself exchanging smiles with Prince Edward, somewhat to my relief, as I thought he'd be less of a challenge than the Duke. He was affable and charming, perfectly easy to converse with. I may have breached protocol by talking too much. We chatted about the theatre which led me on to my sons: Chris's dramatic activities and Peter's reenactment group and political allegiances. I have little recollection of what we ate, and as I was aware of some rule arising from the assorted junk in my memory that you were not supposed to continue eating when a royal person has stopped, I suspect I didn't consume much.

When the time came to turn to Prince Philip I felt rather more confident, and he also was cordial and conversable. We talked about Edinburgh and the personalities who were associated with the university in the sixties. I mentioned the rector of our time, James Robertson Justice, or Sir Lancelot Spratt of the *Doctor* films, a formidable figure with a stentorian voice and crusty temperament. I had once had to visit Justice in a role-reversal situation, with him as patient, myself as doctor. In response to a question he roared in a manner truly reminiscent of Sir Lancelot, 'I do not smoke! What a disgusting suggestion!'

Anyway the Duke laughed uproariously at this story, at which point I caught Robin's bemused glance from the other side of the table.

Then the Queen led the ladies away so that the men could enjoy their brandy, cigars and dirty stories. Later we genteelly promenaded along the corridor where the librarian had placed books and pictures of historic interest and relevance to everyone present at the dinner. Princess Margaret talked with indignation of the stories in the press about the disruptive schoolboy expelled from his class, whose teaching needs were being met by a private tutor.

'He will make such progress, he will go way ahead of his peer group,' she asserted.

Before I could stop myself, I murmured, 'I hardly think so,' and was treated to a frosty stare.

'Of course he will.' The discussion was at an end, by royal decree.

I felt more at ease talking to the High Commissioner for Namibia and his wife. Later in the evening the Queen and Duke took their leave; Prince Edward had vanished but Princess Margaret hovered. I had read somewhere that she liked to hang around until the wee small hours. Robin said to me, 'Well, time to be going.' I murmured that we couldn't leave until she thought fit to go, which, perhaps finding us staid company, she did soon afterwards.

The following week we were invited to a huge banquet at Buckingham Palace for some state occasion. I found out about two days before, when Robin kindly told me that some official had very particularly asked if I would be present. Had I known in time, I certainly would have been.

Peter's graduation was a happy occasion, falling on a gloriously sunny day, and, in contrast to Chris's, free of coincidental domestic disasters. Peter in a smart suit, white shirt and silk tie, wearing his academic robes and mortar, was a fine sight, in keeping with a creditable 2–1 degree of Master of Engineering with Honours. We made a day of it – what the boys used to call a Womble day – with meals and other refreshment at every opportunity.

The shadow Foreign Secretary has access to certain pieces of classified information and it was thought appropriate for Robin to become a Privy Councillor and to be entitled 'Right Honourable'. He was gratified and wanted a family celebration, so I offered to take him and the boys out for dinner. We went to Lancers, a favourite Indian restaurant. Early in the evening I perceived that there was to be a repetition of his cruel marginalisation of me; I could hardly believe that he would be so discourteous on such an occasion, and it was also extraordinary how effectively he did it. I became rather miserable, but was often quiet so no one observed. They wanted to go for a drink afterwards. The last thing I wanted was to stand in a noisy crowded pub, and found the atmosphere oppressive. Robin went off to the bar to get a second round for the three of them; he was recognised by a woman at the bar and began visibly to revel in the chatting-up process. I couldn't bear it. I said to the boys I was finding the atmosphere a little claustrophobic and would go and sit outside. I thought I would rest for a few minutes on a bench outside, then go and find a taxi. However they all came not long after, Robin possibly realising he'd pushed me a little too far.

At the time I didn't appreciate how frequently these unpleasant manipulations were occurring. The pattern is much more obvious with hindsight.

24

Betrayal and the
Beginning of the End

With a few weeks' breathing space between academia and the rough; real world of work, Chris and Peter were both at home for a while that summer. Chris began working in July and looked for a flat in Edinburgh to share with two friends. He had discovered the advantages of sharing his home with female colleagues in the last year at Aberdeen, an arrangement that was unheard of in my student days. His prospective flatmates were Marion and Odette, trainee teachers, lovely girls of whom I became very fond. On occasions over the next year, Chris would bring them round for Sunday dinner and we also were treated to meals in their flat. Delightful, good-natured, with illusions still intact, and wonderful sense of humour, I found an especial pleasure in the company of the boys and all their young friends. Peter's job didn't begin until September, but he busied himself making contact with his future co-trainees, and finding somewhere to stay in Slough.

My birthday fell on a Saturday. We had long wanted to spend a day at a falconry centre in Perthshire, so that is what we did. The day was overcast and wet, not ideal conditions, as we headed north over the Forth Road Bridge. The boys and I were in good humour, Robin was rather silent. On arrival we met the team of enthusiasts (human ones), and after coffee were taken to inspect the resident falcons and other birds of prey, including a very fine golden eagle. There was a demonstration with some small birds, including, I think, a sparrow hawk, with an exciting dive-bombing pattern of flight. We clambered on to a Land Rover and moved off into the hills. Suddenly I remembered I'd left my phone back at the centre; I was on call as usual. It was obviously going to be a pain to go back and I paused, probably looking stricken and indecisive. Robin immediately took charge, saying in his voice of authority that sorry, but we'd have to go back; his wife was a doctor, on call etc., etc. It sounded much more incontrovertible coming from him. So we returned and retrieved the phone, to my relief.

The rest of the day was energetic and fascinating. We were given gloves and taught how to handle the birds, how to launch them in flight and how to receive them back. I'm sure I'm not getting the jargon right. We did some hunting, mainly for rabbits. We had a picnic out in the open, then watched some of the larger birds hunting, including the golden eagle. Our hosts felt that he had not hunted with his usual aggressive dynamism, and therefore we needed a little extra entertainment to get our money's worth. So our guide gave us a demonstration of the Land Rover Discovery as an off-road vehicle. Certainly he pushed it to the limit, driving over rough hilly terrain and up almost vertical gradients. The boys and I loved it, Robin looked a little pale. Then, as I owned a four-by-four vehicle, he let me drive for a bit, keeping to the track at first. Looking ahead, I could see the downhill slope plunging into a valley of mud and water of apparently impassable density. 'Just go on,' said the guide. The hazardous stretch of mire came to meet us, but apart from slithering about a bit, the powerful vehicle ploughed on through it.

Robin had been silent and withdrawn throughout the day, not taking his share with the bird-handling and not responding to the collective enthusiasm and bonhomie. It was obvious that he had something on his mind. I preferred not to know about it. There could be some dire financial disaster looming, but much more likely was some further jealous altercation with Gordon Brown or a spat with some other rival. The boys were accustomed to his moods, and let him alone. We finished the day with a dinner in one of the trendy restaurants opening up around Leith docks, and Robin continued glum and moody, which did not deter the rest of us from enjoying ourselves. At least I was not shut out this time.

The following day, Sunday, 4 August 1996, was the day on which the fates decreed that my life should begin to come apart. I had no forewarning. I had not then even observed his more consistently contrary and difficult behaviour as I've described it. I was doing some desultory tidying up in the kitchen.

Robin came in, shut the door. He said, with no preliminaries, 'Margaret, I'm afraid I've done it again. I've been having another affair.'

I stopped in my tracks. This was the explanation of the dour mood the previous day. I looked at him, not saying a word.

'It's with Gaynor, my secretary. It's been going on for two years now. It's very foolish and I've wanted to end it many times, but she just won't let me. Oh, and by the way, I'm afraid the press have got hold of the story.'

I said, without emotion, 'Well then, you are the most frightful shit, aren't you?'

He embarked on what sounded like a prepared speech. He did love me, he wanted to grow old with me. He had planned to confess at the end of our forthcoming holiday, but found he was unable to keep it to himself.

At this point Peter came charging in. Robin said, would he mind leaving us for a bit, we were talking business. Peter said, Oh, sure, and vanished, without a clue as to the nature of that business. Robin continued, he and Gaynor had been spotted going into some down-market hotel by a porter who had reported it to the press. They didn't have much of a story to go on. Apparently some reporters had been bothering Thelma also, his love from nine years ago, so clearly someone was trying to piece together a sleazy sex story. It could break at any time.

'And that's why you've told me,' I interjected.

He thought the story might be kept until the run-up to the general election next year, for maximum embarrassment.

I was too stunned to marshal my thoughts and feelings; but of one thing I was quite certain: I told him that this spelled the end of the physical side of our marriage. When I had worried about his fidelity in recent years, two thoughts had persuaded me that he would be mad to go astray. One was the thought of press exposure and humiliation: I believed he would never expose himself to this risk. The second was the thought of passing on infection to me. He brushed this aside as beneath his notice.

I didn't begin to understand his mindset, or how his capacity for feeling and sensitivity to others than himself had been so disastrously corroded. I thought he still retained some affection for me, and some feeling that the marriage, which was central to our almost sacred family unit, was important and must be safeguarded. As subsequent events showed, none of this mattered to him any more. I assumed that at the very least he would want to save his marriage for the sake of keeping the voters sweet. I now think that if I'd had hysterics and thrown him out he would have been better pleased, for the fault would then have been mine, I suppose; he would have drawn sympathy, would have had time to restore his gravitas before the election, and the affair would have looked more respectable.

But I never do react with hysterics, and take my duties seriously; and though the marriage was but an empty shell, still it was central to the family and I could not do anything to damage it.

There was little chance for further discussion, with the boys in the house. He may have wanted to be protected from bitter recriminations, and took himself off to London that night.

Now the following Saturday he and I were booked to go off to Spain for our holiday. I continued to feel numb and unable to reach any kind of decision about our future, going through my daily routine on auto-pilot and as always not being able to share my burden of misery with a living soul. I didn't see how we could go away together, but if we didn't go then events would decide themselves. We'd have to explain the change of plan to family and friends; and then the marriage would unravel of its own accord. I could not begin to imagine how Chris and Peter would react to their father's serial and callous infidelity.

I could not find the motivation to pack or prepare for the holiday. On Friday evening we came face to face again, this time just the two of us. He must have been dreading it. I looked at this sorry figure with contempt and he quailed in front of me. I told him that I couldn't see any way out of the morass and was miserably unhappy. Things had gone so horribly wrong and there was no way they could ever be made right again. I didn't want to go to Spain with him, but still less did I want to stay home and face the consequences. I didn't know the person he had become: he had coarsened and hardened and lost all the sensitive, soft, interactive and feeling parts of his nature. He agreed; he recognised what I said as the truth. It was strange how in the total collapse of character there were still glimpses of the good that had once been there: this instance of insight and frankness, for example, and the moment the previous week when he'd recognised my distress about forgetting the mobile phone and put it right.

We decided that going to Spain was the lesser of the two evils. At least it gave time for cooling off, a space to think. I understand the origin of the phrase 'with a heavy heart', for there was a dragging sensation in my breast and a feeling of being perpetually on the verge of tears, which lasted most of the journey. But the very British, self-imposed necessity of not showing your emotions in public ensured I did not break down. By the time we arrived in Santiago de Compostela and had collected the car, I felt more composed and able to converse in an everyday manner. It was odd how habits of a lifetime took over. I spoke to him courteously as I had always done. We had separate beds, which was fortunate, and there was no touching of course, no hugs or kisses or expressions of affection. There was plenty to do and see and my smattering of Spanish was put to good use, for not much English was spoken.

We took our breakfast in a little courtyard where one morning we found our waiter chasing a rat with a hefty stick, and I found myself convulsed with laughter. It was hardly credible. Such are the natural powers of mollification and healing.

After a few days we drove to León, part of the way in reverse of the pilgrims' route to Santiago. Indeed we saw some pilgrims walking along the road. I changed some money and only realised some fifty kilometres further on that the bank had given me the equivalent of dollars, not pounds (my traveller's cheques being American Express). In León I reported this to the central bank, with some difficulty as they only had one English speaker, and they very courteously corrected the error. We stayed at the very splendid Parador Hotel in León, and found a sports centre for swimming and tennis, with which activities we almost miraculously slipped back into the old easy ways of companionship with no lack of topics to talk about, though not yet touching on deep or weighty matters.

For the middle week we had rented an apartment in a tiny, picturesque hamlet perched high up on a mountainside in the unbelievably beautiful Picos de Europa. This was planned as a less active, more contemplative sort of week, to relax, commune with nature, sketch, read, ramble, eat, drink and sleep. It was not exactly ideal in our present situation as there was rather too much time to think. We occupied separate rooms by mutual consent. I thought how happy I could have been here in a more contented frame of mind. Some days needed to be filled; and so we took the cable-car at Fuente De and pursued a rocky, clambering walk. Incredibly we got to a sufficient height to find pockets of snow in the crevices. Robin, as always, had planned a scramble that was far too ambitious for our level of fitness and agility: he wanted to reach the spectacular Mount Naranjo de Bulnes, much beloved of mountain climbers because of its almost vertical gradients. We arrived at a clifftop with a view of this mountain, and it was clear that the next stage would be a very steep downward climb, using a cable that had been stapled to the rock for a hand-grip. We would therefore have to tackle this in an upward direction on the return journey. I told him that this was as far as I was prepared to go. End of discussion. Left to his own judgement he would have pushed himself (and me) to a state of dangerous exhaustion.

We also went for a morning's ride, mainly to see the breathtaking mountainous views. On the Continent I have seldom found horses' welfare maintained at the standard expected in the UK, and I was distressed to see some riders galloping on hard tarmac road. We went on a gentler amble, but the escorts observed that we were riders, and offered to take us for a gallop; I insisted that we only did this on soft ground. Robin was recognised by an English couple who asked if they could take our photograph. For this we stood with our arms about each other, and I wondered if they might be reading about our split in the papers in a week or two.

The spectacular Cares Gorge provided another day trip, where the road is little more than a horizontal notch, a single track, carved in a vertical cliff-face – with no barrier between your car and open space. This was terrifying enough, but when we had to pass another car, courage failed me. I actually got out while he performed this manoeuvre. We parked the car and proceeded on foot, which was much less stressful.

There was a strange incident, into which I may be in some danger of reading too much. One evening in our mountain eyrie, after dinner, I was occupying myself with some needlework and asked if he would read to me. He assented, producing a book of poetry; and read 'My Last Duchess' by Robert Browning.

In this sinister little poem, a nobleman shows off a painting of his last wife, who is now dead. From his chilly dilettantism you gather that she displeased him, as he hints at suspicions of her infidelity and lack of discernment of his value, in some way injuring his pride and rousing his jealousy. And now she has been disposed of, with a strong hint that he authorised her end, as he negotiates with the agent of the father of his next prospective duchess.

> Oh, sir, she smiled, no doubt,
> Whene'er I passed her; but who passed without
> Much the same smile? This grew; I gave commands;

Then all smiles stopped together. There she stands
As if alive.

I had never encountered this poem before, and was amazed that in our present circumstances he was tactless enough to read it to me. Did he not see any parallels? Was he trying to implant suggestions, fear even, in my mind? I quickly put it out of my mind, but recalled it a year later. Reading again the clever portrayal of this hard and haughty man, one other impression is left on one's mind: and that is apprehension for the fate of the next Duchess.

In the quiet of the night, I thought at length about what I should do. Assuming I decided to leave him, I took myself through the steps I should take. I'd ask for compassionate leave, then see a lawyer, talk to the boys, to members of my family. Then I'd go back to work. If I told a few key people, the grapevine would do the rest. I found it impossibly difficult to think of myself as a divorcee, a person who's failed in that most important relationship. Like so many people, I just never believed it would happen to me, in spite of all that had come and gone. Thank heaven for my job and my independence. Thank heaven that I'd never been tempted to rely on his income and so relax my commitments. Because of his instability and unreliability I had never been persuaded to drop my work, or any part of it.

Then at other times I could not bear to face this tragic destructive scenario, and would desperately consider if we could continue as man and wife. On one thing I did not waver. I would never be a wife to him again in the physical sense; never. The very thought was repulsive.

It was clear that we would have to talk soon, so I determined that when we moved on to Haro in the Rioja would be soon enough. If we decided to part, it would be as well to do so near the end of the holiday.

We left our apartment and drove to Potes to leave the key. I dropped Robin off, then because of a traffic jam I had to drive away, turn around and return; all of which took five or ten minutes in the busy Saturday hubbub. He thought I had left him in the lurch, bereft of passport, tickets, money and belongings. We actually laughed over this. Such an idea would never occur to me, more's the pity.

After we booked into the Parador Hotel in Haro, with its monastic architecture, I gave notice that we should talk. We had barely started before I was in profuse tears, the pent-up sorrows of weeks past. He leaped up to close the shutters, afraid of people hearing. He then asked humbly if he could come and hug me; to which I nodded. The physical contact was comforting and may have influenced the immediate outcome of the discussion. He had found it very difficult to cope with the absence of any show of affection. We talked frankly. He had observed with sorrow elderly couples contentedly holding hands, and had thought, I shall never do that. We decided to stay together, to try to improve our relationship. He would give up Gaynor, that was understood. At the time I thought of her as a trivial symptom of our disorder, not really a serious rival. He spoke of our difficulties as if I were equally responsible. He also informed me, rather brutally, that he had no intention of going through life as a celibate, and that our mutual recuperation would depend on a full married life. Thus the guilt was transferred to me for denying him sex, rather than being his for dispensing it so freely and promiscuously. I kept my counsel on this issue.

So that bizarre holiday ended with more harmony than it had started with, and the least glimmer of optimism. I went back to work, Robin prepared for party conference and we went on much as before. He certainly didn't come and say he'd finished the affair. But he treated me with more respect and kindness than he'd done for months or even years. So perhaps that was progress.

I must now go back a little way and talk about Phyllis, who was now nineteen years old, quite an elderly lady, and who had become rather stiff and arthritic and had stopped competing after a period of declining performance. All the same, she had won a points championship as recently as 1995. Instead of schooling I would nowadays take her out hacking in the countryside, often accompanied by Liz on her handsome grey Arab, Bean. We would explore lovely stretches of riverside, woodlands and parks, sometimes disturbing birdwatchers and fishermen, observing all sorts of wildlife and seasonal glories such as carpets of snowdrops or bluebells, wild orchids, profusions of lacy cow-parsley in summer, moist shiny blackberries in autumn. Sometimes we would box up the horses and take them up to the wild heathland of Lanarkshire and have a good gallop. We also discovered the beach at Dunbar, adjacent to the John Muir Country Park, a perfectly idyllic place, for which we acquired riding permits. Cantering along through the incoming waves was exhilarating fun. We usually tried to bring some earth-bound people to help cook a barbecue: a motley crew of husbands, sons and girlfriends.

Since the boys were now financially independent, more or less, the time seemed right to think about another horse. Chris and Peter thought the idea of being replaced by a horse was hilarious – but characteristic. With not too much delay, I found the horse of my dreams: a four-year-old, sixteen-hands bay gelding, half thoroughbred, half Dutch. Linda, a talented and discerning rider, came to advise, and liked him. His official name was Dutch Kindred Spirit, and I called him Sparrow for short. Robin agreed to come and help me collect him one Saturday. Boxing can be a dodgy business with a youngster, but he was very amenable on that occasion. As we drove away feeling waves of relief that we'd got him successfully on board, Robin's phone rang. It was Tony Blair. In high good humour Robin described the role of horse-husband he was playing.

Sparrow needed to be exercised every day, though Phyllis didn't require so much attention, and I was aware that this would prove very demanding. Sparrow went through a phase of very boisterous, naughty behaviour and I began to think I'd bitten off more than I could chew, especially as I continued to ride at seven in the morning, when no one else was about. Linda, bless her, actually came over to give me a hand at this ungodly hour until we'd got things sorted out. Even so, he could be a bit of a tyrant, and some of the stable girls were frightened of him. I lost half a stone in weight about this time with all the increased activity. It's important to take a young horse out hacking and I was delighted at how good and bold he was. Liz and Bean accompanied us, especially when we had to go in traffic, Bean being an excellent schoolmaster; but Sparrow was sensible enough on his own too. Once as we all four set out, an ominous black cloud loomed ahead. In no time, hailstones as big as hazelnuts were clattering round us and bouncing on the horses' backs. Then the thunder began to growl and forked lightning pranced around the horizon. Sparrow trotted calmly on, only reacting with a little flinch if the lightning zigzagged immediately in front of him. When we returned to the stable I asked, 'Where's the search-party then?' They replied, with the robust logic of horsy people, 'Oh, we knew you'd have come back sooner if you'd been in trouble!'

With Christmas approaching, I looked forward to our usual family gathering. Peter would be home for a fortnight and Chris would forsake his flatmates for the same duration. I was confident that Robin was sufficiently chastened not to go back to his old inhospitable habits. I have always loved the planning and preparation that go into Christmas gifts, also the exchange of cards and letters with long-established friends. When the boys were small they were allowed to carry all the presents from whatever hiding place I'd used, and arrange them under the tree; with a surreptitious feel and attempt to guess the contents if they so wished. Now that they chose and even bought most of their gifts, I still wrapped them all, so that there was a sea of parcels spread out enticingly on Christmas morning. Granny once said to Robin that she thought I must have had a very deprived childhood judging by my munificence at this time.

For whatever reason, I had already bought two very lavish gifts to put under the tree for Robin: a set of painted chessmen and a night-scope. The latter is a form of telescope that can be used in the dark for wildlife-watching.

In early December he had to be in Dublin for some official function and suggested I should go along with him, in our renewed spirit of mutual support. This was a terrific idea, as I'd loved Dublin when we were there the previous year, and it was an exciting shopping centre. Although he had engagements, he found time to come round the town with me, and bought me a beautiful soft leather coat for Christmas. As we talked over coffee in Foyle's, the bookshop, I began to feel almost content and secure. Perhaps things could come right after all.

At home only a day or two later, a Sunday, Robin was moody and restless. I asked if anything was wrong.

He asked, rather belligerently, 'Am I going to be celibate for the rest of my life?'

My heart plummeted. I replied, untruthfully as it happened, 'I thought you'd still be carrying on your affair.'

'Well, of course I am.'

We were back at 4 August again; only worse, because there was now no protestation about his affection, only antagonism. And absolutely no attempt to carry out his commitment of breaking off the affair.

He then stood up, with arms folded, and, as if discussing a choice of television programmes, asked, 'Don't you think it would be better for us to go our separate ways now? We've drifted apart, we have different lifestyles. We should face up to it.'

This was two weeks before Christmas, with both sons coming back from their first jobs and looking forward to the security of a loving, happy home and family, and both of them assuming this still point of their turning world would continue as before; and Robin was prepared to destroy all this at a stroke. I was utterly devastated, more torn apart even than in the summer.

He hadn't expected this reaction. Without much warmth, he said again he would end his affair with Gaynor; he would return on Tuesday and confirm he'd done so. He did return, and yet again gave me to understand that all was over between them. He then expected me to shower him with gratitude and adoration. I didn't, I was still too upset. How could I trust him? How could he expect me to believe he would keep his word when she continued as his secretary? He said, wretchedly, he couldn't sack her; and I perceived that she could make life very unpleasant if he treated her badly. Possibly there had been threats. I didn't know, and didn't ask. He admitted also he was afraid of me, but would not spell out why; but it is an emotion that I believe is incompatible with love. His behaviour was very cold, and we were still at odds with each other.

Eventually I said, wearily, 'Let's please get through Christmas as if things were normal. Then you must tell Chris and Peter. If there's to be a revelation in the press, they must not find out like that. We'll talk again then.'

So we shelved the problem. It was not a happy Christmas for me, but the boys' presence was a comfort, and enabled me to put on a brave face. I found an especial poignancy in certain moments, like the Malcolm Sargent Carol Concert at the Usher Hall, which in my state of heightened emotion moved me almost to tears.

The end of the fortnight came, the boys went back to their respective flats. Nothing was said. We celebrated Hogmanay in a quiet way with neighbours. Parliament went back in mid-January and we all got on with our lives as before. Looking back, I believe he was manoeuvring with the intention of provoking me to make the split. He found himself in an impossible situation and this was the only way out that gave him a chance of saving his face. I didn't understand this at the time. The general election was on the horizon and I assumed he would prefer an intact marriage, so, perhaps in a rather undignified way, I hung in there. We saw relatively little of each other, and when we did, were coolly polite. There were no attempts at bonding; indeed he didn't have the time. Before Easter I spent a few days in the New Forest with

Peter, staying at the High Corner Inn. I didn't offer to help with the election campaign but agreed to come to the count, as my absence there would have been remarked. I told him of my hurt when he failed to acknowledge me from the platform at previous counts, and suggested some reference might be appropriate. The campaign was uneventful, and it became clear that the press were pro-Labour, and so presumably for that reason he was safe from embarrassing revelations.

25

The Acme of a Political Career

On 1 May 1997 I exercised Sparrow and did my day's work as usual. Robin and I dined together at Houston House in Uphall, enjoying an amicable if somewhat subdued meal, then set off in my car for the count. As I drove, he turned on the news for the exit polls, which were as optimistic for Labour as all through the campaign. Neither of us exulted; we seemed quelled by world-weariness.

It is best to occupy the hours of enforced waiting, which I did with counting random samples of votes coming from all quarters of the constituency, occasionally stopping for a chat with Jim, Robin's agent, and other supporters. I always tried not to trouble Robin too much as other people liked to have some of his attention on these occasions. There was never any doubt about the result, which was ready to be announced by three in the morning. Spouses are generally expected to go up on the platform, but he made it very clear that he didn't want me there with him. He was effusive in his speech to his workers and voters, and thanked his wife and family for putting up with his frequent absences. I wasn't altogether sure this was better than nothing.

However I congratulated him warmly and joined in the grinning, waving, exultant poses for the cameras. Shortly afterwards Robin sped off to catch a plane for London with Jim, as he wanted to be present at the Festival Hall for the celebrations there. I was not invited. I steeled myself not to feel hurt about this. I knew that I had not been a wife to him for the past nine months, and for him this would be reason enough to treat me distantly. I later saw television coverage of Tony Blair's arrival at the Festival Hall, greeting Neil Kinnock with emotional bear-hugs; and there in the background was Robin, bobbing about, smiling and trying, not very successfully, to be part of the in-crowd.

For the rest of that night I stayed glued to the television, feeling there was plenty to exult about if I put aside my personal difficulties. The end of the self-seeking and dilapidated Conservative administration gave renewed faith in the massed electorate to make a worthwhile decision: to make Scotland a Conservative-free zone, and the health service still salvageable – this was enough to keep me cheerful as I eventually lay down for a few hours of exhausted sleep.

Over recent months I had come to expect that Robin and I could settle down into a brother–sister relationship, one in which I would be prepared to be warm, supportive and even affectionate, but no more. Perhaps this would involve looking the other way if and when he found release with other women, as no doubt he would, and superficially maybe we could display a harmonious relationship.

But from his attitude to me it was crystal-clear that this would not do. He treated me with a sorrowful distance, almost as you might expect of a man whose wife had betrayed him, but whom he did not want to expose. The old guilt transference again. I knew my position as at present was untenable. As a powerful and public figure, he would have the capacity to humiliate me most cruelly, and I felt sure he would do so because he had done it before.

Driving home from the stable on the Sunday after the election, I mulled over these things. I felt bitterly sorry that in this moment of triumph for Labour we could not share our mutual delight. And, further, I knew enough of the demanding role of a cabinet minister and the intensely structured lifestyle, as well as the media attention, to believe that he would find it impossible to continue his affair. If he was not having marital relations with either me or his mistress he could be in serious difficulties and might act foolishly in a state of deprivation. By the time I arrived home I had not consciously reached a decision.

In the kitchen I put the kettle on to boil for coffee before going to wash away the sweat and stable smells. Robin sauntered in. I put out my arms to receive him, and we hugged, though not for long. With his now customary injured air, he tried to extricate himself, but I gently held on, and he allowed me. So we stood, pressed together for some minutes.

He murmured in my ear, 'This is nice.'

Then after a while, 'I don't suppose we could go to bed, could we?'

Without releasing him, I replied, 'I should require some reassurance first.'

His only response was: 'Yes.'

I realised the time was not right for talking, and I should seize the moment. So, without another word, we went upstairs.

His delight in our rehabilitation was considerable and unfeigned. He began to make plans and to press me urgently to keep time for him at weekends.

'We must be sure and keep at least one day a week for each other,' he said.

Badminton Horse Trials took place the following week, and he was enthusiastic about going. A full four days' attendance was out of the question, but we could certainly manage Saturday, cross-country day, and spend two nights in Bath. Meanwhile, his job of Foreign Secretary had been confirmed and I had been introduced to some of his team of bodyguards – whom he referred to as his gunmen – and drivers.

A few days before the election I had accosted one of the managers, reminding him of our verbal agreement over a year previously that my burden of on-call work would be addressed. Although some ineffectual attempts had been made to find a solution, nothing had been carried through. I now announced that I would withdraw altogether from doing on-call at the end of June. I have the utmost sympathy with workers who by the nature of their work are severely inhibited from taking any form of industrial action, and who are finally pushed beyond the limit of human endurance to take that very step. I sympathise, because I have been there. I had the support of my colleagues.

The response was as gratifying as I could have wished. Every manager who had previously brushed me aside sat up and took notice. Dialogue was begun with haematologists in Edinburgh, who quite rightly gave notice to our hospital managers that, while they were prepared to give me support, would not do so open-endedly. St John's haematology department was understaffed for the workload it carried and this must be addressed rationally. They would expect to hear of plans to do so. Another major development was that I would be allowed locums for medical staff holidays in future.

At the end of the week I flew to London and was met at Heathrow by Robin and Paul, the bodyguard. While waiting for my suitcase we sat and had coffee. Paul sat at a discreet distance unless drawn into the conversation. I related how I had fallen off Sparrow that morning in an uncontrolled moment, and we joked about this. Paul asked if I knew Robin's blood group. It is apparently customary to take a unit or two of donor blood for the Foreign Secretary's use in an emergency on all trips abroad, but especially those to troubled spots like Bosnia. Robin had been a donor once, but had lost his card. I promised I would take a sample and get it checked at St John's; for which service I would not charge the Foreign Office. However I had many questions about this practice. How was the blood stored? Who would perform the crossmatch if the blood was to be used, and under what sort of conditions? No answers were forthcoming, though I assumed some prestigious blood transfusion department had been involved in determining the procedure.

Then we joined the car, which of course had privileged parking, drove in style to Bath and checked into the hotel. I noticed that Paul did not carry any baggage, and Robin explained that he had to keep his hands free to grab his gun if needed. Paul related how he had once stayed for a protracted spell in this hotel when he was protecting Salman Rushdie. I had much to learn with this new culture: for instance that the usual rule of ladies first did not apply; also that for his protection Robin had to sit behind his gunman in the car. I perceived that though this system of protection could become irksome, it could also convey an exaggerated notion of care, a sort of nanny security, which could inflate the recipient's self-esteem; a false notion, because of course the protection is for the role, not the individual.

We then dressed and were driven to a favourite restaurant. And Paul came too. To my considerable amusement, he was accommodated at a table some distance from ours; but he was discreet and tactful, and presumably had to diversify his attention. I was in good spirits. I think it was the first meal we had sat down to together since polling night. Conversation between us was lively, and I thought no one would imagine our relationship was of over thirty years' duration. I had a feeling of rejoicing, of regeneration such as I had not felt for many months.

Next morning we set off early, expecting busy traffic on the roads converging on Badminton. Paul supplied me with programmes and identity badges, thus really fulfilling a nanny role! On arrival we were met by a carload of local Special Branch men who also, it appeared, felt obliged to protect the Foreign Secretary. They were disguised in the obligatory waxed coats and green wellies, but somehow stood out like sore thumbs, particularly one man who was about six feet six and proportionately broad. They didn't have Paul's knack of merging discreetly into the background; indeed we were hardly aware of his presence all day.

With a couple of hours before the action started, Robin and I went to look at the trade stands, which at Badminton really are worth visiting, especially if you are in spending mood; which we were, of course, still feeling renewed and ebullient. We indulged in an orgy of celebratory spending, items of dress and artistic pieces for his official residence at Carlton Gardens. I wanted a winter coat, and when I found a smart navy garment with leather trimmings, very expensive, he offered to buy it to put away for my birthday. We left a trail of items to collect, hoping to remember them all at the end of the day.

On the cross-country course we liked to select a number of the more difficult fences and watch a few horses at each, observing the different ways of tackling the obstacle. The gap between fences could be a significant stretch which we usually chose to cover at a sprint so as not to be passed by too many riders on the way. Every time we broke into a run, so did the three security men. We must have presented a comical sight to an onlooker. The weather was pretty awful, with heavy showers, though this did not in any way dampen our spirits. About halfway round the course, the ground being wet and slippery, Robin's feet slid from under him and he fell flat on his back. Instantaneously, it seemed, numerous burly figures leaped out from the bushes and hauled him to his feet. I then became aware that a Range Rover had also been tailing us around, and its services were offered for a brush-down and tidy-up. But Robin was by now sufficiently inured to countryside mud, and was not too concerned. Though he worried about his loss of dignity. He hissed at me, 'Did that look awful?'

'No, of course not; you're far from being the only one to lose his footing,' I assured him.

Towards the end of the day we suddenly became aware that we were no longer being tailed. It was quite an odd feeling. We came across Paul looking rather mortified. He had apparently left us in charge of the other three while he went to the loo to change his muddy trousers, and meanwhile they lost us. We felt a bit like naughty children.

At Heathrow Robin (and Paul) came to see me off. Robin went to get cappuccinos and I drew Paul into conversation, wondering if I could lead him out of his usual reserved discretion. To my amazement I learned that he and his wife were deeply committed to fostering children from the least promising social backgrounds. They had been doing this for fifteen years, alongside their own children. It was not at all the image I had subconsciously adopted of armed policemen. For some reason that day there were more than the usual numbers of submachine-gun-carrying uniformed police at the airport. Robin was verbally attacked by a vociferous young Irishman, who considered that this intensive display of defence was an insult to the Irish people. Paul sat quietly by while Robin dealt with the young hotbrand, who would not go away until he had adequately vented his spleen.

The following weekend Robin dismissed his carers and we went rambling in the Moorfoot Hills on a gloriously bright day. It was good for him to get away from people and phones. We sat down briefly on a grassy summit in the sunny warmth, and he fell deeply asleep for an hour or so. I was accustomed to this habit and had a book with me.

Before the election I had been asked by a GP friend in West Lothian, Dr Dulal Chaudhury, if I would attend the Bangladeshi annual medical dinner which was to be held at the Edinburgh Sheraton on 24 May. I was delighted to be asked and managed to persuade Robin to agree to come, though he was adamant that he would not speak.

His schedule was often crucifying in its intensity, and that Saturday he arrived home with only minutes to spare before we had to leave for the dinner. He was not in good humour, indeed strongly resented being made to go out again. I found the evening a delightful one, and enjoyed meeting Dulal's lovely family and friends. I confessed to having a secret ambition to wear a sari, such an elegant garment. I was sitting a few places from Robin at the top table, and could see he was looking tired. There were no fewer than ten after-dinner speeches, culminating in the guest speaker at the end. After about seven speeches, Robin leaned back and hissed at me that he'd had enough and wanted to leave after the next speaker. I scowled, thinking he couldn't possibly be serious. But at the end of the next speech he began to rise from his seat, giving me a curt nod. I leaned back and whispered urgently that he couldn't possibly go now, he would cause untold offence if he left before the guest speaker, and I would definitely not go with him. He subsided back into his chair looking thoroughly disgruntled. I was glad to have carried my point but incredulous that he could be so childish and petulant on such an occasion, and totally oblivious to the hurt and embarrassment he might cause.

He had undertaken to visit India and Pakistan about this time, including a foray into Kashmir. I was alarmed to hear this because of the list of European travellers who had been kidnapped there. He promised to keep in touch and in particular to phone and let me know when he had left Kashmir and arrived in Pakistan. This he did on Sunday, and I breathed a sigh of relief. Imagine my consternation when I heard on the news that night that the Pakistan government had fallen and that all airports were closed. I rang the Foreign Office the following day and had a message relayed back that he was in the embassy and 'happy as a pig in shit'. The message lacked something in romance and elegance, but I was reassured. He had apparently been apprised of the situation by a phone call from London, before any official at the embassy knew what was happening. Robin's comments were wanted on a news programme in the UK, so he hastily phoned the Pakistani switchboard operator, who was the only person able to give him any details!

I asked Robin if I could come to Hong Kong for the handover ceremonies at the end of June. I longed to be there at such an historic event. He looked dubious and told me that there was no room in the plane, but later relented and said I could go. I liaised with Anne Bullen, one of the private secretaries at the Foreign Office, over the details, finding her pleasant and efficient. I was sent details of Robin's itineraries on a regular basis, and was probably better informed on his whereabouts than I'd ever been in my life before.

He had moved into the official residence at Carlton Gardens, and was rather rude about how gloomy and drab it was. He had asked for a front door key on arrival, which request was met with genuine perplexity. Why would he want a key? He was delivered there by his chauffeur, there was always a caretaker on duty in the entrance hall, and he always had his bodyguard on hand to ask for the wrought-iron gates to open to greet him. He mentioned to me that he sometimes felt like a prisoner in his own residence. I picked up the message that he was lonely. I certainly understood that it was incumbent on me to make myself more available to be with him, and fully accepted that a change in my lifestyle would have to be made. But after the end of June, when I had relinquished the almost constant nature of my on-call work, these changes could begin.

His change of heart and restoration of affection for me was far from complete. He gave a number of private and public parties at Carlton Gardens in those early weeks, and I was never given the option of being there to act as hostess. As before, I only found out after the event, and I perceived his ambivalence was still working within him, excluding me from his life and then acting out resentment against me for being excluded.

The security, or lack of it, associated with our house in Edinburgh was to be urgently addressed. I was visited by an army of men from the Home Office and a security firm to discuss this. As usual I'd had almost no information from Robin, which fazed them somewhat, but I made it clear that as always I would make the practical decisions. The measures proposed were far-reaching, and, though not compulsory, there was a certain amount of pressure to comply. Two outside doors were deemed to be too fragile and were marked down for replacement; all locks were considered inadequate. Every window must have a locking device. Intruder sensors were to be incorporated into every room. A video screen and intercom system were proposed so that we could establish the identity of a caller without opening the door. Panic buttons would be positioned at various key sites, which would be manned by the security people but connected with the police station at Fettes to ensure carloads of Lothian and Borders Police at the front and back of the house in the event of an alert. Since then I must admit to a childish yearning to press the panic button, which so far I have resisted. We were strongly advised to have blast net curtains draped in all the downstairs windows, the idea being that these collect the glass shards in the event of a bomb blast outside, preventing them from scattering and causing disfiguring injury to people in the room. I demurred over this, for I love to look out of the windows at the greenness of the garden, but allowed one at the front of the house. I saw the men casting dubious eyes at the luxuriance of trees in the garden, and forestalled any ideas by saying that my trees were sacrosanct and there would be no felling. There was a complex alarm system to be activated at night and when the house was empty, involving use of PIN numbers and, as far as I could see, huge capacity for noisy disasters if anyone forgot how to deactivate the system. And finally, there was to be a separate post and newspaper box, so that stuff couldn't be pushed through the door. Whoever designed the box never took a Sunday paper or received much mail, for it is ludicrously small.

After we had compromised over some of the less important proposals, a date was fixed in July for the work to start. It would take three weeks, and be completed before our planned holiday in August. I did wonder about the cost of all this to the taxpayer, but presumed it was necessary.

The last weekend in June approached and I received the provisional programme of events for Hong Kong. Anne Bullen phoned to ask if I had a long dress, as I'd need one for the banquet on *Britannia*. I judged I'd need at least three, and a good many other things besides. Space does not allow for the raptures of a lady describing the purchase of clothes and accessories for such an occasion; I have never been so self-indulgent before, and had a truly wonderful time; indeed had to undertake two expeditions before all was complete.

I continued to receive volumes of correspondence related to the trip, and learned that a separate programme would be arranged for me while Robin was tied up with his bilateral meetings and media engagements. I would be accompanied by Jane Cornish, wife of Francis, the future consul-general to the territory. All this added considerably to the delight of looking forward to the event, and the kindly attentiveness to my wishes was in striking contrast to Robin's dismissive attitude. He had told me very sternly not to expect favours as a result of his position; certainly never to expect to use government cars, not even on official Foreign Office business, unless I accompanied him. This was superfluous as I am not one to expect favours or to pull rank, but it was difficult to avoid seeing petty jealousy here. As if he were saying, 'You are not getting free access to all these good things, which I have earned and you have not.'

26

High Profile

On 28 June as I prepared to set out for London en route for Hong Kong, I put all negative thoughts out of my mind, intending to enjoy the visit to the uttermost. I was met at Heathrow, my baggage collected, and conveyed by car to the royal suite where the party gathered in comfort and style to await the flight. Pressmen and cameras were everywhere. Prince Charles and his party travelled on the same flight, and boarded ahead of the rest of us. The time for our boarding was imminent when Robin, casually dressed in jeans, arrived in a flurry and came to greet me, with an unusual show of affection.

Prince Charles's party occupied a separate cabin on the 747 jet. Robin and I were conducted to the front of the first-class compartment. I had never flown first class before, and was enthralled to find how much pleasanter and more comfortable travel in this style is, with room to spread out and dispose your belongings, space to stretch your legs and even lie flat if you so wish. There was individual choice of videos and other entertainment, a freebie pair of pyjamas and wash-bag, and every attention to our immediate comfort by the cabin crew. The thought would creep into my mind that he had at first said there was no room for me on the flight, which was so blatantly untrue.

Also travelling first class were Robin's principal private secretary William Ehrman, who was a mine of interesting information on China and with whom I shared a common interest in books, Minister of State Derek Fatchett, Edward Heath, Douglas and Judy Hurd, Geoffrey Howe, Paddy Ashdown and others. Judy Hurd came and talked to me about Chevening, having heard I was making enquiries about riding or hiring horses there. Dick Allen, Robin's chief protector, also came and introduced himself. He was a charming and conversational man, again the antithesis of what one would expect a protection officer to be.

Robin vanished for over an hour into the second-class compartment to talk to various people. The air hostess wanted to know when we would like our dinner, but I couldn't order it till he returned. I found the frequent attentions of the hostesses rather distracting and overwhelming. Perhaps they sensed this, as after a while they sent a comely young man to me instead, whom I found much more agreeable. Robin, by contrast, positively lapped up their attentions, almost rolling over to have his tummy scratched, and they responded by becoming still more obsequious. After one of these exchanges, he gazed, doe-eyed, at the retreating back, murmuring, 'I'll take that one back with me.'

At the Conrad Hotel where we stayed, our party had an entire floor for its use – the fifty-first – accessible only by smart card, and heavily guarded. Robin and I had a suite of rooms and, from that height, magnificent views over Victoria Harbour from one room and the colourful interior from another. The sitting room was lavishly supplied with bowls of exotic fruit and flowers. Dick occupied the next-door room and the Hong Kong police kept a permanent presence outside our door for the duration of the visit. The man on duty had a desk and, I hope, something to do, for otherwise it must have been excruciatingly boring. Our luggage arrived as if by magic. It occurred to me that if one got used to travelling like this for five years, it could cripple you thereafter in terms of being able to manage on your own account.

Travelling round the island with Robin was accomplished in convoys with not only his own security staff, but the Hong Kong police as well. On our first journey from the airport I was told that in the car behind ours were two machine-gun handlers travelling with the doors open, ready to tackle any would-be assassins. As we drove across Hong Kong, on a Saturday at midday, I wondered at how quiet the roads were; until I perceived that all other traffic had been diverted or stopped to allow us free access. I suppose for security they had to do this. One poor driver had inadvertently slipped through the net and was ruthlessly waved to a stop by outriders buzzing like wasps on motorcycles.

Jane Cornish, who was arranging my unofficial programme, I liked immediately, a warm and naturally friendly person. She explained that I had a car and a driver exclusively for my own use while in Hong Kong and that she carried a mobile phone so that any change in schedule could be instantly relayed to us. I felt rather dazed by this VIP status, but enjoyed it while it lasted.

The first social engagement was the Queen's birthday party at Government House, home of Hong Kong governors for 142 years with a gap for the Japanese occupation. The house was all but ready to deliver up its last governor and his family, with colonial symbols such as the Queen's monograms on the front gates and the Union flag ready to be finally removed in a couple of days. Robin and I drifted through the main hall, talking and admiring, and I caught sight and hearing of Baroness Thatcher, dressed in ominous purple. We moved with the flow into the garden where Chris and Lavender Patten and their family were standing amongst the guests, and where there was a performance of music from the Hong Kong police and pipe bands. A gentleman on my left turned to smile and talk, and I realised it was Prince Charles. He asked if I played any musical instruments, and talked of his attempts on the bagpipes at Gordonstoun.

Soon, there was a dash back to the hotel for a quick change into evening wear, and on to the royal yacht *Britannia* where we were greeted by Prince Charles and Commodore Anthony Morrow. In the reception area where drinks were served before dinner you could easily forget you were not in a firmly founded building; until a slight heave of the floor gave a reminder. I met Tung Chee Hwa, the Hong Kong chief executive-in-waiting, and his wife, who seemed westernised and whose English was excellent. His family business had been in shipping and engineering, and he professed an interest in the engine room of *Britannia*; there was talk of visiting it later in the evening.

At dinner I sat at the top table between Chris Patten and Sir Donald Tsang, Financial Secretary of the colony. Chris talked of his feelings of disaffection when he lost his parliamentary seat at the 1992 general election; it clearly rankled still. Sir Donald Tsang I found I liked very much; he was quite reserved, but happy to be drawn out. I talked of the global HIV pandemic, and how the high costs of treatment would inhibit tackling the disease adequately in Third World countries. I also enthused about the spectacular aviary with showy tropical birds I had seen that afternoon and he very kindly offered to obtain a book for me on birds of the territory.

After dinner the guests were ushered out on deck to listen to the band of the Royal Marines playing a medley of music, based on folk tunes and traditional songs. I stood between Tung Chee Hwa and his wife, both of whom were visibly enjoying the performance. Mr Tung, a genial, smiling man, seemed particularly to appreciate 'Rule Britannia', nodding and bouncing slightly to the beat. I had cringed inwardly when I heard this tune, feeling it was jingoistic and insensitive. He turned to me with an enthusiastic expression, saying that he liked that piece, and please what was its name? I couldn't bring myself to destroy Sino–British relations by strict adherence to the truth, so murmured something about it being a traditional folk-tune. Mrs Tung patted my arm and said confidentially, 'There is something very fine about a man in uniform, that makes a woman's heart glad!' Then we watched the solemn ceremony of beating the retreat.

Mr Tung was to be taken down below to see the engine room, and Robin and I went also in a spirit of curiosity. The access was not designed for slinky long dresses and high heels, but I was nimble enough to cope with the narrow stairways. The room looked like a museum piece with highly polished brass rods and pistons, and everything absolutely spotless. One of the reasons *Britannia* was to be decommissioned was that the engine was so old and out of date that the upkeep was impossibly costly in terms of staff and materials.

As we ascended to the deck we passed a door labelled 'Foreign Secretary', and our attendant remarked that it was a pity we would not have the opportunity to occupy the room.

Back on deck I had an interesting chat with the ship's doctor, Surgeon Commander Alistair Neal, who offered to show me the sick quarters if time allowed. At that point, Robin rather peremptorily distracted me in order to be introduced to Richard Branson. Not paying attention fully I grasped his right hand with my usual firm grip, whereupon the poor man gasped in agony and buckled at the knees. I realised two fingers were bandaged as he had broken a bone or two recently. I was profuse with my apologies and attempts to restore him to a state of well-being. He said with a laugh that as I looked such a slight and delicate creature he thought he could risk offering me his damaged right hand. Robin's sardonic expression indicated how inept this description of me was.

I was thoroughly enjoying myself; and conscious of so doing as we were driven back to the hotel. Robin looked as drained and tired as he often did, his mood in stark contrast to mine. Of course I knew he had a full and intensive schedule and heavy responsibilities. But sometimes I felt impatient that he couldn't lighten up and wear his burden a little more easily; and professionally, really.

The next morning, Sunday, a delicious breakfast was served in our sitting room. Robin was absorbed in paperwork and his thoughts, and was unavailable for light-hearted talk over this most intimate of meals;

a pity, for it was not often that we shared it. The fact that I was having a totally frivolous and indulgent time in contrast to him did not trouble me in the least. Before he left he handed me a package of Hong Kong money.

'What's this for?' I queried, amazed.

'That's the standard daily allowance for you when abroad on Foreign Office business,' he answered.

The amount was substantial and quite superfluous. All my needs were being supplied: hotel, transport, meals. I told him I would return it, to which he said that he didn't know of any mechanism to do so. But I was determined to, all the same. I would consider it totally shameful to come back from such a trip, with such privilege, richer than I had set out.

During the day we received an invitation from the Prince of Wales to spend the night aboard *Britannia*; we were due to dine there again that evening with the international guests. I remembered the regrets that were expressed on the previous evening, and felt quite touched by this courtesy. My response was, yes, please! Quite apart from what politeness demanded, I was thrilled at the invitation.

Back at the hotel I dressed for an early evening reception, and packed evening and night clothes to take with me. It was as well I had been generous to myself when planning my wardrobe as I hadn't taken account of the receptions and other social engagements, and only just had enough changes of outfits. At the reception aboard *Britannia* I met Lady Joan Appleyard (wife of the ambassador in Beijing) and Helen Seaton (wife of the deputy in the British Trade Commission, about to become the British Consulate), both of whom would be my companions on Monday. On that day Jane was required to accompany Cherie Blair who was to arrive with Tony early that morning. Jane's most onerous task was to find a hairdresser for Cherie before the afternoon ceremony.

Robin and I retired to our extremely comfortable nautical quarters where I lay down and put my feet up for half an hour, unaccustomed to the amount of standing around that social chatting entails. The gentle swell and rock was conducive to profound relaxation, and I willed myself not to fall asleep. Then it was time to slither into my evening dress and join the assembled guests for pre-dinner drinks. I endeavoured to engage the Japanese minister and his wife in conversation, since they seemed a little isolated. It was actually very hard work because an interpreter was required, a self-effacing man who hovered like a familiar spirit at your shoulder. William Hague with his fiancée Ffion were circulating, as was Paddy Ashdown, who came and whispered in my ear, 'We all think you're doing very well.' I blinked. I wasn't really aware of doing anything at all except thoroughly enjoying meeting people and being part of the scene. Still, I was susceptible enough to be pleased at his remark.

At dinner I sat between the Foreign Secretaries of Colombia and of Canada, and opposite Baroness Thatcher. She was making much better progress with the Japanese minister than I had done, but later turned her attention to my neighbour, the Colombian minister. My Canadian neighbour murmured, 'She's fighting the Falklands war all over again,' as indeed she was. My Colombian friend talked engagingly of his country and urged me to visit, along with my husband. Out of natural politeness as well as an insatiable appetite for travel, I agreed willingly. I shared this with Robin as we left the table. In more relaxed humour, he laughed. 'Oh, my God, you can't do that. They are out of favour for abuse of human rights. We'll have to back out tactfully!'

Baroness Thatcher was passing, so he introduced me to her. She echoed her remarks made in public earlier that day, that she was cautiously optimistic about Hong Kong's future. Following a mention of Tiananmen Square she remarked, 'They are a cruel race, the Chinese.'

I chimed in, 'I don't think that's true. Any nation with a culture of coercion as well as secrecy—'

But I got no further. 'Very cruel!' she grated emphatically, and sailed away.

There was a repetition of the Royal Marines' performance on shore, so we were ushered again on to the deck to listen. I met Michael Heseltine and his wife with whom we chatted briefly about horses and dressage. Ted Heath was standing in isolation gloomily observing the band; I asked him if he could identify an ethereal melody which kept recurring. He shook his head and looked uncomfortable. Later, as the majority of the guests drifted away, Robin and I were left relaxing with the royal party. I gratefully accepted a long cool glass of fruit juice and talked with Stephen Lamport, the Prince's private secretary, and Susanne Fiennes, the artist. The subject of the Tiananmen Square massacre came up again, in tones of condemnation.

I said, 'I don't think the Chinese are the only people whose army has fired on unarmed citizens.'

There was an uncomfortable silence.

Stephen said, 'You are thinking of India?'

'I am thinking of Amritsar. Also the Black and Tans in Ireland, and Bloody Sunday in Derry in the seventies. I suppose all people are capable of wanton acts of cruelty under certain combinations of circumstances.'

Later I talked with Prince Charles. We got on to the subject of blood transfusion, and he talked of his polo-related fracture and how he had donated his own blood in case of need during surgery. Then he left us and we retired for our historic night aboard *Britannia*.

Next morning Robin had a bilateral with Madeleine Albright, US Secretary of State, and she came aboard for this purpose. While I waited, Commander Morrow asked me to sign the visitors' book. It occurred to me that I would be one of the last to sign, and my modest signature contrasted with some of the other flamboyant and ornate scrawls. The commander drew my attention to names in a book from a previous royal yacht, dating back to 1910; and there in faded ink were the signatures of Czar Nicholas and Alexandra, their son Alexei and their four daughters. It was eerie thinking how their hands had inscribed these very names, before history so cruelly overtook them.

While Robin was engaged on official meetings, I enjoyed strolling through the variegated and fascinating streets with Jane, picking our way between market stalls, finding the array of fruit, vegetables, spices and other groceries on sale fascinatingly different. We visited the Stanley Market, the site of much cash squandering on my previous visit, trying on pretty clothes and hovering over artworks. Lunch one day was at the China Club, notable for a well-to-do atmosphere reminiscent of Shanghai in the years between the wars: genteel and elegant, and we ate with silver chopsticks. On another day, by contrast, Jane, Helen, Joan and I with some other friends took a dim sum lunch in a downtown restaurant that teemed with people and activity. The ladies were lively and amusing company. They talked of their lives as diplomatic wives, and it was clear that very considerable sacrifices were expected of them in that capacity. They were expected to forgo their own careers and be an integral part of their husbands' work lives. It occurred to me that this was precisely the role they were fulfilling so charmingly now. I remarked that the Diplomatic Service seemed to be very fortunate in getting two employees for the price of one. This observation was greeted with some warmth, as this anomalous treatment absolutely cried out to be taken up as a feminist issue, quite apart from any question of under-resourcing. The expectations of the wifely role fixed them in a subordinate and under-achieving position from which there was no escape.

The British farewell ceremony and banquet took place on the last day of June. There was some friction and posturing going on between the Chinese and British politicians over who would boycott which function. Tung Chee Hwa was obliged to follow protocol and meet the Chinese President and Prime Minister, Jiang Zemin and Li Peng, on their arrival in the colony, which meant that none of these dignitaries would be present at the British farewell show or banquet.

Tony Blair, who arrived in Hong Kong that morning, and Robin would boycott the swearing-in ceremony of the new legislature because it was not a democratically elected body, as had been agreed before handover. However, Edward Heath and Geoffrey Howe had announced that they would attend this formality.

As we set out for East Tamar where an immense arena was prepared for the British show, the sky was grey and forbidding. Most of the seats surrounding the arena were covered, but tropical rainstorms had been anticipated and everyone was supplied with an enormous yellow and turquoise umbrella. No sooner had we taken our seats than the heavens opened and the downpour began. Luckily it was very warm. On my left was seated General Sir Charles Guthrie, the most senior commanding officer of all the British forces, resplendent in tropical white uniform liberally adorned with gold braid ('scrambled egg' was my sister's irreverent description as she watched on TV). Although he was seated a few feet from me, I could readily perceive that he had dined well. On my right was my friend Sir Donald Tsang who told me with a benign smile that he had got the bird book for me. Prince Charles and Robin were seated further along, to the left of Sir Charles; also Tony and Cherie who arrived a little late.

The entertainment was laced with a heavy contribution of marching and counter-marching police and service bands, gun salutes, fanfares and other stylised military displays; with a more civil tone from Hong Kong orchestras giving a mix of oriental and western flavours, and literally hundreds of children dancing and singing with all their hearts and souls. They made wonderful aerial floating displays with gossamer sleeves and banners; but unfortunately the persistent rain turned the diaphanous material into heavy trailing appendages. Still, they took it in good part, and with humour began to take delight in the soaking they were getting. Chris Patten made an emotional speech. Towards the end of the programme the Prince of Wales stood up, clutching a handful of notes, to speak. As if on cue the rain, which had been falling steadily, now gathered its forces and really cascaded down. The Prince had to stand forward, clear of the shelter, and within seconds was drenched. I thought someone would leap forward with an umbrella and turned to Sir Donald, ready to be a latter-day Sir Walter Raleigh equivalent if required, but he whispered, 'No, he doesn't want an umbrella.' By the end of his speech, the Prince's notes had been reduced to pulp. The performing children gathered round the departing retinue and Prince Charles commiserated with them, demonstrating in a brief and rather charming cameo that his garments were quite as sodden as theirs.

Once the royal party had departed, a certain atmosphere of tension supervened. For security reasons, guests attending the handover banquet at the Exhibition Centre were to be ushered directly there. But there was also an undercurrent of frenzied negotiation about the precise arrangements for the handover ceremony at midnight that night, concerning which there were differences of opinion between the Chinese and British factions. Robin departed in haste with Tony and other officials, almost leaving me stranded, but I was gathered up by Dale, another of his protection officers, who squired me to the centre. Here there was a reception with a view of a magnificent firework display, which I admired in the company of Leon Brittan, erstwhile Conservative cabinet minister under Mrs Thatcher who resigned over the Westland affair, whom I found at an equally loose end as myself.

Having, one supposes, reached some measure of agreement with their Chinese counterparts, the negotiators returned in force. Cherie Blair, whom I had never met before, gathered me up like a long-lost friend and averred that the deferral of our meeting till now was ridiculous, and we would make sure things were different in the future. I liked her forthright style. She looked around in disgust, saying that there were too many Conservatives in the company. Tony Blair hovered nearby, his eyes ranging over the surrounding people. 'Am I going to meet your husband?' I asked Cherie; so she grabbed him and introduced us. He shook hands and smiled vaguely, but his mind was elsewhere. Kofi Annan (the United Nations Secretary General) strode up to our group and introduced himself, also his lovely Swedish wife Nan. She laughed about the difficulties of teaming her almost identical first and second names.

Because of the hitches and disagreements, the banquet was running a little late and the frenetic atmosphere persisted. On several occasions that evening I found myself scampering along in Robin's wake, trying to keep up. Remembering the time when I saw him stalking ahead of Susan in the students' union, and swearing he would never do such a thing to me, I ruefully realised that here we were over thirty years later and still I had not changed his ways! Finally the enormous assembly was placed and seated, and I found myself between the French and the Russian Foreign Secretaries. The Frenchman told me that he had no English. I had been warned of this, and attempted some stilted conversation in my schoolgirl French. Luckily, Tony Blair was on his other side, so I left them to each other and concentrated on my convivial Russian neighbour, Primakov. His wife was a doctor, a neurologist; he himself was a native of Georgia, about which he spoke with much warmth. He insisted that I should visit Russia with my husband as soon as possible. We then progressed to the topic of whisky, of which he was very fond, and I explained to him the nature of malts and blends. So then I had to write down the names of as many malts as I could remember, and he wrote on my programme, 'From Russia with Love'.

Those of us who were attending the midnight ceremony were ushered into queues, in a manner reminiscent of school Speech Days. I found myself between Lavender Patten and Paddy Ashdown, who explained that the arms carried by the Chinese were archaic and obsolete. The ceremony was clearly designed to be rigidly symmetrical with respect to the military presence and speech-making of the two countries. And at the end, in a moving few minutes, the two national anthems were played, the Union and Hong Kong flags were lowered, followed by the raising of the Chinese and Special Administrative Region flags.

I joined the group of people heading for the quayside to wave *Britannia* away. I had completely lost Robin which was no surprise, but on arrival I saw him stationed at the foot of the gangplank, with the appearance of a host about to see away his honoured guests. This, to me, was not entirely fitting and perhaps rather ostentatious, so I hesitated to join him. But someone, possibly one of the bodyguards, came to escort me over, so I walked across and stood beside him. The Patten family in various states of euphoria and emotion made their farewells and climbed aboard; also the Prince of Wales, by contrast looking highly relieved that it was all over. As well he might. One of the original wishes of the Chinese politicians was that he should walk into the last ceremony followed by the Chinese army with fixed bayonets! Needless to say, this was not allowed.

So *Britannia* sailed away and the crowds waved and cheered.

On Tuesday we attended the Chinese celebratory ceremony, which had the advantage of being dry as it was held inside the Exhibition Centre. The speeches were to me the chief fascination, especially that delivered by Jiang Zemin, the President of the People's Republic of China. I have the translation which is repetitious of such words as 'compatriots' and 'return to the motherland'. The theme both in his speech and in Tung Chee Hwa's was the vision first enunciated by Deng Xiaoping, of 'one country, two systems', to allow the absorption of Hong Kong into China. Jiang Zemin had a rather threatening way of speaking, rising to a violent crescendo when he expected the audience to applaud, and he certainly left us in no doubt about this action. His speech embraced the democratic principles agreed before the handover, and a high degree of autonomy in managing the region's affairs. There was a sense of relief that the agreements had been respected.

Then the UK party packed up and flew home.

27

Protection and Privilege

In the comfort of first-class travel it was easy to get some reasonable sleep. As I dozed someone came to talk to Robin, who responded by saying that his wife was sleeping, so let's move away somewhere and not disturb her. This sounds such a normal, mundane piece of thoughtfulness that you may wonder why I should remark on it. For me, from him, it was very unusual these days, and so I was gladdened and really hoped that for us a new era was beginning.

We arrived in London in the evening and drove to Carlton Gardens by way of a grocer's shop for basic sustenance. This was my first visit to the official residence and I was rocked back on my heels by its magnificent splendour. The first two floors consist of reception rooms, and are designed to impress visiting foreign dignitaries. And so they would: the rooms were of stately proportions, with rich and ornate furnishings, carpets and paintings. The pictures were on loan from London's art galleries, and were circulated periodically. There were two dining rooms, one for large and formal occasions, another smaller one for intimate and friendly dinners. I had not expected anything so grand. The upper two floors were for the Foreign Secretary's own domestic use, and though appointed on a more modern and everyday scale, would still be the height of luxury and desirability as a London home, by anyone's standards. In the main bedroom alone you could have held a party for about one hundred people. I couldn't understand why he had been so derogatory about it.

The following morning after breakfast, he had to go about his duties. I persuaded him to let me have a car to Heathrow, then, with time in hand, set about exploring the house. He was completely ignorant of his own domestic arrangements, except that he knew someone came to clean upstairs, and if he left his dirty clothes lying about, they were miraculously washed and ironed for him. He had never seen the 'pixie', as he called her, and had certainly never paid her. As I poked around the house I heard voices in the hall, so went downstairs to investigate.

Lisa, his social secretary, introduced herself. I asked her about the mysterious cleaner, and we made arrangements between us for the patient lady to receive some money. I also enquired about electricity and heating bills for the upper two floors, which would clearly be rather high. I discovered that none of these costs would be passed on to us. It seemed to me that if he so wished, a cabinet minister could live very comfortably on next to nothing.

I had to come down to earth on my return to Scotland, roll up my sleeves and set to work in the out-patient clinic. I was in a contented mood though, and felt it was good to come back to ordinary living, otherwise one might get delusions of grandeur. The workmen got started with the security arrangements at home. I was told that the place would be immaculate every evening when I came home, and certainly it was, though I believe it might have been alarming to see it in between times.

The holiday we had planned was extravagant and intended to be a further celebration of our renewed partnership. We would travel to Boston, spend a few days exploring there; then drive to Vermont, staying at a well-appointed inn in beautiful countryside. This was intended as something of a rural retreat, rather like the time in the Picos the previous year, which had gone off the rails after his revelations. Afterwards we would fly to Montana and have about ten days' riding on a dude ranch. This would be Robin's first real break since Christmas, since when he had been working intensely in the run-up to the election, and even more so afterwards. He needed to buy some suitable clothes, in particular some new riding gear, but it was impossible to identify time to do so. Certain things, like the green suede chaps, I could get without his body being present. I supposed we might get other essentials in Boston.

The next occasion to look forward to was the weekend at Chevening, on the middle weekend in July. This was our first identifiable free weekend. Many friends and colleagues were eager to know all about it, and kept asking if I'd been there yet. I was contacted by the Board of Trustees' Secretary's Personal Assistant to have the various arrangements explained. Different Foreign Secretaries had used the house in different ways. Douglas and Judy Hurd had used it as a bolt-hole for the family to escape the world and its demands, whereas Malcolm and Edith Rifkind had used it as a base for lavish entertaining. The resident house manager and housekeeper, Paul and Hilda, had found this tough to cope with and were probably pleased when I said I thought we would veer to the Hurd end of the spectrum. Hilda was very happy to cater for small numbers, say up to six, but larger parties would necessitate catering firms, which sounded fair to me. For our first weekend the boys would come to help us explore the delights of the house and grounds, and Robin was keen to invite John and Jenny McCririck to dinner on the Sunday and to stay the night. These were long-standing friends, John being the flamboyant Channel Four racing commentator. I discussed the menus for the weekend with Hilda, who planned to do a mammoth shopping expedition on our behalf, stocking up on basic items for storage. Paul wanted to lay down a small cellar for us but I thought Robin would like to have some say in the composition of this particular luxury.

A friend and dressage trainer, Bill Noble, who came up to Scotland to teach incompetent enthusiasts (and a few competent ones!) like myself, was based in Kent and professed himself willing to bus over horses to Chevening if he and his staff could accompany us. It all sounded symbiotic and promising.

Robin, Chris and I flew down together to Gatwick with Dick in attendance, while Peter was instructed to take a taxi directly to the house; an arrangement that involved much negotiating amongst the security fraternity. Peter and his taxi driver were a little startled to be stopped at the gate by a small army of policemen bristling with machine-guns. They passed muster, and were allowed through, so Peter was standing grandly on the terrace to meet us as we arrived.

It might be deemed appropriate, or even artistic, to protest that I wish I had never visited Chevening, since I was only to enjoy it for one solitary weekend. But I am glad I was there, living, marvelling and experiencing so intensely, anticipating so many future occasions, that I packed many years' worth into those few hours. I have in my possession a list in Robin's handwriting of possible future dates for visits, at least one a month, stretching to January 1998. And no doubt for him, those potentials became actuals; except that he had a different shepherdess with him. But that wouldn't matter too much, as long as someone was there to attend to him. Here was the theme of the film *Le Bonheur* from our student days all over again.

The first evening, with so much for us to admire, Paul and Hilda had some difficulty in leading us through the practicalities of choosing bedrooms – a difficult choice, with so many sumptuous and spacious apartments – and sitting us down to a late supper. Since the Hong Kong trip, Robin had visited Russia, and with him I had despatched a bottle of fine malt whisky for Mr Primakov. By way of return, I received a parcel from Mrs Primakov, containing an ornate, painted, china bird of dubious breed. This was borne away to be added to the treasures of the mansion.

On Saturday morning Captain David Husband (the Secretary to the Board of Trustees) came to greet us and to show us round the house with some account of the historic associations. He knew his subject inside-out of course, and gave a fascinating description. Robin was reluctant to join in the tour, wanting some freedom from duties, which included a brief meeting with the chairman of the board. The entrance hall of the manor provokes particular remark because of a display of ancient weaponry: of muskets, bayonets and pistols, which are however disposed so artistically, interwoven, in geometrical shapes, rosettes or parallel rows, that you do not immediately observe their exact nature. A very fine Spanish oak staircase spirals from the hall, and is supported at five points only, so that if you happen to run up the stairs it shudders alarmingly.

If I had thought Carlton Gardens was very grand, Chevening was more so, but more appealingly arranged for comfort as well as visual appreciation. There were some fine paintings, including a Gainsborough, a beautiful grand piano in the drawing room, artistic arrangements of choice blooms on a scale fitting the spaciousness of the rooms, elegance, taste and historic fascination at every turn. The immense library, housed in five rooms, is a testament to the intellectual leanings of past members of the Stanhope family, who owned the estate for generations; and much of it represents literature of the sixteenth, seventeenth and eighteenth centuries both in English and in European languages. Politics, philosophy and science are also found, including works by Sir Isaac Newton and Charles Darwin. I confess I anticipated many happy, solitary hours here.

The boys were thrilled to find a well-appointed games room with a snooker table, to which they repaired as often as they could, and where they proved that not all their student evenings were spent with their noses in their books.

After lunch I set off for a walk around the lake which extends away to the distance from the lawn behind the house. A pathway meanders in and out of trees and shrubs, never veering far from the lakeside. The still presence of water, the humming of insect life, the drowsy warmth of afternoon sun and the distant sounds of human activities all combined to emphasise the pleasure of solitude. Then I found a secluded window-seat and relaxed with a book. Robin and the boys had acquired some water pistols and disappeared down to the lake with juvenile activities in mind. Some time later I saw them lying on the grass with shirts off, drying out.

An informal dinner was scheduled for eight, and shortly before this hour I put on a dress and sauntered down the staircase. Paul was in the hall looking around with a slightly anxious air. There was absolutely no sign of the other three. I mentioned where I'd last seen them and Paul went off to look. I returned upstairs to peer out from various vantage points, but saw no sign of life. I began to be annoyed, for I had asked Hilda to make baked trout and it is almost impossible to prevent it from overcooking if service is delayed; I felt strongly the discourtesy in being so lax about time. It was Robin's almost invariable habit to be late or to be on the phone when I served up a meal, but I didn't think he would treat other people this way. Finally at twenty past eight I saw them casually ambling up the drive towards the house. I really did not want to create an unpleasant scene and spoil the atmosphere, but I had to let him know how thoughtless he had been. His response was that he had been cross about the formalities that morning, and didn't want to be tied down to fixed times. I bit my tongue and choked back my anger. However, he put his head round the kitchen door and said gaily, 'Hilda, I'm getting a frightful telling-off here!' So we let it pass. I said to the boys later that they should have made sure he was on time, and they were suitably apologetic.

The lake looked romantic and mysterious as night fell and the moon rose over it, and compelled us to go and take a walk. However we had to let the police-post know the plan, as otherwise we would have been set upon by dogs or shot at by marksmen. I wondered what the past Earls of Stanhope would have made of all this.

Next day we played tennis; with an armed police-guard hovering in the vicinity. I was amused at how seriously the local force took their responsibilities, especially as Robin had felt safe enough to dismiss Dick for the weekend.

With our friends the McCriricks coming for dinner, Paul wanted to know if we'd like all due ceremony observed, to which I agreed, as I thought they would enjoy being received with éclat. Robin I thought would probably behave more conventionally as he would seek to impress, and in this I judged correctly, so we enjoyed a most convivial evening with a delightful meal, progressing to a game of snooker and a visit to the library.

The party broke up the next morning, but for Robin and me yet more excitement was in store as we were to lunch with the Prince of Wales at Highgrove House. Dick and the chauffeur arrived in the car in good time, of course. I supplied myself with newspapers as Robin wanted to work, and this necessitated everyone keeping strict silence on the long journey. The July day was hot and I hoped my dress would not crush and crumple too badly. At Highgrove we were greeted with informal courtesy by the Prince, who was as attentive as any host possibly could be to engaging our interest. We viewed the gardens, scented shrubberies and flowery meadows at their very best, clearly a labour of love. We sat beside a pretty, bubbling fountain, a source of attraction to many garden birds, and drank refreshing Pimm's. Over a light lunch, various international issues were discussed. Then we had a look at the stables and admired the hunters.

In order to hasten Robin's return to the metropolis where he had a meeting with the Amir of Qatar, we were to return by helicopter; yet another first for me. Dick materialised from somewhere and we joined our conveyance in a neighbouring field, after bidding farewell to the Prince. Under the clear blue skies the landmarks were clearly identifiable, though the lucid conditions meant heavy competition for airspace from other airborne objects, for which a strict lookout was kept. Our surveillance system seemed remarkably untechnical. Meanwhile, Robin showed his nonchalance by sleeping all the way. At the heliport, he planned to ditch me with my luggage to my own devices, as usual, but Dick was more attentive and had arranged for a car to take me to Heathrow.

For the next ten days I attended to my routine work, getting things shipshape before I left on holiday but without the usual pressures to fit things in on a diminishing time-scale because a locum, Jenny, was coming to take over my duties. The Foreign Office had been badgering me about Robin's blood group as he was going to Bosnia soon, and I finally pinned him down in a chair, put on a tourniquet and approached with a needle and syringe. He hated this, becoming tense and pale. I was afraid he might faint which would reflect adversely on my bedside manner. But I managed to get the specimen without further ado.

On Friday, 1 August I took Muscat to the cattery, then hastened to Marks and Spencer's for one or two last-minute items, congratulating myself when I thought of how vastly different was my state of mind this year from last, when I had set off so unhappily for Spain.

Now if my reader has a logical respect for chronology, I would advise the re-reading of the prologue to which I have come full circle.

28

Media Mistress

People have said that this book should end here. There is a notion that perhaps the book really starts here. My life has been transformed since that fateful day and in ways that would not have been foreseeable. The first change is in the nature of solitude: I have exchanged one variety for another. For years my marital sorrows had been shared with no one, and now suddenly it seemed that all the world was interested, and found its way to my doorstep craving information. Those who have lost a partner will know thoroughly the nature of the newly acquired form of solitude, and it is a very persisting one. When you are so closely linked with another person, there are not two persons, there are three, the third person being compounded of the parts of you both that cleave, body and soul, together. In the past when Robin and I were alone with each other, I have felt the presence of this third quite strongly. I imagine that if your partner dies, that compound third person may remain; but for me, and others like me, the loss was of both of the other two parts of our triumvirate, and the bleakness of the solitude that is left is extremely painful. It is like the pain of a phantom limb; and about as illogical. It is not just that you are single while almost everyone else seems to be part of a pair; it is much deeper and more fundamental than that, something primeval and biological.

As I write it is some ten or eleven months since our split and having thought through all our life together I really do not retain any love or warmth towards him; and no hate either. No emotion. But all the same, I am still imprinted with his image. If I see a picture in the paper or on the television, every aspect, inflection, expression, gesture are so familiar, and deep down inside I still recognise him as my husband. Maybe when he alters with the ravages of time this will change. If this happens I hope it proceeds with all haste.

One totally new aspect of my life was dealing with the press and the media on my own account. Previously reporters were people who came looking for Robin, who were stubborn and a bit of a nuisance, and who would not take no for an answer. To my surprise, I have found them all, whether communicating by letter, by phone or in person, unfailingly courteous.

On Saturday, 2 August as Peter and I took our flight back to Edinburgh, all this was in the future. I could only cope with a few things at a time but I knew the announcement would be made at nine that night and that I could expect to be under siege shortly afterwards. Meantime I would have to shop for basic provisions, and speak to immediate members of the family. I took Peter to Chris's flat and left the two of them to talk things through. They promised to join me that evening with supplies of wine and chocolates, and help cook dinner, then stay the rest of the weekend.

When I'd done the shopping, with my thoughts still in a state of numb suspension, I sat down beside the phone and faced the prospect of some intensely painful duties. I phoned Mum first. I perceived for the first time how dishonest I'd been with all my family and friends in the way I'd portrayed my marriage. When she answered, I said, 'Mum, I've got something rather awful to tell you.'

I heard the inflection of my own voice, and knew she'd be in no doubt that it was something very bad.

'Robin has been having an affair with his secretary. The *News of the World* are running the story tomorrow. And he's decided to leave me.'

Her immediate reaction was that she would come to me that very day. She was terribly shocked. I persuaded her not to do anything so rash, the boys were with me and in a few days I would come to her. We wept a few tears together and I filled in some details.

She said repeatedly, 'I thought you had such a strong marriage. I was so sure that you at least would always be all right, you seemed to lead such a charmed life.'

She admitted she had never liked Robin, he had never treated her warmly, but he had always seemed to love and care for me.

Eventually, worrying about how she would be, left to mourn over me by herself, I had to ring off and speak to Jenny. This was an equally bolt-from-the-blue revelation. But at least the nine o'clock news would spare me the necessity of repeating the process over and over again. Robin planned to pay his mother a flying visit that day, as she also would need to be forewarned.

Already I had found that though it was better to be doing something, it was hard to concentrate or to initiate and carry through actions. Still, with the boys' help I got dinner organised, which they ate. We all drank generous amounts of wine. With a continued feeling of emptiness I heard Peter Sissons make the bleak announcement, followed by a shot of Robin looking strained on the steps of his residence, his eyes expressionless, speaking the words he'd shown me that morning. Though I felt little at the time, the moment was an important turning point, since for me it really spelled the end. Not just acceptance of the inevitable: it was an absolute severance. In particular, the end of my unswerving loyalty to him.

We watched part of a mindless James Bond film, but I was feeling dizzy with tiredness and wine, so went off to bed. Then the doorbell started to ring, which Chris answered. We blessed the security installations, which meant we could speak to reporters and see them without having to open the door. I was up early the next day and as the boys slumbered on, answered the bell myself, which began ringing again at eight o'clock. To queries of how I was that morning, I merely said I had no comment. It was as well they did not realise it was my birthday – a year almost to the day since I first learned of his latest betrayal. Dick and his colleagues had organised a police presence amongst the gathering band of pressmen who were herded a little distance from the house.

I wanted to see the papers. Chris and Peter volunteered to take Robin's car, go and buy copies, then park the car behind the house and return through the garden. With luck the press would not appreciate that we had this separate access and I could use it to come and go freely. The boys clearly relished the drama of the speedy dash up the lane, scattering pressmen to right and left as cameras flashed through the car windows. Luckily our ploy worked, and we were never intercepted at the back entrance.

Chris and Peter had to leave on Sunday night in order to go to work on Monday. Chris promised to enquire at his firm for a suitable lawyer for me. I tried to think and plan a little. I spoke to a colleague at St John's, requested that my holiday be considered compassionate leave and extended to a full three weeks. I arranged for our press manager to put out a statement. In discussions over coffee with my friends at the hospital, we had often debated whether or not the sexual irregularities of highly placed political figures rendered them unfit for their responsibilities. I had always argued that they did not, mentally crossing my fingers and hoping I would never have to prove my sincerity on this point. But now I would have to do just that, and in my press statement affirmed that his private life had no bearing on his political functioning.

Each morning I went out to gather up an armful of papers, as the stories continued to simmer. One day in the newsagent's I picked up a tabloid paper which expressed the view that Robin had behaved nobly in accepting his mistress and repudiating his wife, and contrasted this with Cecil Parkinson. I was so enraged at this misrepresentation of the facts that I stood rooted to the spot, trembling with fury, and scattering my armful of papers on the floor. I was inco-ordinated with anger, but managed somehow to pay, get myself home and ring his bleep, with the terse message to ring back forthwith. I spat down the phone that if he didn't apologise for the way he'd treated me and make it sound good I would go out to the press on the doorstep and reveal exactly how he had engineered our parting. He was very nervous and anxious to placate me, and did issue an apology. Though rather muted I thought.

Still, this particular piece began to clarify to me why Robin had opted to leave me. He was apparently putting his career before all else. I've no idea what ultimatum he received from Campbell and Blair at Heathrow; but they clearly wanted to avoid the image of him having a 'bit on the side' and dropping her as soon as the affair was revealed. The image of a genuine impassioned love affair, and a stale marriage, was one that the public might more easily be persuaded to believe and accept. The cynicism involved in such behaviour was appalling. Also, having read the stories of his love-nest with Gaynor in his own Sutherland Street flat, I fully understood now why he had been so rude about his official residence, which excused his apparent preference for his own place.

He arranged to see me that first week to talk about the terms of our separation. He talked glibly of letting me live in the house as long as I wanted, but should I sell, the value of the house and contents would be split equally.

To this I firmly said no. I had put far and away the greater financial contribution into our house, family and mutual affairs; to say nothing of the practical managing. I had lost marriage, partner, position, prestige, status and I did not see why I should lose half of my home also. I expected to keep the house, contents and to have the remaining mortgage paid off by him. And I expected him to bear the lost holiday expenses.

The corners of his mouth curled up in a little sneer, and he said no more. But when I met Andrew, my lawyer, for the first time, I learned that Robin was sticking to his demand for half of everything.

I rang Peter Mandelson to talk about the impasse over our divorce discussions. I suggested it might be useful if he would visit me, which he did, and he agreed to talk to Robin on my behalf. Soon after, when I spoke to Robin, he recanted and agreed to hand over to me the home in its entirety.

Meanwhile it occurred to me that I had one or two other things that I wanted to say publicly. I talked to the *Sunday Times* about the pressures on me as a senior doctor, particularly those involving out-of-hours responsibilities, and arguing that this was one factor that had kept us apart and contributed to the split. I intended to cause some embarrassment to my employers, and also to point up that senior doctors as well as juniors needed protection. I intended no recriminations, and certainly was not blaming Tory policy, as the headline which blazed across the front page indicated.

As those early days slipped by I received letters from friends who had tried to phone and found the number unobtainable. Some letters were from people I didn't see all that often, but I felt the strength in a friendship that was so immediately and kindly there when trouble loomed. The gratitude and pleasure I felt were intense, the words were balm to my savaged self-esteem. I would sit at the kitchen table and cry over my morning mail. Friends would later describe how astounded they had been on hearing the news; some even thought it was a hoax. Like my mother, they thought our marriage was strong and enduring.

One letter which I hardly expected came from Tony and Cherie Blair. Written in Tony's handwriting, it is very brief and speaks of sorrow that I had been swept up in the media storm and of the distress it must have caused. They were thinking of me, he said. There is absolutely no mention of the marriage or its tragic fate. I'm afraid that, taken in the midst of all the other letters, eloquent in their sincerity, this one grated like sand on raw skin. How insensitive can you be? I wrote back, saying thank you, and I noted that he didn't say he was sorry about the broken marriage, though I presumed he was? A few days later, Peter Mandelson was on the phone again. He had been speaking to Tony in Tuscany and with a combination of mobile phones and distance, found it difficult to gather the gist of why he was so upset about a letter I'd sent. I explained. I told Peter that frankly it was a dreadful, unfeeling letter, and that if Tony ever had to do this again, I hoped he'd get it right next time.

My immediate neighbours braved the press pack and came in to see me. I badly needed someone to talk to, and all my natural reserve was washed away in a flood of unwonted freedom. I was ambivalent, though, about all people at first; needing someone to talk to, but then feeling claustrophobic and wanting to be alone, then going through the cycle again. I began to think through all sorts of implications which had not occurred to me at first. It was expected that Robin would try and maintain strong bonds with Chris and Peter, and with what seemed to me like callous and unseemly haste he arranged for Chris to dine with him and Gaynor at the Caledonian Hotel when they were in Edinburgh; this was less than two weeks after he left me. Of all the hurts, this one was most agonisingly painful. To think of my sons with them as a couple, a foursome, and myself at last effectively excluded: this was the worst, the most bitter pill of all. Knowing Robin's hatred of scenes I knew he would arrange not to be alone with either son, so there would be minimal chance for them to speak frankly to him. I imagined he would continue to behave as a loving father, a source of fun and good things, and would tide things over until the time was gone when censure and criticism were appropriate.

I had expected a phone call from Granny Cook, and after a day or two without any word, called her myself. Poor Granny was in an awful state, gasping and sobbing into the phone that she thought I'd never speak to her again and that she'd lose contact with her grandsons. Of course she had tried to phone me, but Robin had forgotten to tell her about the instant number change. We comforted each other and I affirmed and reaffirmed that there would be no change to our family relationships, himself apart. I promised to come and see her soon, and that I'd get the boys to ring. She said she supposed she would have to meet Gaynor, and apologised to me.

'He's my son, I can't drop him!'

No. I didn't for one moment expect her to do that. I would be the same in her position. Family ties are not so easily dropped – for most of us.

With legal and financial matters put in train, I slung a few things into a bag, shut up the house and set off in my car to drive down south to Mum and Jenny. It felt good to be escaping for a few days and with my mind on driving I could keep my thoughts on an even keel. I tried to listen to books on tape but found I couldn't concentrate. It was a long and tiring drive. I collected Jenny from Glastonbury and we drove through the Somerset and Wiltshire countryside to Trowbridge, always a journey of nostalgia from the days of our childhood. We all had a lot of talking to do. I had taken my letters with me, meaning to answer every one, and for a long time kept this up. Answering was as therapeutic as receiving. I had letters from school and university friends, some of whom I had not had contact with for decades, as well as more recent ones. There were offers to stay, to hide away for a bit, from all quarters of the country.

After a few days I became restive, and felt I should go home. On the drive back I started comfortably enough, but a progressive awareness of my solitariness weighed increasingly on me. I remembered the many times we had travelled home this way as a family, and now I ached with desolation. My concentration was lapsing and I missed my turn off the M74; realising I was in no fit state to be driving, I stopped at a service station at Douglas and got a coffee. For half an hour or more I sat with my head supported by my hands, hopefully concealing the tears that dripped steadily into my cup. I think this was the lowest reach of unhappiness, and it was very bleak. At last, with an effort, I gathered myself together and completed the journey home. I had some phone calls to make; in particular, I needed to do something about the horses, but I was too choked to communicate properly, and gave it up. Ann, my neighbour, came in and, using her Samaritan skills, encouraged me to let it all hang out, have a really good cry, and a good talk, which put me back on the rails again. She invited me to have supper with her and her husband, Gareth, with a little escapism in the form of some wine and travel talk. We were both keen travellers, but my ventures of late had been in comfort and style, while Ann was much more adventurous, fond of back-packing and living rough in far-flung places. We jokingly wondered about making a compromise and going off together somewhere.

The Edinburgh Festival began and seemed like another heaven-sent opportunity for distracting the mind. Peter and Chris took some holidays and we did the rounds of some Fringe performances, and the wonderful street theatre; also some opera and concerts. I accompanied

Ann with family and friends to performances, and met Iain and Kate for lunch and an indulgent afternoon at the Book Festival. It seemed so odd to be enjoying myself. On those hot sunny days I spent some delicious times lounging on pavement cafés with Chris and Peter, just talking about everything and anything, as we had always done.

Robin called round to have his antique-style desk moved and a few other personal belongings. I had packed his clothes for him, knowing he was scarcely capable of doing this himself and all that remained were a few out-of-date political tomes and his university literature volumes. It seemed pathetically little. He tossed his keys down on the table and left.

I am not ashamed to admit that of course I regretted the loss of those privileges that came to me as wife of the Foreign Secretary, though they were way down the scale of afflictions. It did occur to me, however, that until I divorced him there was no reason why I should not visit Chevening with the boys, or even on my own. After making enquiries, he assured me I could do so. But by this time, reason prevailed, and I wrote to Captain Husband saying that it was better to make a clean break and not prolong regrets. I conveyed my gratitude to all the staff who had made the brief encounter so agreeable. He wrote me a very charming letter, expressing his disappointment that he would not meet me with the sons again.

Probably no one realised that the kitchen cupboards at Chevening had been well stocked at my expense. For her first few visits as lady-in-residence, Gaynor will have been living off my bounty; I hope the thought gives her indigestion.

The author and political commentator Allan Massie wrote an article in the *Scotsman* about the pressures to which modern politicians submit and compared them with the more leisurely life of ministers of previous eras. It crystallised my thoughts which I expressed in a brief letter to the *Scotsman*, enlarging on the theme of over-driven politicians. The intense time-pressures which exclude time to pause and think, and which drive a person from his natural pace, coupled with the addiction to praise and acclaim, do induce a form of madness, I believe. I didn't mention Robin at all, but I consider that these factors, evolving from an overweaning and all-absorbing ambition, have eroded his better nature. Possibly these destructive processes affect anyone in power and the public eye. If so, an in-depth study of the interactions of our rulers and the media is long, long overdue. It is conceivably a Catch-22 situation. Someone achieves high office and the media spotlight, and is immediately on the slippery slopes, heading for psychopathy. And arguably the people who present themselves for election and who attain top ranking are a self-selected bunch anyway.

My letter created more ripples than I expected. About two weeks after our split Robin telephoned to ask if he could come and see me. Why? I asked. I just want to see you. Rather reluctantly I gave him a time. I didn't want to see him; I found all contact with him destabilising. He arrived, and settled comfortably in a chair, looking thoughtful – and penitent? He talked about himself; he'd had time these past few days, with nothing much to do except lie low, to think a bit more, to come to terms with things. He said repeatedly that my *Scotsman* letter was right. I was getting worried about where all this was leading. I said that guilt had soured his affection for me; he said, yes, but your letter was right. And then I had the most dreadful fear that he was going to recant, and I could not bear it. Hastily I said he'd have to go, I had an appointment with my lawyer. He gave a little start, as if suddenly awaking; he asked meekly if I'd finished writing to the press now. He hoped things would settle down. Continued stories were very destructive to him. If he was to give up all claim to the house, he would need to hold on to his job in order to recoup his losses. I confirmed, for the present, I had no more plans to speak to the press.

The time was approaching for me to return to work, a formidable thought. Among the many letters which still arrived, a number were from colleagues at St John's, wishing me well for my return. This would take all my mental resources, and I could not face returning to my demanding schedule of early morning riding at the same time. Again, some wonderful friends were on hand to help. Phyllis I seriously thought should be destroyed, as I felt barely capable of looking after one horse, let alone two. But Mary gently took over the task of finding a happy rest-home for her, and having made all the arrangements, transported her there herself. Linda, who had helped me with Sparrow from the beginning, agreed to take him under her wing; we moved him up to her yard in the Bathgate hills, where I rode him as often as I could, knowing that Linda would cope when I couldn't.

The weekend before my start date was difficult and marked by mood swings. As one does, I cast about looking for some alleviation for the painful mental seething. Conscious of the considerable personal satisfaction I gained from positive reactions to my brief forays into the press, I sat down and penned a letter to *The Times*. It was partly in response to articles about the families of high-flying career people. In particular I emphasised that children do not need to suffer in that situation and ours did not; and that though Robin had had an input into their upbringing, it was less than mine. It was hardly controversial, but I knew I would provoke stormy waters for already I was being leaned on to keep quiet. Jim, Robin's agent, had offered to meet me and chum me into work the first morning and I accepted his generous offer. We met and went up to the coffee room, mostly empty at eight in the morning, talking desultorily and with Jim doing his best to be supportive. What malign influence prompted me to tell him of my impending letter to *The Times*, due to appear the following day, I cannot say. But as soon as I let it out, his face darkened and he glowered with fury.

'What made you do that?' he raged.

Gone was the caring, soothing demeanour. I had a copy of the text, which I let him read. He fumed about the effects on the boys, the continuing press stories, the chance of myself getting adverse publicity, the effect on my divorce arrangements. He was every inch Robin's man. There was a bit of me that was both amused and impressed by the power I had. I returned to my office, being lectured all the way. I wished he would go. I needed the time to compose myself before meeting people. He went, at last.

With most people, the lab staff, the secretaries, the nursing staff in wards and clinics, I just behaved as if nothing had happened, and they responded likewise. It was the easiest way for all of us. But this was not possible with my medical colleagues, with most of whom there were strong bonds of friendship. So many came and greeted me in the privacy of my office; they all found ways of conveying solidarity and comfort. Some held my hands, or hugged me, or looked moved almost to tears. Some conveyed deep anger at the way I'd been treated. All found words and expressions that meant everything to me. And there were flowers, tokens and little gifts. It is not possible to find words to express how very much I valued all of this.

The first morning I had to see a new young patient in the day ward, with the usual history, examination, blood and marrow tests. It was going in at the deep end, and it was the best thing to do. Concerning yourself with someone else's problems, and seeking to alleviate, explain, communicate, you forget your own difficulties. I felt almost normal again. On occasions in those early days, as I sat at the microscope or in the clinic, a head would appear round the door and say something like, 'We are thinking of you,' and vanish promptly. The patients were very tactful, finding ways of conveying sympathy without being intrusive: a squeeze of the hand, a pat on the shoulder, a word or two about keeping up the spirits.

With such support, the process was easier than anticipated. One task of considerable sadness I tackled early: all the entries in my diary of combined activities had to be deleted. Commonwealth Heads of Government Meeting, Paris, India, Chevening – the family party at New Year. On the second day, my letter appeared in *The Times* and my comments about family life were quickly taken up by other papers. Robin, about to jet off somewhere, caught sight of an *Evening Standard* headline – and was promptly on the phone. Unbelievably he took a high moral tone and was aggressive about how I'd assured him I wasn't going to talk to the press any more, and how selfish I was being. In my fragile state I didn't scarify him with my retorts; rather the reverse, I fear. The result of this was that, when he'd had time to think, he insisted on putting a gagging clause in the terms of the divorce, to the effect that I should agree never to talk to the press ever again about our relationship or the family. In his lordly way he said that there would be no objection to my speaking about other topics.

But I'd recovered my equanimity by this time, and was furious at the suggestion. I told him I'd rather live in a single end and retain my freedom of speech than submit to any such clause. I spoke to Peter Mandelson, who again spoke to Robin on my behalf. And the insistence on the clause was dropped. I wrote and said I'd no intention of talking about him; I hadn't, at the time. I didn't want him to lose his job. And I did want to keep my home.

Then I met Linda McDougall, journalist and wife of the Labour MP Austin Mitchell, who had asked me to contribute to her book, *Westminster Women*. We had dinner together in Edinburgh, and I did talk very freely, still finding release in pouring out my woes to a sympathetic ear. I was naïve in the extreme, but I couldn't see that this was particularly relevant to the theme of her book, and was surprised that these stories were wanted rather than more serious issues. This was the same night that Diana, Princess of Wales died, which for a while overshadowed everything else. When Linda sent me her piece, I delighted in reading it, but wrote back promptly saying that she couldn't publish that, it was far too destructive. Particularly the bit about his previous affairs. I put a complete veto on that. I said, anonymise it, work it into the text, don't do a separate chapter on the topic.

I'd been in touch with Clare Short, and joined up in London to have a delightful dinner with her, Virginia (her PA), Linda and Angela Eagle who had just 'come out'. Clare gave me a useful piece of advice. She said, you don't want to become known solely as Robin Cook's ex-wife.

Letters were now coming from unknown people who commiserated because of similar traumatic experiences. I also received many letters and phone calls from the media, and felt that the power here could be used creatively. I wrote a piece about the uncomfortable relationship between the NHS and the commercially minded pharmaceutical industry, something I have long felt strongly about, and sent it off to the *Sunday Times*. Meanwhile, having discovered that writing was a new activity which I enjoyed greatly, I began writing about some of my early medical experiences in novel form. But the article didn't immediately appear, and my novel didn't seem to find much favour. I was deeply depressed, and surprised at myself for taking it so badly.

Although going back to work was the best possible therapy for me, it may not have been the same for the patients and possibly not for my co-workers. I knew I was working at much reduced capacity, not surprising considering the media interest continued, and that I was obliged to negotiate with Robin rather often. Both of these influences were stressful and disturbing. The stress translated into physical symptoms of quite surprising magnitude, such as weight loss and disturbed sleep, poor concentration and excessive tiredness. The poor concentration was most worrying but people were patient and no one complained.

Both sons had met Gaynor by now on several occasions. I didn't especially want to know about her, but I did want to know what sort of relationship they would develop with her. Chris wouldn't say much, just that she was shy and very nervous. Peter was much more forthright, saying that she was not a patch on me, could never replace me in their affections or in any other way at all, and I should stop worrying about her. I heard a similar account from another quarter, which shall remain unnamed. Chris went to the races with them both, when Gaynor was made to stay in the car all day so that no pictures could appear of all three of them together. Peter also told me some exemplary tales, illustrating the sort of relationship Robin and Gaynor had, and this gave me a huge sense of relief. If that's what he wants, he's better off where he is, for he'd not get that from me, I thought. So one source of misery was in part alleviated, but life never stands still, and a new realisation surfaced, that no longer was there complete candour and openness between me and the sons. Sure, they would have had plenty of secrets in the past, but now there seemed to be overt no-go areas, and painfully conflicting loyalties.

Just before Ann and I were due to fly off to Ecuador for a hastily planned holiday, I had been aware that my two attempts at writing were not going anywhere, and I had also had a slightly discordant meeting with Chris on his return from the much anticipated stay in Paris with the Aga Khan. These things weighed heavily on my thoughts during the long hours of transatlantic flight. But if I had been able to see into the future, I might have discovered that this would be the last day of protracted or profound unhappiness.

Now that my story is drawing towards the present, I am becoming more selective. I sit and chew my pen, wondering if I want to tell this or that, or if I'd rather keep it hidden. This rehearsing of my history is a departure from my usual reserved character, and I'm relieved to discover I am not completely metamorphosed. There will be just one more significant confession, but numerous other new and exciting things in my life this last year will not be divulged. I'll go under wraps and recreate my incognito.

We arrived, tired and jet-lagged in Quito. We had met others of our group already: Sue from Birmingham and three lads in their twenties from Yorkshire, Gary, Gorky and Mike. At various points on our trip we had an assortment of guides and attendants. We travelled by plane and truck to the tributary of the Amazon where we joined our craft, an elongated, motor-driven, wooden longboat which carried up to fourteen of us, with all our stores and luggage. The overt purpose of the trip was wildlife watching, but naturally we were intent on living rough and having fun also.

Our first camp was along a dark narrow inlet with the magical name of Shushufindi River, in a clearing in the jungle. There were wooden platforms raised three or four feet from the ground, roofed over with palm thatch, with the sides half palisaded, half open. Hammocks were slung with mosquito nets for sleeping; no nonsense about segregation

A SLIGHT AND DELICATE CREATURE

of the sexes. Toilets were wooden seats behind screens, along little paths into the jungle. Wash facilities were bags of water with taps and shower heads suspended behind flimsy partitions. This was quite sophisticated, and as the trip progressed, camps got progressively more basic; in parallel, so did our freedom from inhibition.

Darkness fell swiftly, and as we waited for our supper to be cooked the lads produced a bottle of Southern Comfort. We sat on the hammocks, chatting and sipping and getting mellow. The atmosphere over the dinner table was spellbinding, with the darkness and mysterious jungle noises beyond the reaches of the pools of light created by the candle flames. The food – meat, rice and vegetables – tasted like ambrosia in that setting. Feeling as though beyond the realm of ordinary restrained behaviour, and no doubt assisted by the Southern Comfort, the conversation flowed and became increasingly frank and free. Perhaps everyone there had some sort of trauma to escape from, but the problems were shed in the telling, and the mood was high, with a great deal of comradeliness.

This remarkable evening led to an unforeseen encounter between me and one of our party who shall remain anonymous. It must be enough to say that it was liberating, rejuvenating and transforming of outlook – and in-look – and of expectations for the rest of my life, as well as being altogether delightful in its own right. We were 'an item', as the curious cult phrase has it, for the duration of our time in the Amazon and in Quito. And knowing he was highly unsuitable for a long-term relationship – apart from more cogent reasons, he was seventeen years younger than me – ensured no deep regrets on parting. Ann said that since he looked ten years older than his age and I looked ten years younger, we were compatible in our biological age.

We learned to shoot darts from a blowpipe, Indian-style; how to catch piranhas and disengage them from the hook without getting a finger bitten off; how to row by moon- and torchlight and seek out caymans (small alligators); how to identify hosts of tropical birds, trees and plants. In the dark of the night you could hear beautiful, plaintive, dropping notes of birdsong, spilling down the octaves, which my new friend was able to mimic with thrilling accuracy. One day the heat was so intense that a prolonged siesta in the hammocks was necessary. I wanted a good wash, but the water here was full of piranhas. I slipped down to the boat and had a shower with the help of buckets of water scooped out of the river. Somehow, by this time, modesty hardly

288

seemed to matter. Everyone else followed suit, abandoning shyness with their clothing, but the lads looked uneasy when Ann and I appeared with the cameras.

Returning by way of Lago Agrio we got caught up in a protest action by the local population at the devastation of the rainforest by US oil companies. Installations were occupied, airports shut, roads blocked. Our car was hijacked and the tyres deflated. Back at our hotel we came under siege as the army moved in with tear gas and machine-gun fire. We took some wonderful action shots and had a splendid view from the hotel roof, and a parapet to duck behind when things got too hot. We were eventually rescued by a specially chartered plane and returned safely to Quito. Our second week was spent aboard a tiny yacht sailing round some of the Galapagos Islands, with a wealth of wildlife, especially birds. The tameness and trust of the creatures is almost unnerving. The blue-footed boobies displayed their sensual courtship ritual, while frigate birds already had huge fluffy babies sitting upright in their nests. We swam and sported with sea-lions, dived from the boat and snorkelled in psychedelic tropical populations of variegated aquatic creatures, even with sharks. Ashore there were giant tortoises, iguanas, penguins, sea-lions, pelicans, hawks and doves. Sailing from one island to another, usually a journey of up to four hours in very turbulent waters, demolished my belief that I was immune to seasickness.

We gathered a number of extra friends to our closely knit group this week and as a final fling had a wild night partying in Quito before we all went our separate way; dining, drinking specially concocted margaritas and dancing sinuously Latin-American-style in a nightclub. We had about three hours' sleep before leaving for the long journey home.

In Bogotá, where we had several hours to wait for a connection, I bought an emerald ring, something I have wanted for years. I call it my disengagement ring.

On my return I found a message from the *Sunday Times*, saying they did indeed want to run my article about pharmaceuticals with a little expansion to the text, and I was so overjoyed that I set to work at once.

I got lucky that autumn, because John and Jenny McCririck had won a week's holiday for two in Phoenix, Arizona. With wonderful generosity, John asked me to go with Jenny and have a week's riding in the desert; and 'Whatever else you girls get up to, I don't want to know about!' So in a couple of weeks I was off again. This holiday was very different: a luxury hotel with swimming pools, superb restaurants, bijou shops and all amenities. Besides the riding we spent our time sightseeing and shopping. While I was there, faxes flew to and fro between me and the *Sunday Times* as my expanded article was subjected to the snipping, chopping and chipping that suited the editorial whim. I was ambivalent about the surgery, even though my views were attended to; it was so different from the process of submitting work for professional journals. But I felt good that my views would be read by a wider audience.

Back at work after these two breaks, I was a completely different person, and well on the road back to normality. Above all, I now knew that further relationships were not out of the question. I regained confidence, and had a heady feeling of release from thraldom; also I had shed and left behind a load of bitterness. I even had quite a friendly chat with Robin on the phone, relating our Amazon experiences and joking about how he in his official capacity was nearly called upon to rescue us when we got caught up in the riot. Meanwhile he had been getting into hot water over remarks made about Kashmir on his visit to India with the Queen.

People had warned me that the first Christmas could be difficult. In fact, Chris and Peter were coming home for the full two weeks, including New Year, so I was perfectly happy in anticipation; we would also have Granny Cook to stay for Christmas. I was conscious of being more at peace with myself, more positive and in control than the previous year, when Robin had been so cruelly manipulative just before the festive season.

When Christmas cards began to arrive, I wondered if people would be tactful and avoid robin motifs. I mentioned this to a colleague, and her reaction of ill-concealed horror was delightfully comical, as she hastily withdrew to check on her choice of design, and her relief as she handed me the envelope. In all I received nine or ten robin-adorned cards. I'm sure the senders were completely oblivious of their collective faux pas, and my reaction was one of amusement rather than offence.

At New Year, things livened up considerably in our corner of Edinburgh, because some of our friends from the Amazon trip came to sample a Scottish Hogmanay: Gary, Gorky and Sue. With my family and Ann's, and additional assorted friends, we had quite a gathering.

We all mucked in and made a curry dinner, we introduced the visitors to a wild ceilidh, and at Hogmanay we took the bus to the centre of Edinburgh and joined the street party. In my previous existence the family had been enough, and I never would have done these sorts of things, or even wanted to. I must be a deep-dyed democrat, for it felt very good to be one of the crowd, mingling and merging, and not set apart by the importance of connections.

Epilogue

I had expected the divorce would have been accomplished by now. Early on, Robin had been pushing for haste, but now there always seemed to be some hitch, or he was unavailable for discussions. I asked the Foreign Office to continue sending me the restricted papers indicating his whereabouts, but they refused. Clearly Robin had put a veto on this. One thing that came back to haunt me was the security for his London mortgages being fixed on the Edinburgh home. I remembered my profound misgivings over this arrangement. Robin phoned to say that he had no other security, and could this remain? But I refused. The very idea was ridiculous, and I would not have a moment's peace. He became incandescent with rage and screamed down the phone that I had milked him of everything, and slammed the phone down.

In January, Linda McDougall's book *Westminster Women*, was published and was previewed in *The Times* two days beforehand. There was a leak of some of the material, and one Friday my poor secretary was inundated with phone calls from members of the press, who had picked up on stories of Robin's previous affairs. I was horror-struck and ran downstairs to the hospital shop to gather up some newspapers. The media interest never stopped that day, and one of our managers warned me that there was a group of cameramen in the main entrance hall; he offered me the use of a hospital car because another cluster were sitting in the car park beside my vehicle.

The next day, Linda's unexpurgated article featured in *The Times* magazine. It sparked off weeks of embarrassment for him. Robin phoned, of course, and begged me to do what I could towards damage limitation. I put out a statement again, saying what a wonderful politician he was. I was horrified on my own account, wondering what effect this would have on the divorce arrangements, and really thinking I'd blown it. It was suggested to me that so much of embarrassment was now revealed that he might feel I had no further power to damage him, and why should he hand over the property to me? In addition, I bitterly resented the picture of me that was presented, of a vindictive virago who had at last decided to speak out. I made it clear, in statements to the Sunday papers and in an article in the *Guardian*, that none of this was an interview intended for publication, but a private discussion which I had assumed would be off the record – one MP's wife to another – unless I agreed otherwise.

I spoke to Robin several times that weekend. He said that if reporters managed to identify any of his previous mistresses, he could be forced to resign. And of course the hunt was on for them. Peter Mandelson rang to find out how I was coping. I picked up from him that there would be considerable resistance to the media deciding which and when cabinet ministers should resign, and he did not seem to think Robin was in danger.

On the Sunday, my television interview which paralleled Linda's book appeared. At least I knew I had talked of matters that affect professional women with children, and kept off sensitive topics. I had insisted on avoidance of any questions relating to the marriage. But even here my purpose was thwarted by another voice filling in these details as narrative. I was pretty angry about all this failure to respect confidentiality. However the revelations did me no harm at all, and stories appeared in waves that were supportive of me and condemnatory of Robin. Reporters got hold of his mother, and she, poor soul, made remarks that only added to his misery, including one about how devastated Robin's father would have been. This thought had often occurred to me. I rather think that if he'd been alive Robin would not have left me; his father would have disowned him.

When it seemed as if the stories would settle down and some other scandal take over, Anne Bullen spoke out about her dismissal and Robin's reported wish to bring Gaynor into the Foreign Office. The furore created by this story looked far more dangerous than anything that had gone before. One remarkable result was that Gordon Brown lent his support and this created a new amity between them, which however did not last more than a few months. Then the story about India was dredged up again, and there were questions asked about a lost weekend when Robin briefly flew home in the middle of the trip. This was a storm in a teacup. I have no inside information, but my view is that he came back for personal reasons; while legitimate, it was inconsiderate to those staff who had to accompany him, and it was a wicked and arrogant waste of public money, just for a few hours at home.

To my surprise, the publicity worked substantially in my favour, because Robin explained to me that he would have to appear very keen to get married in order to improve his public image; and of course he would have to be divorced first. He very unwisely made a remark about the superior happiness he'd had in recent months. It was a slap in the face, not just for me, but for the family. In fact it was palpably untrue. Speaking to the Scottish editor of the *Sunday Times*, I allowed more of my true feelings of hurt to be drawn out than I intended. It all appeared on the front page; and Robin was on the phone spitting like a wildcat again. 'Do you want to destroy me?'

When he'd calmed down a bit, he said that he would have to talk of his forthcoming marriage in glowing terms to the press. I said, say what you wish of Gaynor. But just make sure you cast no unpleasant asides on me. He said with feeling, 'I would be happy if I never had to see or hear or think about you, ever again!'

We signed the agreement, and the divorce became effective on Friday, 13 March. I was asked to write a diary for the Scottish *Sunday Times*, and it also appeared in the London edition. I thoroughly enjoyed doing this, and especially being told how good it was. Actually, it was the second diary I had written for them, but the first was rather swamped by the other stories bubbling away in early January.

But for me, the most important consequence of all the disclosures in *Westminster Women* was that I felt to a large extent released from my undertaking not to talk about Robin publicly. The philosophy of that undertaking, as far as I was concerned, was that I should not put him in danger of losing his job, as he had given up to me more than he was legally bound to do. I knew that what I really wanted to do beyond anything else was to write my autobiography, but until now felt I could not do so because it would be so damaging to him. And now he had survived the worst.

So this book was conceived. I have felt the most compelling need to set all this down, and the exercise has been wholly therapeutic. I am sorry if it will cause discomfort to certain people, some of whom I would prefer to spare. But for once I have done a thing entirely for myself. There have been unexpected benefits from the work, particularly a renewed ability to focus my attention on issues without being distracted by emotional or personal matters. And losing yourself in a subject promotes enthusiasm, so the healing process becomes self-propagating.

My opinions on the control of pharmaceuticals had provoked some correspondence and I was pleased to learn that a number of people shared my views. The *BMA News Review* asked me to write a piece on the same subject, which would also carry an opposing view, and this was a good opportunity to use those points that had been edited out of the *Sunday Times* article the previous autumn. I feel very strongly that prescribing practice is influenced far too strongly by commercial pressures emanating from drug companies, and that the profit motive should not influence the development or use of medications. Of course people respond that there has to be some reward for the risk-taking in research and development. This is true, but the argument is not insuperable: there are other powerful motivating forces besides profit-making. Again, vested interests are hard to overcome.

Drug reps target junior doctors in their first jobs, when acquaintance with therapeutics is minimal and the learning curve is steep. It takes a little time before you realise – if you ever do – that this is glorified advertising. There is a body of opinion, which I do not support, that holds the pecuniary rewards of any venture as absolutely sacred. This may be entirely reasonable in the consumer world where the product is optional; a washing machine for instance, or even a work of art. But to my mind, the right of any human being to a proven health-promoting measure, if the need is there, is an infinitely more sacred right. The development and distribution of all medications is a process that is currently entirely in the hands of large, powerful, multinational companies, in which inevitably commercial pressures dictate priorities. Governments worldwide adopt measures to constrain costs but their efforts are puny and ineffective, and one gets the impression that there are divided loyalties because big business and employment are other heavyweights that alter the balance. One has only to look at the story of tobacco companies, which have ruthlessly ignored the evidence of danger to health and who even now actively encourage tobacco sales in Third World countries, to realise how the profit motive can steam-roller other humanitarian considerations. And the analogy with drug companies is not wholly inappropriate, if you look at the scandals which have appeared in the press over the years. Some reports allege that up to thirty per cent of research is not published, giving rise to worries that results may be suppressed for commercial reasons. In this context, the contrast medium myodil and the tranquilliser halcion have hit the headlines in recent years because of known dangerous side effects which went unreported. Third World countries can be particularly vulnerable to inappropriate drug promotion; for instance, anti-tuberculous drugs made available over the counter, thus fostering drug-resistant TB. The new anti-impotence drug viagra is an obvious potential candidate for mishandling. It is already much in demand and there will be immense capacity for inappropriate sales if its use is not carefully controlled.

The more I have thought about this issue in recent months, the more I realise how very much doctors' individual prescribing practices are influenced or even dictated by commercial companies, who infiltrate the research and development arena, the strictly medical scientific information-sharing meetings, take over educational activities at all levels, adopt medical jargon ('evidence-based medicine' is a current favourite), hide naked enterprise under a cloak of ethics. There needs to be a complete re-examination of the entire process, and it will require a very strong and determined government to do it. I was pleased to read of a leaked Labour policy document in June of this year which will insist on more evidence of the cost-effectiveness of drugs before they are released for use.

One of the manifestations of my new up-beat self is that I can concentrate on such issues, and having had further correspondence I hope to go on stirring things up and raising awareness of the need for change. I write this on the very day that the NHS celebrates its fiftieth anniversary and I am vastly more optimistic about its future than I was two years ago. I should very much like to be part of the political process that puts it more securely on the rails again. I firmly believe that if the health service could be more completely buttressed against commercial pressures, many financial problems could be solved, paradoxically enough. Waiting lists would melt overnight if consultants could be persuaded to commit themselves wholly to the NHS and forgo private practice. Private finance initiatives for hospital building are under attack from various professional quarters and it is time the government started listening and reversed the commitments to these improvident manacles.

On a more personal level, having tried to make sense of what has happened in my life, I have arrived at the conviction that I could have done nothing to prevent the sequence of events, and in this knowledge there is peace. I am only one of several casualties of the destructive nature of a distorted lifestyle, which is currently the norm for our politicians. I am well out of it. Someone should be asking questions about whether the present system is the best way to obtain well-rounded, compassionate, balanced, soundly judging people of integrity to govern the country.

But it won't be me. I've got other things to do.

Index

M.C. refers to Margaret Cook and R.C. to Robin Cook.

Albright, Madeleine, 263
Alice in Wonderland, 44–5, 70
Allan, Norman, 133, 146–7
Allen, Dick, 257, 258, 270, 272, 273, 277
Ann (neighbour and holiday companion of M.C.), 281, 282, 287, 288, 289
Annan, Kofi, 266
Annan, Nan, 266
Anne, Princess, 26, 213
anorexia nervosa, 160–1
Antigone, 76–7
Appleyard, Lady Joan, 261
Ashdown, Paddy, 257, 262, 266
Athlene (university friend), 83, 84, 89
Attenborough, Dickie, 189

Badminton Horse Trials, 169, 250, 251–2
Barry (university student), 82, 83–4
Bath, M.C.'s early childhood in, 18–19
Beijing, 220
Ben (drama teacher and boyfriend of M.C.), 76–9, 80–1, 82, 85, 87, 88
Benn, Tony, 163
Beresford, Meg, 168
Bernadette (nanny), 137, 148, 149
Billy (dog), 64–5, 93
Blair, Cherie, 1, 261, 264, 265–6
Blair, Tony, 215; and the breakup of R.C.'s marriage, 2, 3, 278, 279–80; and the 1997 general election, 248; and the Hong Kong handover ceremonies, 261, 264, 265–6

Blyton, Enid, 24
books: M.C.'s childhood reading, 22–3, 24; for English O-levels, 66; read by R.C., 104; *Children of the New Forest*, 156
Branson, Richard, 260
Britannia (royal yacht), 256, 259–60, 261–3, 266–7
Brittan, Leon, 265
Brooker, Mr (vicar), 8, 10
Brown, Gordon, 138, 154, 185, 215, 218, 293
Browning, Robert, 'My Last Duchess', 241–2
Brunhilde (horse), 175, 177–8, 180, 182
Buchan, Janey and Norman, 167–8
Bullen, Anne, 254, 256, 293
Burns Suppers, 89–90, 228–9

Campbell, Alastair, 2, 278
Canadian holiday, 210–11
Carissima (horse), 191
Carlton Gardens (Foreign Secretary's residence), 1, 5, 252, 254–5, 268–9
Carmina Burana, 85
Celia (riding instructor), 172, 174
Chappell, Miss (headmistress), 41, 42, 45–6, 56, 57, 59, 65, 77, 78
Charles, Prince of Wales, 257, 259, 261, 263, 264, 265, 267, 273
Charlie (cat), 28
Chaudhury, Dr Dulal, 253
Cheddar Gorge, 19

Chevening (Foreign Secretary's residence), 1, 257, 282; M.C.'s weekend at, 269–73

China: M.C.'s trip to, 219–20; Tiananmen Square, 220, 262–3; Terracotta Army at Xi'an, 221; and the Hong Kong handover ceremonies, 264–5, 267

Christine, Sister Marie (teaching nun), 35, 36, 37

Christmas carols, 70

Christmas celebrations, 202; (1996), 244–7; (1997), 290–1

Clare (Chris Cook's girlfriend), 225

CND (Campaign for Nuclear Disarmament), 153, 167, 168, 202

Colin (boyfriend of M.C.), 87–8, 90, 94

Coltrane, Robbie, 190

Cook, Chris (son): and the break-up of his parent's marriage, 4, 245–6, 276, 277, 280; birth, 134–5; childhood, 140, 143, 145, 148, 149, 150, 160, 164; appendicitis, 151–2; and horse-riding, 158, 174, 196; character, 170; schooling, 170; and nuclear disarmament, 185; at university, 197–8, 203, 226; and the 1992 general election, 200; and racing, 208–9; twenty-first birthday, 213; dramatic activities, 215–16; and M.C.'s fiftieth birthday, 216; graduation, 222, 223–5; first job, 230, 236; flatmates, 236; home for Christmas, 244–5, 290; weekend at Chevening, 270, 271, 272; at the Edinburgh Festival, 281–2; and Gaynor, 286

Cook, Ina (Granny Cook, R.C.'s mother), 127, 137, 171, 209; M.C.'s first meeting with, 106; helps with childcare, 138, 142, 150; move to Dalkeith, 141–2; hip replacement operations, 147; and family holidays, 154; and M.C.'s fiftieth birthday, 216; and Chris Cook's graduation, 222, 223, 225; on trip to Kilwinning, 228, 229;

and Christmas celebrations, 245, 290; and the breakup of R.C.'s marriage, 280, 293

Cook, Margaret (née Whitmore): R.C. informs her their marriage is over, 1–6; birth, 7; childhood, 14–38, 47–52; photographs of childhood, 15–16, 18, 24–5; and the countryside, 16, 29, 47–8; appearance (in childhood), 17, 18–19; character, 17; at primary school, 23–4, 27–8, 33; childhood illnesses, 25–7; dreams, 27; and needlework, 28; and poetry, 29–30, 31, 44; at convent school (Shepton Mallet), 35–8; and religion, 35–7, 49–52, 69–70; at Sunny Hill School, Bruton, 38, 39–46, 53–5, 56–9, 60–7, 70–2, 73–4, 75–9; learning the facts of life, 43; confirmation, 51; puberty, 53–5; appearance (in adolescence), 54–5, 62; and schoolgirl crushes, 57–8; eyesight, 62; and haematology, 62, 123, 127; school trip to Germany, 63–4; and dancing, 68, 71; appearance (at sixth-form dance), 71; applications to medical schools, 73, 75; boyfriends (in Somerset), 74–5, 76–9, 80–1, 82; holiday jobs, 81–2; boyfriends (at Edinburgh University), 84–5, 87–8, 89–90, 91, 92, 93–4, 99, 110–11; twenty-first birthday, 94; and politics, 97, 184; love affair with R.C., 101–14, 115; and driving, 112–13, 127; correspondence from R.C., 113–14; engagement to R.C., 115; honeymoon, 121, 123; marriage to R.C., 122–3; pregnancies, 129–35, 139–40; birth of sons, 134–5, 142–3; and motherhood, 135–7, 141–2; and breastfeeding, 136, 143; and horse-riding, 138, 157–9, 169–70, 174–5, 182, 191–2, 194–6; relationship with R.C., 152–3, 164–5, 172–3, 175, 185, 199–200, 202–3; and embroidery, 165, 208; fortieth birthday, 169–70; and R.C.'s confessions of extra-marital affairs, 178–82, 237–9; views on the NHS, 187–9, 286, 295–6; discovers breast lump, 199–200; visit to India, 204–5; foot injury, 209–10; fiftieth birthday, 216; silver wedding anniversary, 216, 217; suspects R.C. of having another affair, 219; deterioration of relationship with R.C., 227, 231–2, 234–5; dines at Windsor Castle, 232–4; birthday visit to falconry centre, 236–7; and R.C.'s affair with Gaynor, 237–42, 245–7, 249–50; last holiday with R.C. (in Spain), 239–43; considers plans for leaving R.C., 242; at the Bangladeshi annual medical dinner, 253–4; and the Hong Kong handover ceremony, 256, 257–67; and R.C. as Foreign Secretary, 256; weekend at Chevening, 269–73; present feelings towards R.C., 275; and the press, 275–8, 279, 282, 284, 285, 289, 292–3, 294; on solitude, 275; and divorce proceedings, 278–9, 284, 285, 292–3, 294; on the lifestyle of politicians, 282–3, 297; and writing, 286, 294–5; holiday fling, 288, *see also* Edinburgh University medical school; holidays; homes; medical career; music

Cook, Peter (Grandpa Cook, R.C.'s father), 127, 137, 140, 160, 171, 209, 293; background, 106; M.C.'s first meeting with, 108; and food, 124; move to Dalkeith, 141–2; and family holidays, 154; illness, 203; death, 212–13

Cook, Peter (son), 238; and the breakup of his parent's marriage, 3–4, 245–6, 247, 276, 280; childhood, 27, 148, 149, 150; birth, 142–3; and horseriding, 157, 158–9, 174, 195, 196; character, 170; schooling, 170; illnesses, 173–4, 183; at university, 197–8, 198, 203, 205, 226; in Canada, 210; in Grenoble, 222–3, 225, 226, 228;

twenty-first birthday, 222; first job, 230, 236; graduation, 234; home for Christmas, 244–5, 290; weekend at Chevening, 270, 271, 272; at the Edinburgh Festival, 281–2; and Gaynor, 286–7

Cook, Robin: as Foreign Secretary, 1, 250–6, 269–73; tells M.C. their marriage is over, 1–6; as student at Edinburgh University, 92–3, 98, 116; love affair with M.C., 101–14; appearance, 103; character, 104–5, 152–3, 201–2, 215, 239; outbursts of temper, 105, 198, 229–30; attitudes to money, 106, 124, 146, 148, 197–8; relationship with his parents, 106, 154, 164–5; and the medical profession, 107–8; and country life, 108; letter to M.C. (after their engagement), 113–14; engagement to M.C., 115; and M.C.'s residency at the City Hospital, Edinburgh, 118–19; job applications, 120–1; teaching post at Bo'ness academy, 121, 123; marriage to M.C., 122–3; adopted as Labour Party candidate for Edinburgh North, 124; and guilt transference, 124, 193, 243, 249; general elections, (1970), 125–6; on Edinburgh City Council, 127–8, 131, 132; and the WEA (Workers' Educational Association), 127, 128, 141; parliamentary candidate for Central Edinburgh, 133–4; and birth of son Chris, 134–5; and M.C. as a mother, 136; and cars/driving, 138, 148, 170–1, 172; and horses, 138, 157–9, 169, 172, 195–6, 202, 244; maiden speech, 142; as M.P. for Edinburgh Central, 142, 156, 163; and present-giving, 148, 171; and the Western European Union, 150–1; as a father, 152–3, 165; relationship with M.C., 152–3, 164–5, 173, 175, 185, 199–200, 202–3, 256; and the Scottish Minorities Group, 153–4;

Cook, Robin: as Foreign Secretary – *cont*
heavy drinking, 154, 176, 181, 183,
193; in the shadow Treasury team, 156;
and hunting, 159; and racing, 159,
208–9; and the Ditchley Foundation
conference, 162–3; parliamentary candidate for West Lothian, 163–4; and
M.C.'s medical career, 164; and the
European Parliament, 167–8; and Neil
Kinnock, 167; and nuclear disarmament, 168, 184–5; political rivals,
168–9; and cooking, 171, 183; weight
problems, 171–2, 184; sexual difficulties, 172, 180; in the shadow
cabinet, 173, 184, 201; and depression,
176, 181; confesses to extra-marital
affairs, 178–82, 237–9; and the poll
tax, 190; and privacy, 190; racing
column in the *Glasgow Herald*, 198,
203, 209; as an M.P., 201–2; on television, 202; buys flat in London, 205–
6; on *Through the Keyhole*, 207–8; and
the Labour leadership election (1994),
214–15; and M.C.'s fiftieth birthday,
216; silver wedding anniversary, 216,
217; as shadow Foreign Secretary, 217–
18, 219, 234; and M.C.'s friends, 219–
20; deterioration of relationship with
M.C., 227, 231, 234–5; and the Scott
Report, 230–1; speeches, 231; dines at
Windsor Castle, 232–4; visit to falconry centre, 236–7; affair with
Gaynor and effect on M.C., 237–42,
245–7; and the 1997 general election,
248–9; resumption of marital relations,
249–50; at the Bangladeshi annual
medical dinner, 253–4; in Kashmir,
254; and the Hong Kong handover
ceremonies, 256, 257–67; M.C. takes
blood sample from, 273; relationship
with Gaynor, 286–7; trip to India, 290,
293–4, *see also* holidays
Cornish, Jane, 256, 258, 261, 263
Cornwall, M.C.'s holiday job in, 91–2

Corries, The, 84
Crofton, Professor, 115
Cryer, Bob, 168

Dalkeith, Earl and Countess of, 125–6
Dalyell, Tam, 121, 163, 164
Darwin, Charles, 271
David (medical colleague of M.C.), 133,
146, 147
David (R.C.'s personal assistant), 2
Davidson, Arthur, 183
Day, Miss (schoolteacher), 27–8
Deng Xiaoping, 267
Devlin, Bernadette, 120
devolution, referendum on (1979), 154
Diana (friend), 74
Diana, Princess of Wales, 285
diplomatic wives, role of, 263–4
Ditchley Foundation conference, 162–3
Doble, Mrs (schoolteacher), 34, 35
Donald (boyfriend of M.C.), 99
Doubtful Misfortunes of Li Sing, The, 58–9
Douglas-Hamilton, James, 98

Eagle, Angela, 286
Eatwell, John, 194
Ecuador, M.C.'s holiday in (1997),
287–9
Edinburgh Festival, 281–2
Edinburgh University medical school,
82–8, 89–99; M.C.'s application
accepted, 75; Freshers Week, 82–6;
digs, 83; female friends, 83; and Scottish Nationalism, 83, 85, 95, 96–7;
M.C. counselled by senior student,
85–6; dissecting room, 86, 90; lectures,
86; musical society choir, 86, 93;
physiology and biochemistry practicals, 86–7; rectorial elections, 86;
social life, 86, 87–8, 89–91; Christmas
holidays, 88, 93; Charities Week, 90–
1; holiday jobs, 91–2, 94–5; exams,
92, 94, 107–8; debates, 94, 97–8, 101;
clinical studies, 95–6; M.C. wins class

medal, 107; and the contraceptive pill, 108–9; 'Final Phase' of course, 109–10

Edward (M.C.'s first boyfriend), 74–5, 78, 99

Edward, Prince, 232, 233, 234

Ehrman, William, 257

Elaine (nanny), 161–2

Elizabeth II, Queen, 193, 232, 233

Elizabeth (nanny), 149, 151

Ellis, Osian, 57

European Parliament, 167–8

Exmoor, holidays in, 192–3

Fairnbairn, Nicky, 109

Falklands War, 165

Fatchett, Derek, 257

Fiennes, Susanne, 262

Fitzpatrick, Mr and Mrs, 159

Florence, trip to (1984), 167–8

Follett, Barbara, 189, 208

Follett, Ken, 189, 196–7, 208

Foot, Michael, 156, 167

Forest Brook Farm, holidays at, 156–7, 165

Foulkes, George, 109, 134

Fowler, Fiona, 155

Fowler, Norman, 155

Fraser, Raymond, 105

Free Presbyterian Church of Scotland, 95

French, Ted, 132

Frost, David, 208

Fry, Stephen, 189

games: in M.C.'c childhood, 21, 25, 37–8; Monopoly, 165; R.C.'s games with his children, 165; at Christmas, 202

Gaynor: R.C.'s affair with, 3, 237–9, 243, 245–6, 278, 280; meets R.C.'s sons, 286–7; and Anne Bullen, 293

general elections: (1970), 125–6; (1974), 140–1, 144; (1979), 154; (1983), 165–6, 167; (1987), 176; (1992), 199–200; (1997), 246, 247, 248–9

George (university student), 84

Geraldine (pupil at Sunny Hill), 42, 60, 65

German prisoners of war, in postwar Britain, 15–16

Germany, school trip to, 63–4

Ghali, Boutros Boutros, 224

Giselle, 23

Griffiths, Nigel, 140

Grossman, Loyd, 208

Guthrie, General Sir Charles, 264

Gwenda (schoolfriend), 39, 43

Hague, William, 262

Hallowe'en, 144–5

Harry (bodyguard), 2

Harvest Festival, 49–50

Haskell, Miss (maths teacher), 65

Hattersley, Roy, 168–9

Heath, Edward, 126, 140, 163, 257, 262, 264

Henderson, Hamish, 89

hepatitis, outbreak in Edinburgh, 125

Heseltine, Michael, 262

Highgrove House, 273

Hilda (house manager at Chevening), 269–70, 270–1, 272

Hogmanay celebrations (1997–8), 290–1

holidays: with Edward (boyfriend), 74; M.C. as a student, 92, 100; Ullapool (with R.C.), 131–2; New Forest, 156–60, 165, 169–70, 182–3, 193–4, 200, 208, 219; Lake District, 180–1; Exmoor, 192–3; India, 204–5; Canada, 210–11; Hungary, 216–17; China, 219–20; Ireland, 226–7; weekend in Grenoble, 226; Spain, 239–43; planned US trip (1997), 269; Ecuador, 287–9; Phoenix, Arizona, 289–90

Hollick, Clive (now Lord Hollick), 182–3, 194

homes (of Robin and Margaret Cook): flats in Edinburgh, 121–2, 127; the Mill in Clermiston, 143–5; security

homes (of Robin and Margaret Cook) – *cont*
  for house in Edinburgh (when R.C. becomes Foreign Secretary), 255–6, 269
Hong Kong, 220, 221; handover ceremonies (1997), 254, 256–67
horses and horse-riding, 138, 169–70, 174–5, 182, 191–2, 194–6, 281; Sparrow, 1, 5, 244, 248, 250–1, 283; on Somerset farms, 48; and R.C., 138, 157–9, 169, 172, 195–6, 202, 244; in the New Forest, 157–9; Wendy, 174–5; Winkie, 174, 175, 182, 184, 191; Brunhilde, 175, 177–8, 180, 182; Lucky, 183–4, 191, 196; Carissima, 191; Phyllis, 191–2, 194–5, 203–4, 209, 232, 243–4, 283; in Hungary, 217; in Spain, 241; Badminton Horse Trials, 250, 251–2
hospitals: Ballymoney, Northern Ireland, 99–100; Victoria Hospital, Kirkcaldy, 111; City Hospital, Edinburgh, 115–20; Western General, Edinburgh, 121, 129, 130, 132–3, 133, 206, 207; Bangour General Hospital, West Lothian, 146–9, 161–2, 187, 193; St John's, Livingston, 193, 196, 201, 206–7, 218–19, *see also* medical career
Howe, Sir Geoffrey, 154, 257, 264
Hungary, holiday in, 216–17
hunting, 159
Hurd, Douglas, 257, 269
Hurd, Judy, 257, 269
Husband, Captain David, 271, 282

India: M.C. visits, 204–5; R.C.'s trip (as Foreign Secretary), 290, 293–4
Ireland, holiday in, 226–7
Irmgard (German friend), 64
Irvine, Derry, 226

Jack (boyfriend of M.C.), 110–11

Jean (university friend of M.C.), 83, 92, 192
Jeanette (nanny), 136, 137
Jiang Zemin, 264, 267
Jim (R.C.'s agent), 248, 284
Justice, James Robertson, 86, 233

Kaldor, Mary, 168
Kane, Jack (Lord Provost of Edinburgh), 127, 135
Kashmir, R.C. in, 254
Keay, John, 109
King's School, Bruton, 57; drama group, 76–7
Kingston, Mr and Mrs, 31–3
Kinnock, Glenys, 167
Kinnock, Neil, 167, 184, 190, 194, 199, 248
Kirkcudbright, visits to R.C.'s parents in, 108, 128, 139–40
Kureishi, Hanif, 196

La Bohème, 57
Labour Party, conferences, 123
Lamport, Stephen, 262, 263
Le Bonheur (film), 99, 270
Leslie, Mr (music teacher), 41–2, 46, 61
Li Peng, 264
Linda (M.C.'s horse-riding companion), 244, 283
Lisa (R.C.'s social secretary), 269
Liz (M.C.'s horse-riding companion), 243–4
Lucky (horse), 183–4, 191, 196
Lynn (nanny), 150, 160, 161

Mac (boyfriend of M.C.), 91, 92, 93–4
MacCaig, Norman, 91
McCormack, Mr (cardiac surgeon), 116
McCririck, John and Jenny, 270, 272–3, 289–90
McDougall, Linda, *Westminster Women*, 285–6, 292–3, 294
Mackie, Lindsay, 102

Mackintosh, John P., 109
Macnamara, Kevin, 150
Madame Butterfly, 23
Major, John, 199
Man, Isle of, 15
Mandelson, Peter, 279–80, 285, 293
Margaret, Princess, 232, 233–4
Margaret (school friend of M.C.), 33
Margarita, Crown Princess of Romania, 138–9
Martin (university friend of M.C.), 88
Mary (M.C.'s aunt), 7, 51, 73
Maureen (girlfriend of R.C.), 110
Maureen (school friend of M.C.), 27–8
medical career: postgraduate exams, 127, 128–9, 132, 147; consultancy post at Bangour, 147–8, 161–2; medical record reorganization, 162; demands of, 206–7, 218–19, 230, 250, 279; M.C. asks for compassionate leave, 277; returning to work (after the marriage break-up), 283–5, 284, *see also* hospitals
medical colleagues (of M.C.): political attitudes, 124–5; attitudes to her maternity leave, 137; and work demands/stress at St John's, 206–7, 250; and M.C.'s marriage breakup, 284
Minnie (South African nanny), 11–12, 13
Mitchell, Austin, 285
money matters, 106, 124, 144, 146, 148, 197–8; and the divorce settlement, 278–9
Morag (university friend), 83, 84, 90, 91–2, 100, 102, 110, 113
Morrow, Commodore Anthony, 259, 263
Muggeridge, Malcolm, 108
Mullins, Mrs (German teacher), 61, 63, 72
Munro, John, 129
Murray, Mrs (landlady), 83, 85, 88
Muscat (cat), 225, 274

music: piano-playing, 27, 31, 32, 37, 45, 58, 62, 66, 71, 75–6, 78–9; lessons at Sunny Hill school, 45, 61; M.C. plays church organ, 68–70, 88; folk-singing, 84; Edinburgh University medical school musical society choir, 86, 93; and the Cook family, 165
'My Last Duchess' (Browning), 241–2

Nancy (university friend), 83, 90, 92
nannies, 136, 137, 149–50, 160–1; Minnie (in South Africa), 11–12, 13
Naranjo de Bulnes, Mount (Spain), 240–1
Neal, Surgeon Commander Alistair, 260
New Forest holidays, 156–60, 165, 169–70, 182–3, 193–4, 219
New Year celebrations (1997–8), 290–1
Newton, Sir Isaac, 271
NHS (National Health Service): market reforms, 187–9; and the pharmaceutical industry, 286, 295–6
Noble, Bill, 270
Northern Ireland: M.C.'s residency at Ballymoney, 99–100; Bloody Sunday, 129
nuclear disarmament, 153, 167, 168, 184–5

Onassis, Jackie, 214
O'Neill, Martin, 109, 125
opera, 57
Oswald, Tom, 133
Owen, Bill, 196

Paisley, Reverend Ian, 100
Parkinson, Cecil, 278
Patten, Chris, 259, 265, 267
Patten, Lavender, 266
Paul (bodyguard), 250–3
Paul (house manager at Chevening), 269–70, 270–1, 272
pharmaceutical industry, and the NHS, 286, 295–6

Philip, Prince, Duke of Edinburgh, 193, 232, 233

Phyllis (horse), 191–2, 194–5, 203–4, 209, 232, 243–4; suffering from colic, 223–4, 225; retirement, 283

piano-playing, 27, 31, 32, 37, 45, 58, 62, 66, 71, 75–6, 78–9

poetry: of R.L. Stevenson, 29–30, 31; comical, 44, 66–7

poll tax, 190

Powell, Chris, 183

Powell, Enoch, 139

Prescott, John, 185

Primakov, Yevgeny, 266, 271

Prime of Miss Jean Brodie, The, 111

private health care, M.C.'s views on, 188–9, 296

radio: in M.C.'s childhood, 23, 48–9; Singing Together programme, 29, 84

Rayner, Claire, 189

Regan, Gaynor see Gaynor

Rendell, Ruth, 208

Rifkind, Edith, 269

Rifkind, Malcolm, 98, 101, 269

Robertson, George, 109

Rodgers, Bill, 163

Ross, Sandy, 125, 126, 141

Rushdie, Salman, 251

Rushton, Willie, 208

Sandy (boyfriend of M.C.), 90

Santiago de Compostela, 240

schoolteachers: at Warton primary school, 23–4; at Doulting village school, 34, 35; at the convent school (Shepton Mallet), 35, 36, 37; at Sunny Hill School, Bruton, 41–3, 45–6, 53–4, 56, 57, 59, 65, 76–8

Scotsman, M.C.'s letter to the, 292–3

Scott Report (on arms-to-Iraq allegations), 230–1

Scottish Minorities Group, 153–4

Scottish Nationalism, and Edinburgh University, 83

Seaton, Helen, 261

Sessions, John, 189–90

Sexey's School, Bruton, 40, 57

sexuality, 57–8

Shore, Peter, 156

Short, Clare, 286

Sissons, Peter, 277

Skye, Crofters' Aid Scheme, 95

Smith, John (Labour leader), 185–6, 200, 201, 213, 214

Social Democratic Party, 163

Somerset: M.C.'s childhood in (Chelynch), 30, 31–8; M.C.'s holiday job in Frome, 81–2; Christmas holidays (from university), 88, see also Sunny Hill School, Bruton

South Africa, M.C.' parents and early life in, 9–13

Spain, last holiday together in, 239–43

Sparrow (horse), 1, 5, 244, 248, 250–1, 283

Steel, David, 153

Stevenson, R.L., poetry, 29–30, 31

Stewart (boyfriend of M.C.), 84–5, 89–90, 92, 98

Strang, Gavin, 139

Strasbourg, trips to, 150–1

Straw, Jack, 156

Sue (red-haired friend), 41, 47

Sue (schoolfriend): at convent school, Shepton Mallet, 37; at Sunny Hill School, Bruton, 38, 44, 60, 65, 66, 67, 71, 72; and piano-playing, 45; and puberty, 54; and elocution, 58, 62–3, 70–1; and the King's School drama group, 76, 77

Sunday Times, M.C.'s writings on medical issues, 279, 286, 289, 290

Sunny Hill School, Bruton, 38, 39–46, 56–9, 60–7; journey to, 39–40; pupil relationships, 39, 60–1; uniform, 39; morning assembly, 41–2; teachers, 41–

3, 45–6, 53–4, 56, 57, 59; curriculum, 43–5; sports, 44; music lessons, 45, 61; Speech Day, 45–6; Latin lessons, 53–4; cultural events, 56–7; and schoolgirl crushes, 57–8; biology lessons, 61–2; German lessons, 61, 72; O-level year, 65–7; sixth form, 70–2, 73–4, 75–9
Sunny Hill School, prep, 40–1
Susan (girlfriend of R.C.), 98, 103–4, 106, 266
Suzhou, 221

Taylor, Edward, 101
Thatcher, Margaret (later Baroness), 154, 155, 187, 259, 262
Thorns, Miss, 45, 66
Through the Keyhole (television programme), 207–8
Tiananmen Square, 220, 262–3
Times, The, M.C.'s letter, 284, 285
Topcliffe, Yorkshire, M.C.'s early childhood in, 15–18
Trollope, Anthony, 104, 171, 208
Trollope Society, 208
Tsang, Sir Donald, 259, 264, 265
Tung Chee Hwa, 259–60, 264, 267
Tunstall, Mr (vicar), 33, 35–6, 36–7, 49, 51–2, 56; sermon on the Sabbath, 52; and M.C. playing the church organ, 68, 69, 70; gives M.C. book on Christian sex ethics, 82
Tunstall, Mrs, 49, 82

Vaughan, Gerald, 155
Vera (friend of M.C.'s mother), 10
viagra, 296

Wallace, Captain Ronnie, 159, 192, 193
Walter (German prisoner of war), 15, 16, 64
Warton, Lancashire, M.C.'s childhood in, 20–30

Wendy (horse), 174–5
Westminster Women (McDougall), 285–6, 292–3, 294
Whitmore, Jenny (M.C.'s sister): birth, 11–12; childhood, 14, 16–19, 28–9, 32, 48, 52; schooling, 33, 38; nursing, 64; marriage, 72–3; pregnancy, 75; and father's death, 214; and M.C.'s fiftieth birthday, 216; and the breakup of M.C.'s marriage, 276, 281
Whitmore, Joyce (M.C.'s mother), 136; family, 7–8, 14, 15; marriage to M.C.'s father, 8–9; nursing career, 8, 11; in South Africa, 9–13; appearance, 22; and books, 22–3; and M.C.'s childhood, 25; and the facts of life, 43; and the village shop, 52; and cigarette smoking, 81; and M.C.'s university holidays, 92, 93; and communism, 97; domestic responsibilities, 124; golden wedding anniversary, 197; and the death of M.C.'s father, 213–14; and M.C.'s fiftieth birthday, 216; and the breakup of M.C.'s marriage, 276
Whitmore, Lewis Arthur (M.C.'s father): family, 7, 14–15; marriage to M.C.'s mother, 8–9; in South Africa, 9–13; and M.C.'s childhood, 15, 20–2, 24–5, 49, 52; appearance, 21; and school events, 46, 59; and religion, 49; illness, 55–6; character, 65; and politics, 97; golden wedding anniversary, 197; eightieth birthday, 203; death, 213–14
wildlife: in Somerset, 47–8; in the New Forest, 157, 219; in the Galapagos Islands, 289
Windsor Castle, dining at, 232–4
Winkie (pony), 174, 175, 182, 184, 191
Wishart, Ruth, 185–6
Woods, Donald, 196–7